Learn the subject...
Study right...
Master your classes...

Are you **REA**dy? It all starts here.
Master high school Earth Science
with REA's comprehensive study guide.

Visit us online at
www.rea.com

AUTHOR & STAFF ACKNOWLEDGMENTS

Charles O. Brass, B.S., Instructor, University of Chicago Special Programs

Joseph Conklin, B.S., Consulting Meteorologist, Pleasantville, NJ

Fran Decibus; Slim Fayache, Ph.D., Instructor, Rutgers University

Kevin Hanson, M.Ed., Adjunct Professor, St. Cloud State University

Pamela Phillips, M.A., Instructor, Hayden High School (Alabama)

We would also like to acknowledge **Vincent Biancomona**, B.S.; **Kenneth Dallow**, M.S.; **Johanna Holm**, B.A.; and **Michael Sporer**, B.S., for their editorial contributions to this book.

In addition, we would like to thank REA's **Pam Weston**, Vice President, Publishing, for setting the quality standards for production integrity and managing the publication to completion; **Diane Goldschmidt**, Associate Editor, for post-production quality assurance; and **Christine Saul**, Senior Graphic Artist, for cover design.

The *High School* TUTOR®

EARTH SCIENCE

The Staff of Research & Education Association

Research & Education Association
61 Ethel Road West • Piscataway, New Jersey 08854

THE HIGH SCHOOL TUTOR®
EARTH SCIENCE

Printed in the United States of America

Library of Congress Control Number 2005901274

International Standard Book Number 0-87891-975-9

THE HIGH SCHOOL TUTOR® and REA® are registered trademarks of Research & Education Association, Inc., Piscataway, New Jersey 08854.

REA'S HIGH SCHOOL TUTOR® SERIES
Designed with You in Mind

REA's High School Tutor® series gives you everything you need to excel in your high school classes, especially on midterms, finals and even pop quizzes.

Think of this book as access to your own private tutor. Here, right at your fingertips, in a handy Q & A format, is a great companion to your textbook. You'll also find that the High School Tutor® lends greater depth to classroom lectures. You've heard all about the theorems, the timelines, the big ideas, and the key principles; this book equips you to break it all down into bite-size chunks.

To obtain maximum benefit from the book, students should familiarize themselves with the tips below.

Larry Kling
High School Tutor Program Director

HOW TO USE THIS BOOK

Earth Science students will find this book to be an invaluable supplement to their textbooks. The book is divided into ten chapters, each dealing with a separate topic. The information is presented in question and answer format to match the format of the tests and quizzes teachers are likely to use. By reviewing the questions and the provided answers, students can prepare themselves for actual test situations.

HOW TO GRASP A TOPIC FULLY

1.   Refer to your class text and read the section pertaining to the topic. You should become acquainted with the themes discussed there.

2.   Locate the topic you are looking for by referring to the Table of Contents in the front of this book.

To learn and understand a topic thoroughly and retain its contents, it will generally be necessary for you to review the problems several times. Repeated review is essential to gain experience in recognizing the themes that are most relevant and selecting the best solution techniques.

HOW TO FIND A QUESTION TYPE

To locate one or more questions related to particular subject matter, refer to the index. The numbers in the index refer to *question* numbers, not to page numbers. This arrangement is intended to facilitate finding a question rapidly, since two or more questions may appear on a page.

If a particular type of question cannot be found readily, it is recommended that you refer to the Table of Contents in the front pages and then turn to the chapter that is applicable to the question being sought.

In preparing for an exam, it is useful to find the topics to be covered on the exam in the Table of Contents, and then review the questions under those topics several times. This should equip you with what might be needed for the exam.

CONTENTS

CHAPTER 1

OVERVIEW OF EARTH SCIENCE

The Study of Earth Science Defined

● PROBLEM 1–1

Describe the scope of the study of earth sciences.

SOLUTION:

The general study of the earth sciences encompasses all scientific fields. The complete earth scientist strives to have a diverse background in all areas of science. Such background includes the broad science areas of biology, chemistry, and physics. Because it is such a diverse science and draws on so many fields of study, the vocabulary, techniques, and concepts of earth science often cross the gray boundaries that we perceive to separate the sciences. An earth scientist needs to be familiar with all areas of the physical and life sciences and works to make connections between present findings and past research. The earth scientist works to better understand the present and the past history of Earth, as well as looking to the future of our planet.

● PROBLEM 1–2

Describe the role of prediction within the realm of the earth sciences.

SOLUTION:

From meteorology to planetology, prediction is a cornerstone of science.

What, when, where, why, and how are all questioning tools used to understand the natural world and universe around us. With a basic understanding of the elements of nature, science allows for predictions of future events based on past observations and evidence. The weather for a particular area can be hypothesized based on past climate and weather. Geologists can estimate time windows for volcanic eruptions using data from past events such as seismic activity, slope bulge increases, gas volumes, and concentrations of gasses emitted from volcanic vents. The past is a key to today, but perhaps the past is an even greater tool in science for the prediction of events that will occur in the future.

The Branches of Science Within Earth Science

● PROBLEM 1–3

Outline the various branches found within the earth sciences and identify which type of scientists work within each branch.

SOLUTION:

The study of earth sciences includes all aspects of the physical earth. This includes the oceans and atmosphere, mountains and valleys, volcanics and earthquakes, and the evolution of earth systems—past, present, and future. The rocks and waters of Earth are studied by geologists as well as the minerals and resources that support our civilizations. The earth sciences also include research in areas far beyond the sphere of our tiny planet. Planetologists speculate and study about far off worlds and moons. Astronomers peer into deep space to gather evidence of the origins of the universe and celestial bodies. They help us to look to future exploration with anticipation and wonder. Lessons learned here can be applied to far off worlds to gain insight to cosmologic events in space and how they may relate to Earth.

● PROBLEM 1–4

Describe at length how an oceanographer, meteorologist, geologist, and astronomer could contribute to a comprehensive understanding of earth sciences.

SOLUTION:

Living on a planet whose surface is covered by 70 percent water, the oceanographer has an extensive role in developing an understanding of the connections between earth and the oceans. The number of areas to be considered is so vast that the field of study can include formation of shorelines, the features of the sea floor, and the processes that caused the formation of the ocean basins. Additional areas of study include tides and currents, air-water interaction, water chemistry, heat transfer, weather and climatic affects and interactions, organisms, environments, and resources. The topics listed are not limited to the domain of oceanography, but are interconnected and thus important to a comprehensive study of oceans.

Even if we try to ignore the weather, we are likely to fail as meteorology will in some way directly impact our lives. Traditionally, this area of the earth sciences is divided into two disciplines. Meteorology is concerned with the daily short-term fluctuations in atmospheric phenomena. The composition and structure of the atmosphere, incoming solar radiation, ocean interaction with air, evaporation, heat transfer, cloud formation, and precipitation are all topics of interest within this area of study. Climatology is defined as the long-term effect of weather on a given area. The causes of climate and climatic variation are of primary interest in this area of study. The long-term affects of weather can be better understood by connecting and understanding global system interactions. The past and present climates of Earth are areas of interest to meteorologists, as well as predictions of possible future climatic changes.

A deep understanding of the planet Earth is needed to explain the natural aspects of earth. The primary goal of the geologist is to understand the changes that take place on and below the surface of the planet, and to understand the reasons and causes of those changes. Physical geology is the study of earth materials, surface changes, internal structure, and the forces that cause those changes. The geologist strives to know structures and form, as well as the historical past and possible future events of Earth. Wind and water are processes that contribute to the shaping of Earth and thus are important factors to understand. Resources and reserves are areas germane to geology as well.

To contemplate the complete past of the universe is indeed a grand endeavor. The knowledge gained in the study of the past can help space scientists to better understand cosmology in the present and perhaps predict events and changes in the future of the universe. Closer to home is the study and understanding of planets and moons, asteroids, comets, and meteorites. Perhaps the greatest contributions of these researchers to the knowledge of Earth is the increasing body of information available on terrestrial (earthlike) and jovian (giant gas) planets. The comparative geology allowed due to the huge mass of data for comparison has increased awareness of Earth's features and internal and external processes that cause those features.

● PROBLEM 1–5

Explain how a physicist, chemist, and biologist can apply their training and knowledge to expand the understanding of the earth sciences.

SOLUTION:

Physics can be simply defined as the study of forces, motion, energy, and their effects on matter. The pure physics of a scientific laboratory transfers easily to the physical world called Earth. Crustal motion, earthquakes and volcanism, atmospheric and oceanographic motions, heat flow in magma and water, and solar output and electromagnetic spectrum are just a few of the many areas where physics plays a part in the earth sciences. Few scientific endeavors are confined within the bounds of a "pure" science. Science and the earth sciences in particular are eclectic in nature. That is, input from many sources and disciplines is needed to provide the whole big picture of Earth.

Chemistry is simply stated as the study of the properties and composition of matter in the natural world. Matter is defined as the physical material of the universe that occupies space and has mass. The earth and all the geological features we see are the result of physical and chemical changes. The core of the Earth through radioactive decay provides heat to generate gigantic convection cells. Those cells in turn manipulate the crust of Earth as huge crustal plates collide. The pressures and temperatures produced cause magma to form. Those magmatic bodies affect the surface of Earth as geologic landforms are produced and precious resources are deposited. Not only are crustal processes of importance to a chemist but those of the atmosphere and hydrosphere are of interest as well. The chemistries of the oceans and air are also germane to the chemist. Again, the earth sciences prove to be eclectic in nature as many disciplines contribute to the big picture of understanding the nature of Earth.

Defined as the study of living organisms, biology proves to be another valuable tool to assist in the development of a comprehensive understanding of the earth sciences. The most obvious application in geology would be the study of paleobiology or the fossil record. Another application of biology within the realm of earth science is in the understanding of the deposition, formation, and location of fossil fuel resources. In areas of resource management and pollution, the ecological and environmental aspects of biology prove to be critical. Knowledge of ocean life can be combined with geologic and oceanographic information to provide a more complete picture of the complex environment we call the ocean. Once again it must be stated that the sciences are all interconnected in a complex web of knowledge. The boundaries that define disciplinary borders become gray with the passage of time and the accumulation of information. The sciences are all intertwined both in purpose and substance as the universe and Earth become better known and understood.

● PROBLEM 1–6

Define the purpose of the following earth science specialties: volcanology, glaciology, seismology, marine geology, planetology, and climatology. What types of training will assist scientists in these fields of study?

SOLUTION:

a) Volcanology—The volcanologist needs to draw from many specialized fields of study to undertake a complete study of volcanic formation and eruptions. Knowledge of chemistry will allow for an understanding of magmatic composition and out gassings from the magma. Subtle changes in the composition of gases may hint at future changes in store for any particular volcano. Basic geology will provide some historical background. A knowledge of physics and mathematics will prove to be very useful to model past and present data into a workable hypothesis of future events. Computer analysis is of paramount importance in this field as in any area of science. The mass of data being accumulated has to be quickly and accurately analyzed so that assumptions and predictions can be made about future volcanic events.

b) Glaciology—Knowledge of basic geology is very important to a glacial

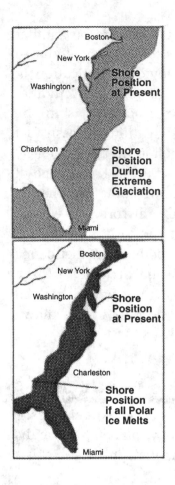

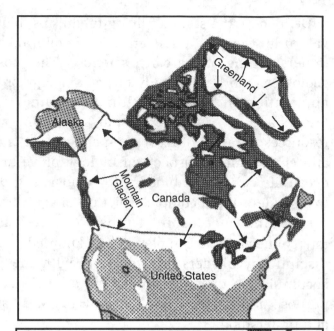

expert. The land forms, lakes, and general topography of a region are tell-tale signs of past glacial events. An understanding of climatology and meteorology are essential for understanding past fluctuations in glacial surges and retreats. Global fluctuation in climate is responsible for changes in the total percentage of ice covering Earth today. To predict future changes in glacial masses, models need to be conceived and adapted. Any subtle change in sea level would affect millions of people. A rise in ocean waters could inundate coastal communities, while a falling sea caused by glacial growth and advance could leave important ports high and dry. These changes in glacial coverage could also have dramatic impact on crop growing belts and world agriculture. The correlation between glaciers, climate, and humans is a most important field of study for many of the reasons listed above.

c) Seismology—The surface of Earth is an ever-changing place. The shifting of the crust directly affects millions each year. Recent examples of tectonic activity in Japan and the United States points out the importance of a thorough understanding of crustal movement. Earthquakes occur all over the surface of Earth and have also been recorded on other bodies in our solar system. The potential for economic and human disaster is enormous. The major goals in the understanding of earthquakes are the prediction of three important pieces of information. The prediction would include the potential place an earthquake would occur, the predicted magnitude or size of the quake, and the time frame in which the shaking could be expected. Knowledge of all areas of the sciences is crucial to fully understand this most complex and potentially lethal reaction created by the enormous stresses that occur within the earth.

d) Marine Geology—The marine geologist is sometimes called the geological oceanographer. This scientist uses the tools and knowledge of both fields to further understanding of the sea floor, land forms and their formation. An understanding of tectonics assists this type of science specialist. Also needed is knowledge of tides, currents, and geomorphology of sea floor features. Knowledge of paleoclimates helps in the

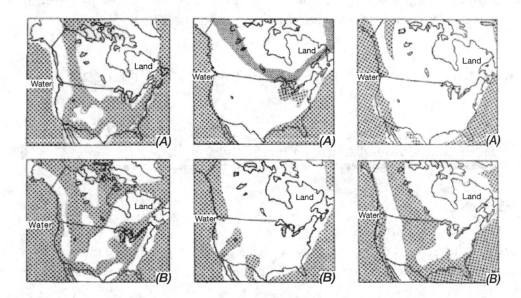

understanding of sea level fluctuations and changes in coastal topography. The use of computers and modeling also assists the marine geologist as the volumes of new data to be assimilated and understood is massive.

e) Planetology—The study of our solar system begins with an extensive knowledge of our planet, Earth. We have found many similarities between Earth and our surrounding neighbors. The composition of other moons and planets has provided insight into the processes that formed our planet. Rivers and erosion, glaciers, volcanics, and tectonics are some of the phenomena observed in our exploration of the solar system. The staggering amount of data collected in recent decades is still being processed and reevaluated. Ideas are formulated and hypotheses changed due to new input and understanding. The possible visual and mathematical observation of a new solar system beyond our own has broken open the future possibilities for planetologists.

f) Climatology—Weather can be defined as the short-term changes in the atmospheric conditions near the surface of Earth. Climate, on the other hand, consists of the long-term conditions that affect land masses, plants, animals, and humans. Rainfall and temperature are two of the components of the study of climatology. Past and future trends in climate are a concern of this science. Modeling and computers are fundamental in working with systems and trends within the atmosphere of Earth. The air and its interaction with oceans and land masses increase our understanding of complex patterns and systems. The influx of solar energy is also of primary importance in the study of climatology. Knowledge gained can be applied to atmospheric systems on other planets and moons as well. As more information is gained and understood, greater application of climatic models can be made for Earth and all bodies in the solar system.

Scientific Method—How Scientists Attack Problems

● PROBLEM 1–7

What is the purpose of the scientific method?

SOLUTION:

"Scientific method" is a general term used to describe the lines of inquiry and reasoning that scientists use to solve problems and explain observed events or phenomena. The method may include inductive and/

or deductive reasoning based on observation and analysis of information. The heart of the method is the hypothesis which is an educated guess that seems to explain the phenomena. If a hypothesis can, over a period of time, withstand criticism and the burden of proof, then it may become a scientific theory or even a scientific law.

● PROBLEM 1–8

What is the scientific method, and how do scientists use it to attack problems and find solutions?

SOLUTION:

A scientist may approach a problem from several directions, but most angles of attack start with a hypothesis. The hypothesis is a well directed, educated proposition or solution that is tentatively assumed to be correct. Once the hypothesis is stated, the scientist then will test it for validity as compared to observed facts, experimentation, and observations. The true strength of the hypothesis is not so much the mass of evidence to support it but rather the ability of the concept to withstand attack and criticism once the hypothesis is published for peer review. If the concept/idea can over a period of time withstand the pressures and scrutiny of the scientific community and still prove to be valid, then the hypothesis can be used to predict the outcomes of future experiments.

● PROBLEM 1–9

Why define or be concerned with the scientific method and how might the average person use the scientific method to solve everyday problems?

SOLUTION:

The scientific method is not just a body of knowledge, but is more a manner or mode of thinking. The sense of wonder that humans intrinsically possess seems to provide a natural funnel for the process called the scientific method. The attempt is made to observe and gather information and data as it relates to an event. Analysis and synthesis of information is critical. This information is then processed to help infer a solution to a given problem or perhaps just a general understanding of the observed event. The method is also used to make many other "everyday" decisions as information is processed and conclusions made in the day-to-day world. The strength or validity of the decision (hypothesis) depends on the volume and accuracy of data used to process the decision. Sometimes the hypothesis is correct and a good decision is made. At other times the decision is poor possibly due to bad data, or just a poorly constructed hypothesis. In any case, the decision maker must start the thought process over and build a new working hypothesis.

The decision-making process for a person includes observation, gathering fact, prediction, and trial and error. These are all steps that scientists follow. The purpose is to make a decision based on a hypothesis. Perhaps the decision is not a good one and the hypothesis proves to be null. Then the process starts over as the hypothesis is revised and new data is considered to help make the decision. Any decision a person makes, from a simple walk across the street to the purchase of a new car, requires a hypothesis based on observation and evidence.

● PROBLEM 1–10

Explain how a scientific theory is different than a hypothesis.

SOLUTION:

A hypothesis is an educated guess based on observation and evidence. The facts as they are understood are interpreted and a "guesstimate" is made. The hypothesis is then tested against the real world to see if it will hold up to scrutiny. The survival of any hypothesis depends on the strength of the data to support it. If, over time, a hypothesis withstands criticism from the scientific world, it then may be considered to be a theory. A theory is an accepted truth that becomes a cornerstone for the work of others. Occasionally, the "truths" through time, criticism, or new information are found to be untrue or inaccurate. If this is found to be so, the theory can be modified or thrown out. Generally, a theory withstands the test of time very well with possibly some slight modification. Science considers concepts and ideas with great scrutiny before they approach theory status. By the time an idea reaches that plateau, it is generally accepted as a scientific truth.

Describe some important functions in scientific thought.

SOLUTION:

Observation and analysis are very important functions in the scientific world. The function of science is to make the mysterious understandable for all. The process that makes the real world understandable is that of critical thought. A mystery is only a mystery until the puzzle is solved through inductive or deductive thought. Data is accumulated and organized and used to support a proposed hypothetical solution. This can allow others to investigate and draw their own conclusions. The interplay of ideas and hypotheses is fundamental to scientific thought, and is welcomed by mainstream scientists. The publication of papers and presentation of ideas at conferences allows mass exposure of new ideas to the scientific population. Through discussion and adjustment, ideas either evolve and become strengthened or are discarded.

Explain how earth scientists attempt to explain the past history of the Earth while researching in the present.

SOLUTION:

James Hutton is generally accepted as the founding father of geology. He described a universally accepted principal that the "present is the key to the past." This concept is known as uniformitarianism. With this idea, scientists can use the environments and elements of Earth today and compare this world of today to that of the past. The assumption is that the basic principles of the physical world are the same throughout geologic time and that comparisons of today to the past can provide insight into past geologic events. Uniformitarianism is useful for understanding the Earth's past and also for predicting future geologic events. The processes we see today will also apply to the future.

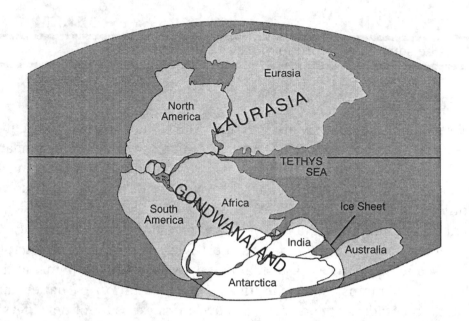

Explain why some scientific concepts might not be readily accepted though they may appear to be factually sound.

SOLUTION:

An example of this can be seen in the lack of acceptance of the early theories of plate tectonics first called continental drift. German scientist Alfred Wegner proposed in 1915, that all continents were joined in the past to form a supercontinent he called Pangaea. Wegner based his theory on several important pieces of evidence. First were fossils of a reptile called Mesosaurus that were found on two separate continents, which he deducted could only have lived on both land masses when they were directly connected. Similar fossils of plants also supported the supercontinent theory. Tropical plant fossils found in Greenland and Antarctica suggested that past climates in these areas were much different than today. Further evidence of glacial action in tropical and desert areas where glaciers do not exist today helped to support his ideas. The final clue to the structure of Pangaea could be seen in the similar rock structures found on separate continents. Strata of rock found in Africa and South America supported the theory as did similar rock units in Greenland, Western Europe, and North America. Though Wegner's theory seemed to have much supporting evidence, he could not explain why or how the continents moved. The lack of a mechanism or driving force for continental drift doomed the acceptance of this radical theory. Many closed their minds to the new idea, and it was forgotten until the mid 1950s when new evidence from the deep ocean floor was discovered.

A more recent example of this phenomenon is a new theory as to the extinction of dinosaurs at the end of the Mesozoic Era. Many possibilities have been suggested as to the cause of the demise of these great animals. Theories include changing climates, both warmer and cooler, which would have affected the living environments as well as the vegetative food sources. Some propose that the breakup of Pangaea would be enough to shift climates and weather and cause massive extinction of the dinosaurs. Others suggest that the zenith of these species was simply over and that the extinctions were inevitable for species that had achieved the pinnacle of evolutionary success. A newer theory suggests that the cause of the massive die off is extraterrestrial in origin. The theory proposed by father and son team Walter and Luis Alvarez identifies a collision between Earth and a large rocky chunk of space debris as the cause of the Cretaceous extinctions. The asteroid collision would have ejected massive amounts of particulates into the atmosphere. The dust may have blocked solar radiation and drastically altered climate worldwide. This so called "nuclear winter" would have resulted in the extinction of most of the species alive on Earth according to its authors. This theory is being subjected to the same scrutiny that all new ideas are, and some people may have rejected it without full consideration.

● PROBLEM 1–14

Explain how science and technology have changed the world for the better and describe the challenges and problems they have presented us for the future.

SOLUTION:

The wonders and discoveries of science have changed the status of humanity greatly in modern times. Our ability to manipulate the natural world has allowed us to change our lifestyle and dramatically alter civilization. It is obvious that we no longer live and toil as our ancestors once did. Much of this change is due to the input of science and the influence of new technology. Examples of this can be easily seen in agriculture, communication, transportation, and medicine. The other side of the technological coin however is the responsibility which comes with new discovery. New technology can also bring with it new problems. Environmental issues now command international focus. Ozone depletion and greenhouse gasses are hot topics of debate. Global warming or cooling, depending on which set of data is being presented, provides much scholarly dialectic. Energy and resource use is critical to modern civilization, yet the depletion and eventual disappearance of these is a major concern to society. Science has an obligation to society and mother earth to balance technologic change with environmental responsibility.

● PROBLEM 1–15

Describe the correlation between science and scientific technology.

SOLUTION:

Science is the process in which the real world is observed in an attempt to understand sequence and connections in nature. Ideas and discoveries are then translated by humans into what we call technology. Scientific technology is the application of science for the benefit of the general population. The television, microwave oven, and the car are common examples of this scientific application. Computers, nails, electricity, medicine: these are also examples of technological application of science. To solve a problem, science and technology provide answers.

SHORT ANSWER QUESTIONS FOR REVIEW

Choose the correct answer.

1. The survival of the planet Earth could possibly be based on the study of the (a) eclipse occurrences. (b) sun and moon relationships. (c) solar system. (d) galaxies.

2. A theory can be defined as (a) an educated guess. (b) an invention of the human mind. (c) a possible idea that would lead to scientific explanation. (d) a scientific explanation.

3. A person who studies the stars is called a(n) (a) astrologer. (b) astronomer. (c) astrophysicist. (d) star searcher.

4. One of the disciplines used by geologists to better understand the materials formation and the working of the earth's processes through time is (a) carbon-14 dating. (b) geochronology. (c) paleontology. (d) both (b) and (c).

5. A natural philosopher who first studied the relative position of the land and sea fluctuations and realized it took place over a long period of time was (a) Plato. (b) Leonardo. (c) Aristotle. (d) Democritus.

Fill in the blanks.

6. The scientific method is based on a _____ which is generally referred to as an educated guess.

7. _____ must be recorded completely and correctly to insure correct data that can be duplicated and verified.

8. _____ is the study of conditions in the free atmosphere anywhere away from the ground.

9. A person who studies the lay of the land (mountain, valleys, lakes, and streams), their placements, and distances from a certain point is called a _____.

10. A theory of Earth's origin that studies the shifting of plates at Earth's core is _____.

Determine whether the following statements are true or false.

11. Earth science deals with the origin, composition, and physical features of Earth such as geology, geography, meteorology, and oceanography.

12. Aerology is a branch of mineralogy.

13. Meteorology is the study of Earth's atmosphere that includes the day-to-day variations of weather conditions as well as weather conditions over an extended period of time.

14. The principles of scientific research and experimentation is called the scientific method.

15. Geology is the study of mineralogy that includes the identification of minerals, but not a study of their properties, origins, and classification.

ANSWER KEY

1. c
2. d
3. b
4. d
5. c
6. hypothesis
7. observations
8. Aerology

9. topographer
10. continental drift
11. True
12. False
13. True
14. True
15. False

CHAPTER 2

TOPOGRAPHY

Topographic Maps and Contour Maps

● PROBLEM 2-1

Of what use are topographic maps to earth scientists?

SOLUTION:

A topographic map consists of contour lines connected to represent equal elevation above sea level, and thus show the contrasts of height of an area through its hills and valleys. The map becomes a model for the geography and underlying geology of the region represented and thus is an important tool for the earth scientist. The map, on a smaller, more workable scale, can be a valuable tool for planning and research in a classroom or lab. Data gathered and ideas proposed from using the topographic map as a scale model can then be transferred to the real world to assist the scientist with research.

● PROBLEM 2-2

What can a topographic map indicate about the geology of a region and describe how the past history of an area may be interpreted through a topographic map.

SOLUTION:

The elevation or lack of elevation can be an indicator of the underlying

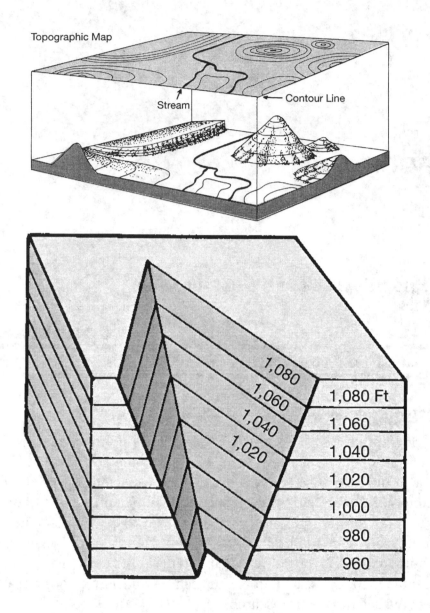

Topographic Map

Stream

Contour Line

1,080
1,060
1,040
1,020

1,080 Ft
1,060
1,040
1,020
1,000
980
960

geology of an area. Conical peaks suggest a volcanic area, whereas dendritic tree branch type drainage indicates sedimentary or glacial deposits. The type of drainage, slope, or vegetation in an area is also a general clue as to the types of rock structure found beneath a given area. An earth scientist can determine much about an area based on the observable topography.

A large contour interval indicates uplift through tectonic activity. This would suggest close proximity to a plate boundary. Areas lacking a large relief could be considered to be inactive and have been erosional surfaces for some time. Various types of erosional patterns will also define the rock

18

structure below as resistant and nonresistant rock types have characteristic surface drainage as well as landforms and topography.

Primary Highway, Hard Surface		Index Contour
Secondary Highway, Hard Surface		Supplementary Contour
Light-duty Road, Hard or Improved Surface		Intermediate Contour
Unimproved Road		Depression Contours
Railroad: Single & Multiple Tracks		
Railroads in Juxtaposition		Boundaries: National
		State
		County, Parish, Municipality
Buildings		Civil Township, Precinct, Town, Barrio
School, Church, & Cemetary	cem	Incorporated City, Village, Town, Hamlet
Buildings (Barn, Warehouse, Etc.)		Reservation, National or State
Wells Other Than Water (Labeled as to Type)	o oil o gas	Small Park, Cemetary, Airport, Etc.
	water	
Tanks: Oil, Water, Etc. (Labeled Only if Water)		Land Grant
Located or Landmark Object; Windmill		Township or Range Line, United States Survey
Open Pit, Mine, or Quarry; Prospect		Township or Range Line, Approximate Location
Marsh (Swamp)		Perennial Streams
Wooded Marsh		Elevated Aqueduct
Woods or Brushwood		Water Well and Spring
Vineyard		Small Rapids
Land Subject to Controlled Inundation		Large Rapids
Submerged Marsh		Intermittent Lake
Mangrove		Intermittent Streams
Orchard		Aqueduct Tunnel
Scrub		Glacier
Urban Area		Small Falls
Spot Elevation	× 7369	Large Falls
Water Elevation	670	Dry Lake Bed

● PROBLEM 2–3

A topographic map has a contour interval of 100 feet. Between point A and point B there are seven contour lines. What is the change in elevation between points A and B on this topographic map?

SOLUTION:

The change in elevation would be calculated by multiplying seven times the contour interval of 100 feet. The change in elevation is thus 700 feet from point A to B. The relief of the map is not indicated by this problem as the question does not include information about the base elevation of the map. The large contour interval does indicate that this is an area with a rapid change in elevation as a contour interval of ten or 20 feet would be used in an area with lesser relief.

● PROBLEM 2–4

City A rests on a contour line that indicates 2,300 feet. City B rests on a contour line for 1,950 feet. If the contour interval of the map is 50 feet, how many contour lines would be counted between city A and B?

SOLUTION:

The change in elevation between cities is 350 feet. By dividing the difference in elevation by the contour interval, the number of contour lines (seven) can be calculated.

● PROBLEM 2–5

Why would a contour map use a contour interval of 80' per line?

SOLUTION:

The 80 foot interval is necessary because of the rapid increases and decreases in elevation found on the map. Any interval less then 80' would have resulted in so many lines being on the map that they would blend together in a blur. It may have been prudent to even use a larger interval such as 100' per contour. The appropriate interval must be selected based on the elevation changes found in the area of the map.

Use the following topographic map section to answer problems 2–6 through 2–9.

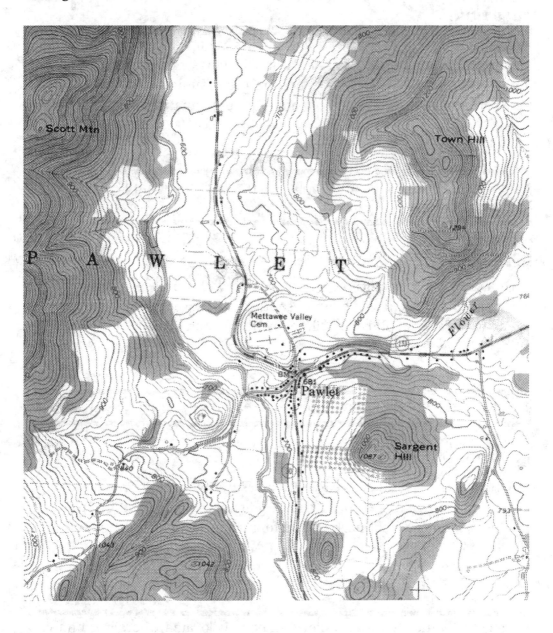

What do the tight contour lines on Scott Mountain represent as compared to Sargent Hill?

SOLUTION:

The closeness of the contour lines shows Scott Mountain to be a steep terrain as compared to Sargent Hill. The close proximity of the lines indicates a rapid change in elevation on the mountain. The wider spaces between the lines on the hill indicate a more gradual change in elevation.

● PROBLEM 2-7

On a map such as this topographic map, which direction is which, and how can one tell?

SOLUTION:

Unless otherwise indicated up on a map will represent north. West is left, east is right, and, of course, south is at the bottom of the map. A majority of maps of all types will follow this general rule.

● PROBLEM 2-8

What do the initials BM represent as seen on the west side of Pawlet?

SOLUTION:

A bench mark (BM) is a carefully measured elevation above sea level. The numbers to the east of BM represent the actual elevation in feet of 681 feet Another bench mark can be found southeast of Sargent Hill at an elevation of 795 feet.

● PROBLEM 2-9

Predict why the Mettawee Valley Cemetary is located where it is on this map.

SOLUTION:

Due to a lack of contour lines in this area of the map, it can be assumed that the topography is level and unobstructed. There is also no river or stream in the direct area so flooding from the hills is not a concern.

Use the following topographic map section to answer problems 2–10 through 2–12.

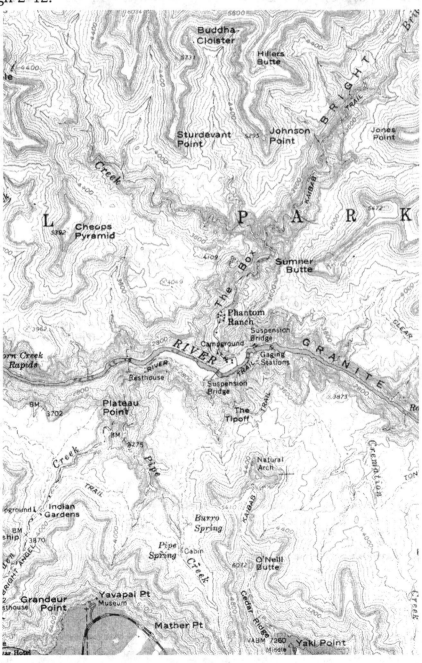

Locate the highest elevation on this map section. What leads you to believe that it is the highest elevation?

SOLUTION:

Town Hill shows an elevation of 1,294 feet at the X on the southern peak of the hill. It could be assumed that this is the highest elevation on the map. Be sure to check the elevation of Scott Mountain before making an assumption about the 1,294 elevation. Notice on Scott Mountain that the contour lines in the northwest corner of the map show elevations of 800', 900', 1,000', and so on. By counting the number of lines between the hundred foot intervals, it can be deduced that each line represents 20' in the real world. Starting at the last known contour line of 1,000 feet, count the number of contour lines and multiply by 20'. The elevation of Scott Mountain is about 1,600' according to this topographic map.

● PROBLEM 2-11

Locate the BM to the west of Plateau Point. What does the elevation there tell you when compared to the elevation found at Yaki Point in the south central part of the map?

SOLUTION:

With a contour interval of 80' per contour line, the change in elevation in just this distance of about two miles is 3,500'. The tight packing of the contour lines is a give away as to the rapid elevation change on this map.

● PROBLEM 2-12

Speculate as to the nature of the deep valleys and rivers found on this topographic map.

SOLUTION:

Even without knowing that this area is found within the Grand Canyon, it is possible to speculate as to the reasons for such a rough landscape.

The sharp buttes and points indicate rapid erosion possibly by a massive uplift in the area. As the river starts to erode back down to base/sea level, the canyon walls are eroded and steep slopes form.

Map Reading and Usage

● PROBLEM 2–13

What is the historical reason for the study of maps?

SOLUTION:

It has been very important throughout the history of civilization to map boundaries and other territories. The expansion and acquisition of new lands has been of utmost importance to all civilizations. Maps have been very useful to humans as a method to keep track of positions, movement, and resource location. The map, as a tool, has proved to be invaluable to humans as a method to categorize information into a small model representation of the real world.

● PROBLEM 2–14

Evaluate the significance of maps and explain the advantages and disadvantages of map reading and usage.

SOLUTION:

As small scale models of the real world maps are significant to many disciplines in the sciences. Geologists depend heavily on topographic and geologic maps. Oceanographic and hydrographic maps are invaluable for research as are weather and climate maps. City planners look to maps to determine areas for industrial and home zoning, recreational areas, flood control, and ground water flow, as well as soil management problems. Maps can be used by many types of people for multiple purposes and therefore are very valuable tools for scientists.

The main advantage of map usage is that a smaller representation of the object studied is represented by the map. The purpose of a model such as a map or globe is to scale down an area into terms that are easier to understand, or to see the "big" picture on a smaller scale. This can in many cases make an area, state, country, or planet, easier to comprehend as far as real size, landforms, shape, and topography.

A main disadvantage of maps is that the scale is reduced and thus much of the fine detail may be lost due to the size reduction. The advantages and disadvantages must be weighed and considered when using any model. Scientists feel the advantages are worth the inconvenience that may arise if one understands the drawbacks of the map type being used and for what purposes that type of map was selected.

● PROBLEM 2–15

Describe a few of the map types used by scientists and explain why scientists might use those types of maps.

SOLUTION:

Basic map types include road and topographic maps. Other types of maps include ocean and lake current maps, bathymetric, and environmental hazards maps. Weather and climate maps are of great assistance to the general population also. Of a more specialized nature are infrared, magnetic, and gravity anomaly maps. The range of map types is great, and each map style is significant to the type of research being conducted.

Of the types of maps already discussed, all types are valuable to scientists. The strength of a map is not based on the particular map itself, but on an interdependent comparison with other maps containing important information. The three-dimensional interference of any map along with the experience of the scientist will allow for an accurate interpretation of data and concepts. All types of maps and globes can be used by a scientist, and many different types are used.

● PROBLEM 2–16

Of what general use would a map be to a scientist in a new geographic area?

SOLUTION:

Aside from general location and orientation in the new situation, other useful data could be obtained from the map, no matter what type it was.

A highway map would help to suggest the landforms and topography of the area. It could also outline vegetation, drainage patterns, and population locations. From these bits of information a general idea of soil type, drainage, geologic substructure, and possible tectonic activity could be inferred.

● PROBLEM 2-17

Do we use longitude or latitude to determine direction east or west?

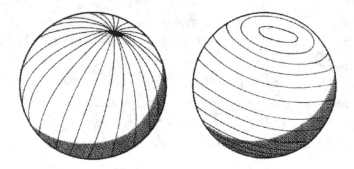

SOLUTION:

Lines of longitude stretch the "long" distance from pole to pole and divide the Earth into sections that are either east or west of a set designation. Latitude lines divide the Earth from the equator to the poles both north and south.

● PROBLEM 2-18

In the past decade a relatively new science known as Geographic Information Systems (GIS) has grown in scope and importance. Relate the functions and goals of GIS.

SOLUTION:

Global interest in GIS has grown rapidly since the early 1980s. GIS is a way to integrate information in a way that facilitates decision making. GIS allows an operator to design and develop a database that can be used to address a number of different topical areas. Current areas of study by various GIS systems include: tropical deforestation, acid rain, rapid urbanization, overpopulation, hunger and famine, diseases, and the impact of changes in global climates.

● PROBLEM 2–19

How did Geographic Information Systems integrate into the scientific community and help researchers better understand problems and issues?

SOLUTION:

The strength of GIS is that it allows an operator to develop and design a digital spatial database. This pool of information assists analysis and can be used to generate maps, graphs, and reports. The computers and software used make the entry and storage of data easier than before, and users can cover more diverse areas. Some specific areas that are being studied under GIS include satellite data, government planning and zoning, municipal property access, land records, parcel mapping, and areas of public safety.

● PROBLEM 2–20

What advantages does GIS present over more traditional geographic and cartographic methods?

SOLUTION:

GIS is not simply mapmaking through computers. The hardware and software can isolate data on any or all information in the database. Some areas that could be analyzed for data include locations, conditions, trends, patterns, and modeling. The database can produce reports, spreadsheets, and maps. The strength of GIS systems is the ability of the system to link data sets and allow for in-depth data evaluation.

● PROBLEM 2–21

How are some countries currently using Geographic Information Systems?

SOLUTION:

Currently Great Britain uses GIS for land registration as well as keeping environmental database information up to date. Utility system operation and efficiency are also monitored and updated. Perhaps a most ambitious undertaking is the development and upgrading of a topographic database of England. China and Japan are monitoring and modeling environmental changes and issues. Canada uses GIS for forestry applications and measuring timber volumes, types, and accessibility. The results and predictions are published or reported to the appropriate agencies. In the United States, the census bureau invested $170 million in GIS technology to assist in taking, analyzing, and reporting the 1990 census. Studies are underway to analyze U.S. transportation networks and usage. Topologically Integrated Geographical Encoding and Reference (TIGER) is used by both the census bureau and the geologic survey to access their data. Other applications include fish and wildlife planning, management of forests, coasts, and recreational and agricultural areas, as well as mineral inventories and energy management.

● PROBLEM 2-22

Predict the future of Geographic Information Systems use throughout the world in the next decade.

SOLUTION:

GIS experts foresee billions of dollars being spent in the next decade in the U.S. alone. Being a relatively new field in science, demand is growing for operators and GIS systems for many different technological fields. The prices of hardware and software are diminishing and the tools of GIS are becoming commonplace in business, government, and education. Considering the breadth of topics and data that can be analyzed, it is not surprising that this field is expanding at such an explosive rate.

Road Maps

● **PROBLEM 2-23**

What type of information would one expect to find on a road map, why would it be valuable for earth science, and list specific types of information an earth scientist could interpret from road maps.

SOLUTION:

A geologist may have the most use for standard road maps of all the earth scientists. This type of scientist will be looking for areas of exposed rock called outcrops where samples can be easily observed and collected. The geologist may collect rocks and minerals in this manner. A paleontologist who studies fossils may also collect fresh samples from roadcuts.

Aside from the basic location information available on a road map, some additional information can also be interpreted. The legend of this type of map is very significant to interpretation, as is the location structures and other types of features. The legend will include information on the road types, scale, parks, historical features, and natural wonders.

The most obvious types of data that can be interpreted from a road map include the location of cities and municipalities. Additional information will include locations of drainage and water systems. Also important are elevations, populations, and road systems. From this type of map area drainage and river and lake orientation could also be interpreted. The hydrologic information listed could also be used to infer rock types and geology below. An earth scientist can use the basic road map information to coincide with other types of map information to create a broad and clear picture of the area under study.

● **PROBLEM 2-24**

What are some of the problems associated with the use of road maps?

SOLUTION:

A basic understanding of the limitations of road maps is essential. This type of map can be of use, but cannot be an exclusive source of information. The scale of such maps will make the small area represented a close approximation for the real earth. This information used with geologic and environmental maps will allow for greater interpretation of the area.

● **PROBLEM 2–25**

If a road map has a scale of one inch equals 50,000 inches, how far apart in miles is city A from city B with a map distance between them of 5.5 inches?

SOLUTION:

The distance between cities A and B, in inches, is equal to the product of 50,000 (scale per inch) and 5.5 (275,000 inches). We divide by 12 (inches/foot) to find that this distance is 22,916.67 feet. Dividing by 5,280 (feet/mile), we find the distance to equal 4.34 miles.

● **PROBLEM 2–26**

A highway map legend includes the information: 1" = 1,013,760". In miles, how much distance is represented by one inch on this map?

SOLUTION:

The process to convert inches to miles is a simple one. First, the number 1,013,760 needs to be converted to feet by dividing by 12. Next, the total number of feet needs to be converted to miles by dividing by 5,280 feet per mile. The scale listed in the legend of this highway map indicates that one inch on paper equals 16 miles in the real world.

Geologic Survey Maps

● **PROBLEM 2–27**

Explain the types of information that may be revealed by geologic maps.

SOLUTION:

Geologic maps represent the rock formations of an area as they would be seen with all the vegetation and topsoil scraped off. The bedrock formations below the soil and plants have been mapped by using drill logs from geologic survey crews as well as the records of private companies searching for water supplies deep underground. All the data available is correlated to give a three-dimensional model of the rock types and rock structures below the surface of the earth.

● **PROBLEM 2–28**

How are geologic map models used for resource exploration? Explain how a geologic map could be used to identify the age of rock units in an area and describe how geologic ages of rock strata are determined for geologic maps.

SOLUTION:

This type of modeling is used for resource exploration within various rock units. Natural gas and petroleum traps, coal formations, minerals, ores, and many other natural resources may be found in this manner. The geologic map may also be used to infer the contacts between rock units where movement may occur. The forces that cause earthquakes and volcanoes can be better understood when a geologic map model is used for analysis of the region and the forces that cause these events.

The purpose of a geologic map is to identify the location and age of sub-surface rock units and the contacts between those units. An integral part of the geologic map is the legend used to identify the relative age of rock layers of the area as compared to the ages of other rock units in the map area. The major purpose of a geologic map is to determine the relative geologic age of rock units in a given area.

The relative and absolute ages of rock layers are checked and compared over the course of many years. As new techniques and concepts are introduced, the accepted values of the dates for fossils and rock strata are refined and adjusted to the increased precision of the new techniques. The dates for these rock units are determined through radiometric dating of radioactive isotopes and their decay rates. The change of a radioactive parent element to a daughter element is measured and ratios of the elements compared. The absolute dates obtained are then compared to the relative dates of any fossils found in the area. These relative dates are compared to other fossil assemblages containing the same types of fossils and the ages are compared as well. These fossils can also be radiometrically dated for another cross reference as to the geologic dates.

● **PROBLEM 2-29**

How might a person benefit from information contained in a geologic map if he or she wishes to build a home or industry?

SOLUTION:

The basic information included in a geologic map could help a consumer to make a decision about the purchase of land in a given area. Data contained in this type of map could include faults, fractures, and active geologic areas within the region. Other information might include groundwater supplies, water access and flow, and environmental areas of concern to the consumer as well. To feel comfortable with the purchase of land in an area, many geologic factors should be considered and evaluated.

● **PROBLEM 2-30**

Geologic mapping in the solar system has been a goal of the space program for decades. What purpose would this information serve to earth scientists?

SOLUTION:

The mapping of other planets and moons has given earth scientists an opportunity to do extensive comparative geology. The principle of uniformitarianism can allow for planet and moon comparisons within our solar system. The new planetary data gained from Pioneer, Viking, and Voyager has allowed science to peer out at the solar system and do comparison planetology to better understand Earth and the evolution of planets.

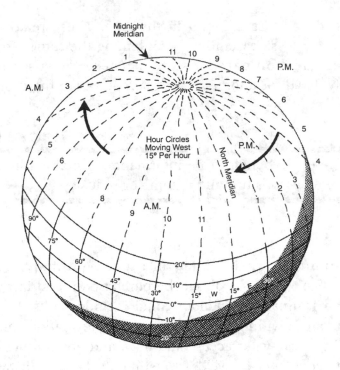

Globes

● PROBLEM 2–31

Of what use to scientists are globes?

SOLUTION:

The usefulness of globes as small models is universal. The globe is a small scale, three-dimensional representation of a planetary body. The smaller size makes it easier to visualize the entire surface. A globe can be used for locations on Earth as well as for comparison to other planetary globes.

● PROBLEM 2–32

What are the advantages and disadvantages of using a globe versus using a map?

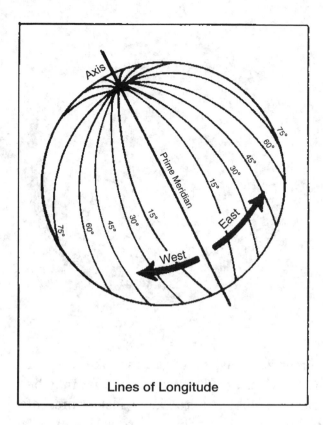

Lines of Longitude

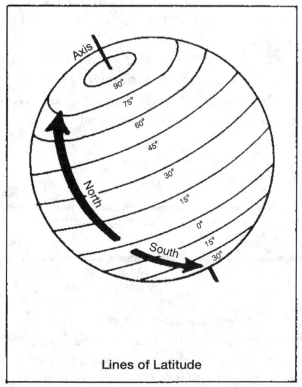

Lines of Latitude

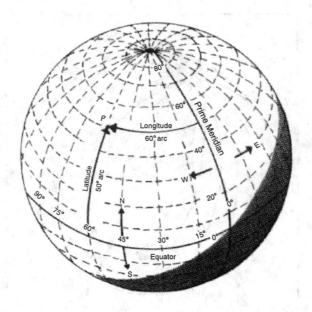

SOLUTION:

The three-dimensional aspect of globes makes them useful tools because they can provide actual world comparisons that may be easier to visualize and understand. The globe is a true large-scale representation of Earth with little distortion that one might find when working with a large-scale map. A map may provide useful information as well and could be used in conjunction with a globe.

The small size that makes a globe a valuable tool also provides some drawbacks. The loss of scale will also provide a loss of the fine detail that a smaller scale map would provide. As with any tool or model the strengths and weaknesses should be understood so that the correct tool is used for the job at hand.

● PROBLEM 2–33

Why would you need both latitude and longitude to determine exact locations on the globe?

SOLUTION:

The exact location of a place or object would have to be reported so that location east or west was known as well as location north or south. Latitude and longitude grid systems divide the Earth so that a specific location anywhere on the globe can be pinpointed with a certain degree of accuracy. The location north/south from the equator and east/west from the prime meridian can be accurately reported and an object's location can be determined.

● PROBLEM 2-34

A globe has a scale of 1":10,000,000". What does this indicate about the scale of the globe?

SOLUTION:

This scale indicates that one inch on the surface of the globe represents 10,000,000 inches in the real world. To work out the math, 10,000,000 would need to be divided by 12 inches/foot. The resulting number would then need to be divided by the number of feet per mile, 5,280. The resulting math shows that on this globe one inch equals 157.8 miles on the surface of the globe. Standard earth globes have a scale roughly set at about 1:41,849,600, or 660 miles per inch.

● PROBLEM 2-35

How do globes as models of a planetary body assist scientists?

SOLUTION:

Earth scientists have just begun to understand the geology of other planetary objects in our solar system. The reconnaissance missions to other planets and moons have delivered a wealth of information that is still being analyzed and interpreted today. Our new understandings of crustal movement and plate interactions on Earth have been used for comparative geology with Mars, Venus, the Moon, and the moons of Jupiter and Saturn.

● PROBLEM 2-36

How might information found on planetary globes be used in the future?

SOLUTION:

Many experts feel that the new information gained from our space missions and probes will keep scientists busy well into the twenty-first century. This planetary information has been transferred to small scale models called globes. These models can be used for quick and easy reference for planets and moons. This new data can also be used to better understand the geology of our planet through comparison and contrasts of landform features.

SHORT ANSWER QUESTIONS FOR REVIEW

Choose the correct answer.

1. An axis is (a) a connecting line at the equator. (b) a connecting line between the poles. (c) a connecting line between orbits. (d) a pole.

2. As a study of the surface of the earth, topography consists of an understanding of (a) altitudes. (b) elevations. (c) mean sea level. (d) all of the above.

3. Many geologists use maps as model representations of the surface of the earth. These maps consist of (a) latitude and longitude. (b) declination and hashures. (c) all of the above. (d) none of the above.

4. Latitude is the distance in degrees north or south of the equator. The latitude of the equator is zero degrees, and the poles are at 90 degrees. Longitude is the distance in degrees east or west of the prime meridian. The meridians are semicircles drawn around the globe from pole to pole. Which statement is true? (a) The distance between latitude lines increases as you move toward the poles. (b) The distance between longitude lines increases as you move toward the poles. (c) The distance between latitude lines decreases as you move toward the poles. (d) The distance between longitude lines decreases as you move toward the poles.

5. On the map below, which letter shows the location of Hardy's Mountain?

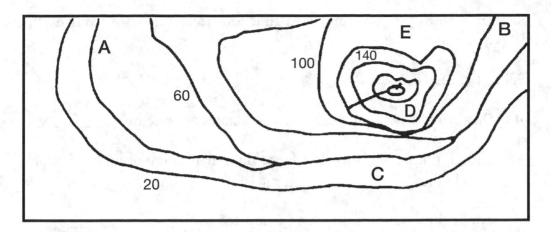

6. Which of the following is usually used with a topographical map? (a) Photograph (b) Flashlight (c) Compass (d) Brush

Determine whether the following statements are true or false.

7. An alidade is the name of a surveying tool.

8. Contour lines are used in mapmaking. Contour lines give exact elevation above sea level and show the shape of the land at the same time. When contour lines cross, this indicates the top of a hill or mountain.

Items 9 and 10 refer to the following map.

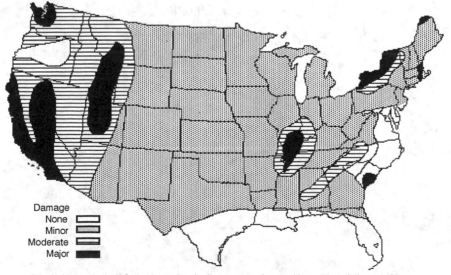

Seismic risk map for the U.S. showing earthquake damage areas of reasonable expectancy in the next 100 years (Derived from U.S. Coast and Geodetic Survey, ESSA Rel. ES-1, January 14, 1969.

9. Data from the map indicates that few states are safe from earth-quakes.

Fill in the blanks.

10. Data from the map indicates that few states are safe from _____.

11. The proportion or ratio of distance on a map to the distance in reality is called _____.

12. The highest point in the world is located in _____.

13. The highest altitude on Earth is Mount Everest, which is _____ feet above sea level.

14. A _____ map might be a handy tool for an engineer.

ANSWER KEY

1. b	8. False
2. d	9. True
3. d	10. earthquakes
4. d	11. scale
5. d	12. Asia
6. a	13. 29,028
7. True	14. topographic

CHAPTER 3

THE LITHOSPHERE

The Layers of the Lithosphere

What is the lithosphere?

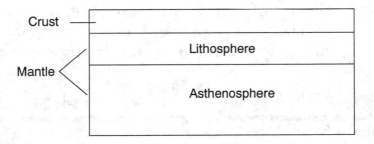

SOLUTION:

The outer 80 to 100 kilometers of the Earth is called the lithosphere. It is composed of the crust and the outermost portion of the mantle. The lithosphere is distinguished from other parts of the Earth by its rigid, brittle characteristics. Due to the rigidity, the lithosphere has little flexibility, and this causes many breaks and much movement in the crust. These breaks form plates which move toward, past, or away from each other due to convection currents produced below them in the mantle.

Describe the crust.

SOLUTION:

The thin, rocky outer layer of the Earth is the crust. Composed primarily of sedimentary rocks, the crust is layered and brittle. It varies in thickness from 5 to 8 km beneath the oceans to 24 to 48 km under the continents. The major surface area of the crust is found under the oceans of the Earth.

● **PROBLEM 3-3**

What is diastrophism?

SOLUTION:

The process in which the Earth's crust changes either slowly or rapidly is known as diastrophism or tectonism. Folding and faulting are the two main methods of diastrophism. Folding is the exertion of pressure upward on the crust usually resulting in mountains. Faulting is the process of plate movement in which uplifting, compression, or lengthening of the crust occurs. Faulting causes earthquakes when sudden movements occur.

● **PROBLEM 3-4**

Describe the asthenosphere.

SOLUTION:

The asthenosphere is an area of the mantle found below the lithosphere. It is a solid which has the property of plasticity. Plasticity is the ability of a solid to flow like a liquid. Glass and some plastics have this characteristic. Areas of the asthenosphere which are closer to the hot, liquid outer core are more fluid than those which are closer to the lithosphere.

● **PROBLEM 3-5**

What is isotasy?

SOLUTION:

The hypothesis that the solid crust is at equilibrium with itself and with the other layers of the Earth is a concept known as isotasy. The solid lithosphere moves over the molten asthenosphere in order to maintain an equilibrium to be established between the solid and liquid portions of the Earth. This forms the plastic zone, which is evident due to the area of the crust which does not break easily. The upper brittle crust breaks under pressure. The area below it, before reaching the asthenosphere, flows more easily yet it is not a liquid. This zone of plasticity allows the crust to be folded instead of broken when under plate stress. The process of gaining equilibrium is called plate movement. During plate movement, changes in the continents occur.

● **PROBLEM 3–6**

What are the differences between continental crust and oceanic crust?

SOLUTION:

Continental crust is believed to be much older than oceanic crust. Continental crust is over two billion years old. On the other hand, oceanic crust is only about 160 million years old. Low density granite composes most continental crust. Basalt, a high density rock, composes oceanic crust. These differences are probably due to the constant destruction of oceanic crust by subduction.

The Structure of the Earth

● **PROBLEM 3–7**

Explain the structure of the Earth.

SOLUTION:

The Earth is composed of three main layers: the core, the mantle, and the crust. The crust is the outermost layer. It is about 24 to 45 kilometers in thickness under the continents and 5 to 10 kilometers under the oceans. The Mohorovicic Discontinuity separates the crust from the mantle.

Divided into two parts, the mantle is a total of approximately 2,900

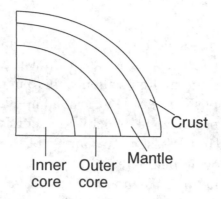

Inner core   Outer core   Mantle   Crust

kilometers thick. The upper mantle is divided into the lower portion of the lithosphere, which is very brittle and rigid. Below the lithosphere is an area of molten rock called the asthenosphere. Dividing the mantle from the core at a depth of approximately 2,800 km is the Gutenberg Discontinuity.

The outer core is a thick liquid of about 2,250 kilometers in thickness. The inner core is a solid believed to be composed of iron and nickel. It is about 1,200 kilometers in thickness.

● PROBLEM 3–8

How are the divisions of the accepted model of the Earth's structure determined?

SOLUTION:

The divisions of the Earth's structure are not easily seen since scientists cannot venture into the depths of the Earth. Scientists use information about earthquake waves to determine the differences in the phase of the materials in the Earth. Earthquake waves behave differently in different phases of matter. All waves produced by an earthquake travel through the crust without any hindrance. At the area between the crust and the mantle, body waves slow considerably. This area is termed the Mohorovicic Discontinuity.

At about 2,900 kilometers below the surface S waves stop or are deflected, and P waves slow down. This area is considered liquid since it has been found that the transverse wave movement of the S wave cannot travel through a liquid. This defines the area known as the Gutenberg Discontinuity, which separates the mantle from the core.

Describe the composition of the core, the mantle, and the crust.

SOLUTION:

The core is composed of two parts: the solid inner core and the liquid outer core. Due to the believed average density of 11 g/cm^3, the core is thought to be mostly metallic. Scientists theorize that the core is composed of mostly iron and nickel. The liquidity of the outer core is believed to be caused by the radioactive elements breaking down in the core, producing intense heat.

The mantle consists of rock with an average density of about 4.5 g/cm^3. This density indicates that iron and magnesium are the predominant elements found in the mantle.

Many different elements producing a variety of compounds are found in the crust. Rocks composed of minerals in various stages of weathering are found in the crust. In spite of the amount of knowledge available, not all of the crust has been studied, because major portions of the crust is found under the oceans at depths not easily attainable by scientists.

● PROBLEM 3-10

What is believed to have caused the heating within the Earth?

SOLUTION:

Radioactive elements such as uranium and thorium produced a great deal of heat as they decomposed. The heat buildup over time produced molten rock. The outer layers cooled after some of the heat escaped. This caused the outer core to remain molten rock. The inner core solidified because heavier metals with high melting points were deposited by the convection currents.

● PROBLEM 3-11

Describe the convection of magma.

SOLUTION:

The magma has been heated by radioactive elements within the core of the Earth. It then begins to flow through cracks in the rock layers of the Earth. As the magma cools, gravity pulls the heavier materials down. This process produces a convection current in the magma. These currents are usually found in convection cells. These cells are believed to cause the fluid motion of the asthenosphere.

● PROBLEM 3–12

How were the continents originally formed?

SOLUTION:

Most scientists believe that the Earth began as a molten mass. The heavier materials were pulled to the center as lighter materials moved to the outer areas. Once on the surface these materials cooled producing land masses. The heat from the core caused these newly formed landmasses to move. As they drifted they collided and parted many times over billions of years, finally producing the continents of today.

● PROBLEM 3–13

Describe how the configuration of bedrock is determined.

SOLUTION:

In order to determine the configuration of bedrock, outcrops of rock are studied. These outcrops are grouped into formations. Formations are rock layers which have similar characteristics. Contacts are rock layers which separate adjacent formations. Once these characteristics are determined, a geologic map can be made. The geologic map shows the configuration of bedrock.

● PROBLEM 3–14

What is the attitude of rock layers?

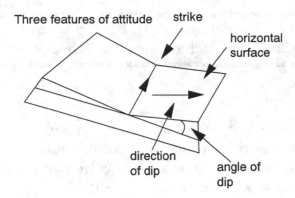

Three features of attitude — strike — horizontal surface — direction of dip — angle of dip

SOLUTION:

The attitude of rock layers is the orientation of an individual layer of rock. It is defined using three features: strike, the direction of dip, and the angle of dip. The strike is the angle an imaginary line has with the horizontal plane of the ground. The direction of dip is measured perpendicular to the strike. It is the direction the rock layer is from the horizontal. The angle of dip is formed by the rock layer and the horizontal surface. Combined, these descriptions are the attitude of a rock layer.

Wegener and Plate Tectonics

● **PROBLEM 3–15**

What is plate tectonics?

SOLUTION:

Plate tectonics is the concept that the upper portion of the Earth is composed of solid plates which move over the molten portion of the Earth, the asthenosphere. The solid portion, called the lithosphere, is broken into six major plates and many minor ones. These plates move toward, away from, or past each other forming the landmasses, earthquakes, mountains, and volcanic activity.

In 1960, an American geologist, H. H. Hess, proposed a theory called sea-floor spreading. What is the evidence which supports his theory?

SOLUTION:

The theory of sea-floor spreading, named by Robert Dietz in 1961, is based on the knowledge that the Mid-Oceanic Ridge is an area of great turmoil. Earthquakes and volcanoes occur frequently along the ridge, which runs through the major oceans of the Earth.

Molten rock from the mantle moves upward through the ocean's thin crust, forming the Mid-Oceanic Ridge. This movement causes the sea-floor to spread away from the ridge. Proof of this movement is the magnetic remnant in the iron rock formed along the ridge. This magnetic characteristic changes as the Earth's magnetism changes.

Another method of proving the theory of sea-floor spreading is the dating of rocks on the ocean floor. The older rocks are away from and on the bottom of the Mid-Oceanic Ridge; this is an indication that the sea-floor is spreading by the addition of new rock at the ridge.

● **PROBLEM 3–17**

Alfred Wegener restated the theory of continental drift in the early 1900s. Explain the theory.

SOLUTION:

The theory of continental drift states that the thin continents move over a molten layer of Earth beneath them. This movement began with the cooling of the Earth to form its solid layers. The continental drift theory today states that a large continent called Pangaea once existed. After this continent broke apart the sections began drifting, producing the continents known today.

● **PROBLEM 3–18**

What evidence exists to substantiate the theory of continental drift?

Much evidence indicates that continental drift does occur, and that at one time a giant continent called Pangaea existed. Similarities of species and fossils among the continents indicates that at one time the continents were joined in some manner.

Coastlines of the continents match as if they were the pieces to a jigsaw puzzle. South America and Africa seem to fit together. The Sierra Mountains of South America geologically match the Cape Mountains of South Africa. In North America, the Canadian Appalachian Mountains match with the Hebridges Mountains of Great Britain.

The glacial ice sheet that existed about 300 million years ago covered the southern portion of the southern hemisphere similar to the way the ice sheet covers Antarctica today. This indicates that the southern portion of the southern hemisphere landmasses must have been exposed to a polar climate. It is believed that they drifted north, away from the polar region.

● PROBLEM 3-19

What are magnetic anomalies?

SOLUTION:

Magnetic anomalies are changes in the magnetic direction of rocks produced along the Mid-Oceanic Ridge. These rocks are produced from the molten rock deep within the Earth. Lines parallel to the magnetic field of the Earth are formed in the rock as they cool. Moving away from the ridge causes changes in the direction of the lines. The changes indicate that the magnetic field of the Earth has changed over the years. The last change occurred about 700,000 years ago.

Pangaea, Laurasia, and Gondwanaland

● PROBLEM 3-20

Explain the formation of Pangaea.

SOLUTION:

Scientists believe that about 250 million years ago two large continents existed. These two continental masses moved toward each other until Laurasia, the northern continent, and Gondwanaland, the southern continent, collided. This collision produced large mountain ranges which ran along a single continent called Pangaea. Pangaea, meaning all-land, formed and later began breaking into smaller landmasses. The theory of continental drift restated by Alfred Wegener in 1912 explains the movement of continents throughout the history of Earth.

● PROBLEM 3-21

Explain the biological and geological evidence supporting the theory that Pangaea exists.

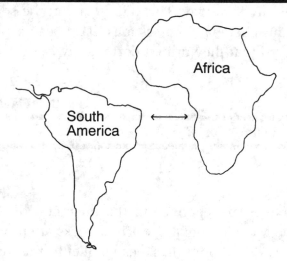

SOLUTION:

There are similarities of living species and identified fossils found in the continents of today that are the same. Fossils of the same type of reptiles are found in South America and Africa. Fossils of the same type of plants are found in India and Australia. These finds indicate that the landmasses were once connected.

There is a unique variety of garden snail found in the eastern part of the United States and western Europe. This snail is only found in the areas that were apparently once united.

The shapes of the continents and the mountain ranges of the continents allow a matching of the coastlines. Mountain ranges in North America and Europe match in strata and fossil remains in a manner that supports the idea that at one time these areas were joined.

Glacial evidence in the southern portion of the southern hemisphere indicates that the area was once exposed to a polar climate similar to that of Antarctica. Since both the southern portion of Africa and Australia show this characteristic, it is believed they were once united as a single continent.

● PROBLEM 3–22

What evidence supports the theory that Gondwanaland and Laurasia existed?

SOLUTION:

Mountain ranges are produced at the time two continents collide. There are mountain ranges on the North American continent which are similar in appearance and strata as those in western Europe. These mountain ranges are similar to those produced by the collision of two continental plates, such as the Indian plate subducting under the Eurasian plate. These two plates are producing the Himalayan Mountains. The mountain ranges in eastern North America and western Europe are not located at a subduction zone. Since they were probably produced by subduction it is believed they were once part of the same northern continent, Laurasia. In order for these mountain ranges to be produced, another continent must have existed. This continent is called Gondwanaland and existed as the southern continent which collided and subducted, producing the mountain ranges of the northern continent.

● PROBLEM 3–23

What modern continents formed from Laurasia and Gondwanaland?

SOLUTION:

Laurasia, the northern continent, and Gondwanaland, the southern continent collided to produce Pangaea. As Pangaea separated, the area that was Laurasia became North America, Europe, and Asia. Gondwanaland became India, Australia, Africa, South America, and Antarctica. These continents drifted to their current positions and are continuing to drift. It is believed that at some time in the future a new Pangaea will be formed as the continents reunite in the area known as the Pacific Ocean, which is slowly growing smaller.

The Major Plates of the Earth

● PROBLEM 3–24

What is a plate? What are the types of plate boundaries and where are most of them found? Why?

SOLUTION:

A portion of the rigid crust between 50 and 150 kilometers thick, which is believed to move, is called a plate. These plates are believed to move over the liquid asthenosphere. Geologists have identified approximately six major plates and 19 minor plates.

Three types of plate boundaries have been identified. Divergent boundaries are found where two plates are moving away from each other, such as the boundary found in the Mid-Oceanic Ridge. A convergent boundary is where two plates collide. One plate moves under the other plate, usually producing mountains. When two plates slide past each other a transform fault is found. This type of boundary is evident by the appearance of faults, such as the San Andrea's Fault in California.

Most plate boundaries are found along the oceanic crust at the coastlines of the continents. Since the oceanic crust is very thin and brittle, it is easily manipulated by the asthenosphere. The movement under a continental plate is much easier for the oceanic plate, which is less dense. Due to this type of movement a number of earthquakes occur along the coastlines.

● PROBLEM 3–25

There are six major plates of the lithosphere. Name them and explain their movement.

SOLUTION:

The six major plates are all characterized by large pieces of the Earth's lithosphere. The Eurasian plate consists of most of Europe and Asia. It is

Diagrams showing the movement of the three types of plate boundaries

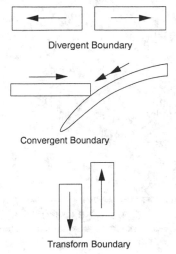

Divergent Boundary

Convergent Boundary

Transform Boundary

moving eastward toward the westwardly moving American plate. Between the two plates, moving northwest, is the Pacific plate.

The African Plate is moving under the Eurasian plate in a northeasterly direction. On the eastern coast of the Eurasian plate, the Indian plate is moving under the Eurasian plate in a northerly direction. The largest plate, the Antarctic plate, is moving away from the Pacific plate. The study of these plates is called plate tectonics.

● PROBLEM 3-26

What was the contribution made by Alexander von Humboldt to the theory of plate tectonics?

SOLUTION:

In 1801, Alexander von Humboldt observed that the major continents fit together as a puzzle. Mountain ranges and coastal shapes enticed him to develop a theory. He hypothesized that the Atlantic Ocean was a large valley produced by erosion. This idea was not widely accepted; however, the observations he made were used by later scientists to develop the theory of sea-floor spreading and the theory of plate tectonics.

What is the evidence that the plates exist on Earth?

SOLUTION:

The occurrence of earthquakes and volcanoes were mapped over a period of years. A pattern formed indicating that there was something causing movement in the areas around oceans. The volcanic activity and earthquakes appeared in similar rings. The idea that the continents moved was asserted by Alfred Wegener. If the lithosphere was broken into plates and moved on the molten asthenosphere, then the volcanic activity and earthquake pattern would outline the plates. Accepting this idea allows scientists to explain the processes which cause earthquakes and volcanoes.

The Movements of the Earth's Plates

● PROBLEM 3-28

What causes plate movement?

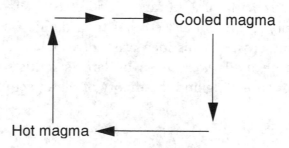

Movement of magma by convection current is shown

SOLUTION:

A convection current produced within the molten portion of the mantle is believed to produce the plate movement of the lithosphere. The convection current is produced by the heating of the mantle rock by its radioactive elements. As the rock is heated it moves up toward the lithosphere where it cools and begins to be pulled back toward the center of the Earth by gravity. This current is continuous, causing the movement of the plates.

● PROBLEM 3–29

Explain the three types of convergent plate boundaries.

SOLUTION:

A convergent boundary occurs when two plates collide. When two continental plates collide, mountain ranges are formed. The Himalayan Mountains are an example of two continental plates colliding. Subduction occurs when an older oceanic plate is pushed under a younger oceanic plate. A subduction zone occurs at this area. The collision of an oceanic plate and a continental plate usually produces mountains. When the oceanic plate moves under the continental plate volcanic eruptions occur, forming a volcanic mountain range. As a continental plate moves under an oceanic plate, folded mountains occur.

● PROBLEM 3–30

By what type of plate movement is the Mid-Oceanic Ridge produced?

SOLUTION:

The Eurasian plate and the American plate are moving away from each other at the Mid-Oceanic Ridge. This causes a boundary called a divergent boundary. At a divergent boundary hot magma moves upward, producing a mountain ridge. This mountain ridge on the ocean floor is called the Mid-Oceanic Ridge.

How is an oceanic trench produced?

SOLUTION:

An oceanic trench forms when a subduction zone produces a deep trench under the ocean. Such a trench can be up to 11 kilometers deep, over 1,500 kilometers long, and as much as 100 kilometers wide. The largest is the Mariana Trench, formed where the Pacific plate is moving under the ocean boundary of the Eurasian plate.

● PROBLEM 3–32

What is a rift?

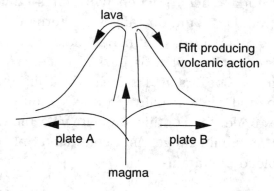

SOLUTION:

When two plates are moving apart a rift is formed. At a rift, volcanoes can form as the magma moves up. Iceland is a product of volcanic activity from a rift in the Atlantic Ocean.

● PROBLEM 3–33

What is continental accretion?

SOLUTION:

When rock material is added to continental boundaries by plate collisions, continental accretion occurs. The west coast of North America contains pieces of ocean crust. The area around Alaska is younger than the adjoining area of North America. These types of facts support the theory of continental accretion.

The Types of Volcanoes

● PROBLEM 3–34

What are the visual differences between the three main types of volcanoes?

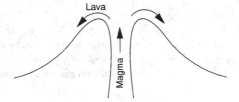

Shield cone volcano

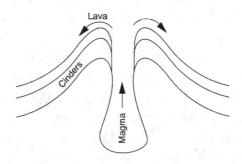

Composite cone volcano

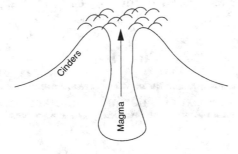

Cinder cone volcano

SOLUTION:

The visual differences between the three main types of volcanoes are related to the type of eruption and debris that occurs. A shield cone is formed from a quiet eruption of thin lava. This forms a gentle slope with a broad base.

A steep-sided, narrow-based cone is evidence of an explosive ash eruption. This type of eruption produces a cinder cone. A cinder cone is basically a pile of ash and cinders left from the eruption.

When an eruption combines flowing lava and spewing ash, a composite cone is produced. Layers of rock and ash combine to form a steep-sided broad-based cone, sometimes called a stratovolcano.

● PROBLEM 3-35

What three products are produced by volcanoes?

SOLUTION:

Volcanoes produce two types of lava. Pahoehoe is hot and thin, causing fast-flowing lava under a hardened crust. The surface becomes uneven as it cools. Aa lava is cool, thick, and covered with clinker and is therefore slow-moving. Rough rocks are produced by the cooling of aa lava.

Gases are produced by volcanoes. These gases—water vapor, carbon dioxide, and hydrogen sulfide—are dissolved in the magma. After reaching the surface, the lava cools and releases the gases into the atmosphere.

The third type of material produced is rock. Tiny particles of volcanic dust are released by volcanoes. When the particles are less than 2 millimeters (about the size of sand) they are called ash. Cinders are the rock particles that are several centimeters larger than sand. Rocks one meter or more in size are called bombs. These rocks are ejected as a liquid and harden while in flight.

● PROBLEM 3-36

Describe the categories extinct, dormant, and active volcanoes.

SOLUTION:

There are three categories of volcanoes: extinct, dormant, and active. An extinct volcano is one that is not likely to erupt. A dormant volcano is one which is not erupting but could erupt at any time. An active volcano is erupting at the present time.

How many active volcanoes are known.

SOLUTION:

There are about 600 active volcanoes in the world. Most are found in belts or narrow regions. In the Pacific Ocean, the largest belt, called the Ring of Fire, is found. Smaller belts are found in the Mediterranean Sea and in eastern Africa.

Describe the process of volcanism.

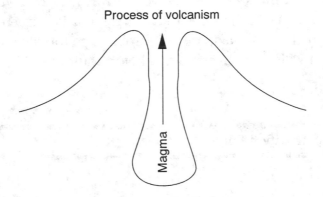

Process of volcanism

Magma

SOLUTION:

Volcanism is the process of magma moving to the surface of the Earth. The magma moves by convection currents to the crust out toward the surface. This process produces volcanoes.

What causes the viscosity of lava?

SOLUTION:

Viscosity is the property of fluid which causes the fluid to resist movement; the more dense a fluid, the higher the viscosity. Chemical composition and temperature determine the density of the lava and therefore determine the viscosity. Lava with low silica composition is thin with low viscosity and flows swiftly. The higher the silica levels in the lava the slower the flow of the lava. Higher temperatures cause the density of a fluid to decrease, so that at higher temperatures the lava is less viscous. The faster-moving thin lava is usually hotter than the slower moving thick lava.

● PROBLEM 3-40

Compare and contrast volcanic craters and calderas.

SOLUTION:

Both volcanic craters and calderas form at a vent of a volcano. When lava hardens around a vent, a crater is formed. If a vent becomes completely covered with hardened lava a caldera is formed. A vent may become hardened when magma flows out and the top collapses. This also forms a caldera which can become filled with water, forming a crater lake.

● PROBLEM 3-41

Can volcanic activity be predicted?

SOLUTION:

Volcanic activity can usually be predicted through certain changes which occur in the geology of the area. There is usually an increase of heat from the magma, indicating it has moved up into the volcano, and eruptions are probable as the temperature increases. Earthquakes or the emission of gases also indicate the possibility of volcanic eruption.

● PROBLEM 3-42

What is an island arc?

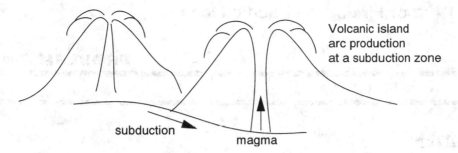

Volcanic island
arc production
at a subduction zone

subduction

magma

SOLUTION:

An island arc is a group of volcanic islands formed by subduction. An ocean plate sinks into a trench producing volcanic activity. This activity builds an island chain along the boundary. An example of an island arc is the Aleutian Islands.

● **PROBLEM 3–43**

What are flood basalts?

SOLUTION:

Flood basalts are thin lava flows from fissures in the Earth. This lava does not produce a volcanic cone, instead it covers large areas. Flood basalts originate in the upper mantle.

● **PROBLEM 3–44**

What is a volcanic neck?

SOLUTION:

A volcanic neck is the central plug of an extinct volcano. Due to its composition a volcanic neck does not erode easily. The volcanic neck may remain intact long after the outer portions of the extinct volcano are weathered away.

The Ring of Fire in the Pacific Ocean

PROBLEM 3-45

What is the Ring of Fire?

SOLUTION:

The Ring of Fire is an area surrounding the Pacific plate. The subduction plate movement causes the production of volcanoes. Since the Eurasian plate and the American plate are both moving toward the Pacific plate it is being forced under them. This causes a large area of subduction. The Pacific plate is then surrounded by the volcanic activity. This area of volcanoes surrounding the Pacific Ocean is known as the Ring of Fire.

● PROBLEM 3-46

How is the Ring of Fire related to the many earthquakes which occur along the Pacific Ocean?

SOLUTION:

The ring of volcanoes which give the Ring of Fire its name is an indication of plate movement along the boundaries of the Pacific plate. Earthquakes also generally occur along plate boundaries. There is a large amount of earthquake activity along the same ring that forms the Ring of Fire. This is another indication that there is plate movement along the Pacific plate.

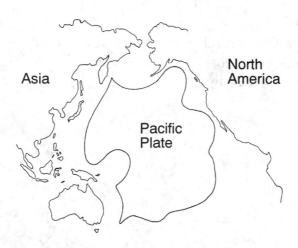

Asia

North America

Pacific Plate

Where are most active volcanoes located in the Ring of Fire? Why?

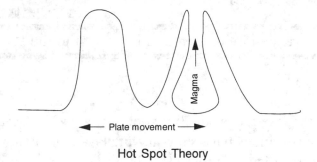

Hot Spot Theory

SOLUTION:

The most active volcanoes, other than the Hawaiian volcanoes, are found at the northwestern edge of the Pacific Ocean. This is probably due to the Pacific plate moving under the Eurasian plate. The movement of the Pacific plate under the Eurasian plate causes the Pacific plate to form new magma, forcing the hot magma back up to the surface.

● **PROBLEM 3-48**

Explain the hot spot theory and why it is accepted that the Hawaiian Islands are products of a hot spot.

SOLUTION:

The hot spot theory explains the formation of volcanoes in the middle of a plate. An opening in the oceanic crust allows magma to come to the surface. As the lava cools, a volcanic mountain forms. As the lava builds, an island is produced. Slow-moving plates can form large islands, while fast-moving plates can produce small seamounts, which did not reach the surface of the ocean.

The Hawaiian Islands are made up of several islands. These islands are aligned in a northwesterly direction from the island of Hawaii. Each of these islands is a volcanic mountain, but only the island of Hawaii and a new island forming southeast of Hawaii have active volcanoes. This chain of islands is in the middle of the Pacific plate. The line of islands is like an arrow pointing in the direction the Pacific plate is moving. This evidence indicates that there is a hot spot under the islands which forms a new island as the plate moves.

● **PROBLEM 3–49**

What type of volcanoes are formed at the hot spot in the Pacific Ocean?

SOLUTION:

Most volcanoes formed over the hot spot in the Pacific Ocean are shield volcanoes. These volcanoes have slow-moving lava which allows the build-up of several layers of igneous rock. This build-up forms seamounts which eventually rise to the surface of the ocean.

Plate Movement and Earthquakes

● **PROBLEM 3–50**

What produces most earthquakes?

SOLUTION:

As plates move over the asthenosphere, strain is placed on the lithosphere. Due to the rigidity of the lithosphere, stress is built up until rocks move or break, producing a fault. As the rocks break, energy is released in the form of waves. These waves move through the Earth and along its surface, producing earthquakes.

● **PROBLEM 3–51**

What are faults and define the major types of faults.

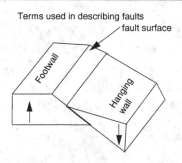

Terms used in describing faults

fault surface

Footwall

Hanging wall

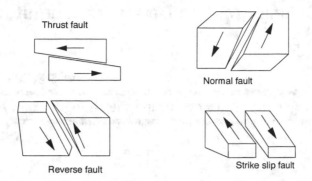

Thrust fault

Normal fault

Reverse fault

Strike slip fault

SOLUTION:

Faults are cracks in the Earth formed by plates moving next to each other with neither giving way. Usually this movement originates in the asthenosphere. A fault plane is the surface of the rocks which have moved. The rocks which are above the fault plane form a hanging wall. The rocks below the fault plane are called a footwall.

There are four types of faults. A normal fault occurs as a result of the downward movement of rock along the fault line. This causes the development of opposite forces. The crust is literally pulled apart.

A reverse fault occurs when the rock above the fault moves upward along the fault line. Thrust faulting is a type of reverse fault which occurs when the fault plane is at an angle to the rock. Reverse faulting, and especially thrust faulting, occur at subduction zones.

Strike-slip faulting occurs when forces parallel the boundary of the plates. Usually this type of faulting occurs at plate boundaries moving next to each other. Strike-slip faulting is associated with transform faults.

● **PROBLEM 3-52**

What type of faulting is produced at the San Andreas Fault?

SOLUTION:

Strike-slip faulting of the Pacific plate moving northwest past the North American plate which is moving west produced the San Andreas Fault. This type of fault is called a transform fault. A transform fault generally occurs where plates do not move under or away from each other.

65

The Use of Seismograph to Determine Magnitude of Earthquakes

● **PROBLEM 3-53**

How is a seismograph used to determine the strength of an earthquake?

SOLUTION:

A seismograph is an instrument used to measure the vibrations produced by the movement of waves through the Earth. These waves are produced by the release of energy during an earthquake. The energy causes a pen to move on the seismograph, producing marks which indicate the strength of the energy. The greater the energy, the larger the marks produced on the seismogram and the larger the marks on the seismogram, the stronger the earthquake.

● **PROBLEM 3-54**

Describe the Richter scale.

The Richter Scale
1   Usually not noticed
2   Detected only by instruments
3   Barely noticed
4   Felt by most people, little damage
5   Generally felt, some damage
6   Moderate damage
7   Major earthquake
8+ Great earthquake

SOLUTION:

The Richter scale enables scientists to relate the magnitude of an earthquake to others. Charles Richter developed this method of measuring the energy output of an earthquake. The scale uses a logarithmic function for determining the strength of the earthquake. Each whole number represents 31 times the strength of the preceding whole number for energy received by a seismograph. The same scale is used for the energy released by the earthquake at the epicenter. The energy released by the earthquake increases ten times between each whole number.

What is the Mercalli scale?

SOLUTION:

The Mercalli scale was developed by Guiseppe Mercalli. It uses Roman numerals to indicate the amount of damage caused by the earthquake. Mercalli had no seismographs in the 1890s to determine the strength of an earthquake. Using damage produced and reactions by observers, he developed the Mercalli scale.

● **PROBLEM 3-56**

Explain how the seismograph records the strength of an earthquake.

Seismograph

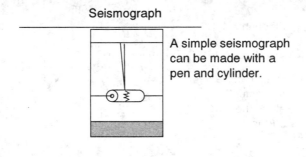

A simple seismograph can be made with a pen and cylinder.

SOLUTION:

A seismograph records the energy produced by an earthquake. The energy of the wave is proportional to the amplitude squared. As the energy increases, the amplitude of the recorded waves increases. Each type of wave is recorded with the time of arrival. This allows seismologists to determine the strength and the distance from the earthquake origin.

● **PROBLEM 3-57**

Which scale of earthquake strength is used most often? Why?

SOLUTION:

The Richter scale is most widely used by scientists. It enables the scientist to measure accurately the energy produced by an earthquake. Records can then be kept and understood by scientists around the world.

The Types of Waves Produced by Earthquakes

● PROBLEM 3-58

Explain the three waves produced by an earthquake.

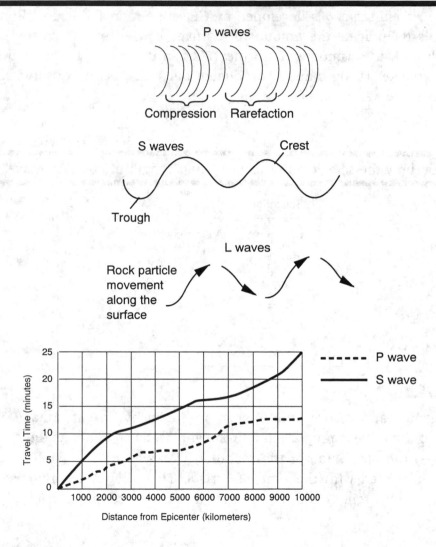

SOLUTION:

The three types of waves produced by an earthquake are differentiated by their speed and the material through which they travel. The first waves to be produced are the primary, or P, waves. The P waves travel through solid and liquid rock at an average speed of 6 km/s. As the wave moves, the particles in the rock move back and forth in the same direction the wave is traveling.

Secondary, or S, waves travel only through solid rock. At an average speed of about 4 km/s, these waves produce an up and down movement of the particles which is perpendicular to the wave movement.

The most dangerous type of wave is the L, or surface, wave. These are the most destructive, although the movement is slow compared to the other two. The wave formed moves the particles in the rock much as a wave in the ocean moves.

● PROBLEM 3–59

What are the two main differences between P waves and S waves?

SOLUTION:

S waves shear the rock at right angles to the movement of the rock. This requires an elastic quality in the substance being broken. Liquids and gases do not have an elastic quality perpendicular to the surface; therefore, S waves cannot travel through liquids and gases. P waves travel through any type of material. Rate of travel is the major difference. S waves are slower than P waves.

● PROBLEM 3–60

Describe a tsunami.

SOLUTION:

A tsunami is a large wave produced when an earthquake occurs beneath the ocean floor. In open ocean, the tsunami is only about one meter in height. As the tsunami moves to shallow water near land it can grow to a height of fifteen meters or more. Tsunamis are also called tidal waves.

● PROBLEM 3–61

How does monitoring earthquake waves help scientists describe the interior of the Earth?

SOLUTION:

Each type of body wave travels through different phases of matter. The secondary wave travels only through solids. Since it does not travel through the outer core, it is believed that the outer core is liquid rock. The primary wave can travel through the entire Earth. This allows scientists to make assumptions about the central core. If the outer and inner core is a liquid, then the P wave would travel faster through the entire core. Using the speed of the P wave and assuming the outer core is liquid, the time the P wave would exit the other side of the Earth can be predicted. Knowledge about the outer core and the speed of the P wave allows scientists to predict that the inner core is a solid.

● PROBLEM 3–62

What type of earthquake wave causes the most damage? Why?

SOLUTION:

Surface waves cause the greatest amount of damage from an earthquake. These waves travel along or close to the surface. This wave motion causes buildings and other structures to be destroyed. It literally causes a wave like that of the ocean to be produced on the surface of the Earth.

● PROBLEM 3–63

What are body waves from an earthquake?

SOLUTION:

Body waves are the waves which travel through the interior of the Earth. There are two types of body waves. Primary, or P, waves are compressional waves. Particles in a primary wave move back and forth in the same direction as the wave movement, allowing them to travel through any phase of matter. Secondary, or S waves have particles moving at right angles to the movement of the wave. This type of movement forces the S waves to travel only through solids.

● PROBLEM 3–64

What are seismic waves?

SOLUTION:

Energy released by an earthquake produces waves; compressional waves and transverse waves are both produced. These waves are called seismic waves.

● **PROBLEM 3–65**

What are after shocks?

SOLUTION:

After shocks are produced by the movement along a fault. This movement is usually not as severe as the first shifting of the plates. After shocks can occur for more than a year after a major earthquake.

Determining the Focus and Epicenter of Earthquakes

● **PROBLEM 3–66**

How is a seismograph used to determine the epicenter of an earthquake?

—Surface of Earth

● Focus of earthquake

SOLUTION:

The epicenter is located on the Earth's surface above the origin or focus of the earthquake. The difference between the arrival time of the primary wave and the secondary wave allows seismologists to determine the epicenter of an earthquake. The greater the distance from the epicenter to the seismograph, the longer the time interval between the S and P waves.

By using seismographs at different locations, seismologists can estimate the position of the epicenter. Primary waves travel at about 6 km/s and secondary waves travel at about 4 km/s. Knowing the difference in arrival time permits the distance the waves travel to be estimated. Using three or more seismographs at different locations, the epicenter can be determined by intersecting lines which follow the direction of the waves. The intersection of the lines is probably the epicenter of the earthquake.

● PROBLEM 3–67

Describe the focus of an earthquake and define the methods used to determine the focus of an earthquake.

SOLUTION:

The focus is the place in the Earth where the initial energy of the earthquake is released. The focus is generally deep in the crust or upper mantle of the Earth.

Usually, to determine the focus, the epicenter must be found. By measuring the difference in the speed of the body waves, scientists can determine the general location of the epicenter. Once triangulation determines the epicenter, the focus which is directly below the epicenter, can be found. The actual distance beneath the surface is difficult to determine, but it can be estimated by the damage at the surface.

● PROBLEM 3–68

Describe the epicenter of an earthquake.

SOLUTION:

The epicenter of an earthquake is directly above the focus of the earthquake. The focus is the place in the Earth where the earthquake occurs. On the surface, directly above the focus, is the epicenter.

Prediction of Earthquakes (Future)

● PROBLEM 3–69

What are some methods used in an attempt to predict earthquakes?

SOLUTION:

Earth plates move every year, however, some areas along the plates do not move. This causes a build-up of pressure in specific areas along the plate boundaries. When this pressure is released, an earthquake occurs. Seismologists use seismometers and lasers in an attempt to measure the yearly movement and determine where this sticking of plates occurs.

Seismometers and lasers are setup along plate boundaries to measure the slightest vibrations and strain on the Earth's crust at the boundaries in different locations. This information is then analyzed to determine any changes in the movements that may occur before an earthquake. Many other observed changes occur before an earthquake, such as an increased concentration of radon in well water, the decrease of electrical resistance of the surface of the Earth, the slowing of P waves, increased bulging or elevation of the ground, and the abnormal behavior of animals and birds.

● PROBLEM 3-70

What changes in the seismic waves of small earthquakes allow prediction of large earthquakes? How does the appearance of radon deep in water wells indicate an earthquake is about to occur?

SOLUTION:

Small earthquakes are those not felt by humans. They occur almost daily in areas with a large amount of earthquake activity. By monitoring the waves produced by these quakes, scientists can determine that a more severe earthquake will occur. The P waves of the small earthquakes begin to slow in speed for as much as a month, then suddenly return to normal prior to a severe earthquake.

Radon is a short-lived gas produced by the radioactive decay of radium. Scientists believe that the rocks in deep wells are placed under stress, causing the release of the gas from the rocks. This stress is a precursor to earthquake activity.

● PROBLEM 3-71

Why would bulging of the ground indicate the possibility of an earthquake?

The ground bulging indicates that a process of uplifting is occurring under the surface. These changes are probably due to plate movement or magma movement from the asthenosphere. Movement of the plates or magma can cause earthquakes.

● **PROBLEM 3–72**

What is a possible method of preventing or lessening the severity of an earthquake?

SOLUTION:

Since water is a poor transmitter of earthquake waves, scientists have attempted to put water into fault areas where earthquakes will occur. It has been discovered that the severity of earthquakes has been lessened by the water. The rock absorbs the water, keeping it from being placed under the stress necessary for the transmission of earthquake waves. It is believed that the possibility exists to prevent earthquakes. The problem is that the areas of the most severe earthquakes have large areas of stress which would cause difficulty in preventing an earthquake; however, the lessening of the strength has been proven in areas of California and Russia.

Major Landforms of the Lithosphere

● **PROBLEM 3–73**

How are landforms on the lithosphere produced?

SOLUTION:

Crustal movement produced by the pressures on the lithosphere causes formations in the crust to occur. These formations are eroded causing distinct physical features on the Earth such as mesas, buttes, hat rocks, and many of the features associated with the Grand Canyon. These physical features are called landforms.

What are the major landscape features?

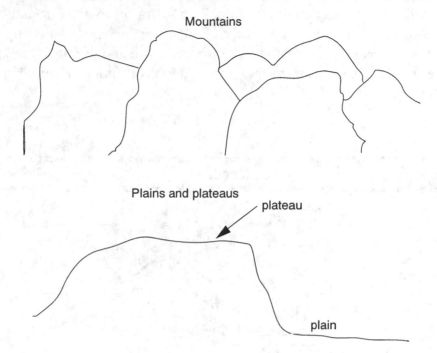

Mountains

Plains and plateaus

plateau

plain

SOLUTION:

There are four major landscape features: mountains, plains, plateaus, and rivers. Mountains are sections of the Earth's surface which have been pushed upward by geologic or volcanic forces. A mountain must rise at least 600 meters above the surrounding surface. A plateau is a horizontal section of the Earth's surface which has been pushed up. Rivers are formed by water cutting through rock layers producing a deep valley. A plain is similar to a plateau in that they are both raised sections of land. A plain, however, is lower in elevation than a plateau.

● PROBLEM 3–75

What are the types of mountains?

SOLUTION:

Mountains can be a singular unit or they can be in a series called a mountain range. When there are a number of ranges together they form a mountain system. A mountain chain is formed as mountain ranges form a long unit. Mountains are formed in three main processes.

Volcanic mountains are generally formed at plate boundaries where subduction occurs. When large pieces of crust are uplifted, fault-block mountains are produced. Fault-block mountains usually reach high altitudes. Folded mountains are areas of rock which are pushed up and fold over. Most folded mountains are formed from sedimentary rock with marine fossils. These indicate that the material of folded mountains was once part of the ocean.

● PROBLEM 3-76

How are folded mountains produced?

Folded mountain formation

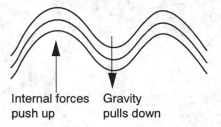

Internal forces   Gravity
push up   pulls down

SOLUTION:

Folded mountains are produced when magma or a plate pushes the sedimentary rock of crust upward. Gravity pulls the rock back down, folding the strata over. This process produces folded mountains such as the Appalachian Mountains.

● PROBLEM 3-77

Describe the formation of fault-block mountains.

SOLUTION:

When large blocks of crust are moved along faults, a fault-block mountain is produced. The Sierra Nevada Mountains are an example. As the surface buckles under pressure, blocks of crust are pushed up forming mountains.

Describe the formation of dome mountains.

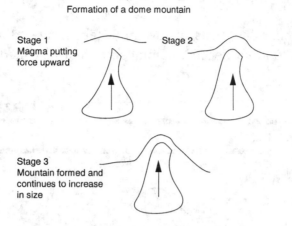

Formation of a dome mountain

Stage 1
Magma putting
force upward

Stage 2

Stage 3
Mountain formed and
continues to increase
in size

SOLUTION:

Magma moving upward but not onto the surface of the Earth pushes the crust up. This produces a dome mountain.

The Adirondack Mountains is an example of dome mountains.

● **PROBLEM 3-79**

What are anticlines and synclines?

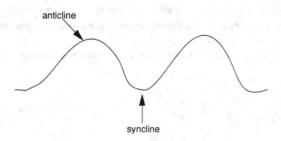

anticline

syncline

SOLUTION:

When rock layers are folded, dips and rises are produced. The dips are called synclines and the rises are called anticlines. These folds are found in the rock layers of folded mountains.

Describe a batholith.

SOLUTION:

A batholith generally forms inside mountain ranges. Batholiths extend over large areas to great depths. A smaller version is called a stock.

● **PROBLEM 3-81**

Describe a laccolith.

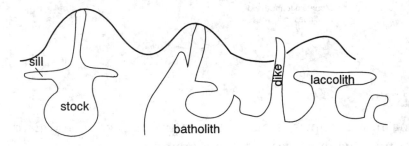

SOLUTION:

Laccoliths are dome shaped structures formed between rock layers. Smaller structures can also be produced. A horizontal small laccolith is called a sill. A vertical structure is a dike.

● **PROBLEM 3-82**

Describe landforms produced by glaciers.

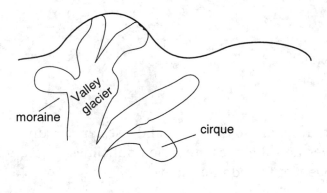

SOLUTION:

Glaciers leave distinct features behind. Valley glaciers can produce a U-shaped valley by smoothing the steep-sided valley through which it travels. As a valley glacier hollows out, a depression cirque forms. A cirque lake is produced when the glacier melts, filling the cirque.

Drifts are produced as rock deposits are released from a melting glacier. Drifts can be in the form of tills or outwashes. A till is a mixture of all rock sizes deposited. An outwash is deposited rock left as water moves away from the glacier.

● PROBLEM 3-83

What are Eolian landforms?

SOLUTION:

Eolian landforms are sandstone deposited by wind. Wind transports sand which collides in the air, producing very smooth surfaces. Usually the grains are small and uniform in size. Sand dunes form the most common Eolian landforms. Dunes produce sedimentary rock as the sand mounds up, solidifying under pressure. These rocks forms can be several meters thick.

Weathering and Erosion of the Land

● PROBLEM 3-84

Explain the processes of physical and chemical weathering.

$$CO_2 + H_2O \rightarrow H_2CO_3$$

$$CaCO_3 + H_2CO_3 \rightarrow Ca(HCO_3)_2$$

Chemical reaction of calcite with carbonic acid

Physical weathering

water enters cracks in rocks   water freezes expanding   breaking rock into peices

79

SOLUTION:

The process of physical weathering breaks apart rocks without altering the chemical composition of the rock. The primary cause of physical weathering is due to the pressure placed on rock by water.

The most common form of water that breaks rock is ice. Freezing water expands, causing rocks and soil to break apart. This allows erosion and changing of the surroundings to occur. Other forms of physical weathering include permafrost, salt wedging, and the invasion of rocks and soil by plants and animals.

New substances are produced through the reaction of the minerals in a rock with another substance. This process is called chemical weathering. Many reactions can cause chemical weathering.

Carbonization is the process of carbon dioxide in the air mixing with rain to produce carbonic acid. When this reaches the ground it breaks down minerals such as feldspar, gypsum, and mica into clay. When calcite, which forms limestone, reacts with carbonic acid it dissolves quickly. This forms caves in areas of large limestone deposits.

Another type of chemical weathering is hydration. This occurs when water dissolves a mineral and then combines with elements within the mineral. This usually allows the rock to be broken down further by mechanical weathering.

Oxidation is the process of combining oxygen with the elements within minerals. Iron (III) oxide, or rust, is an example of oxidation. This is what gives iron ore its reddish-orange color.

Other acids and gases are released into the atmosphere by man and nature which can contribute to the chemical breakdown of minerals.

● PROBLEM 3-85

What affects the rate of weathering?

SOLUTION:

The slow process of weathering is affected by many factors. Two of the major factors are the type of parent rock and the climate of the area. Hard parent rock which contains quartz will weather slower than softer rock. The more humid the climate the faster weathering occurs. Since water is the major weathering agent, the more abundant the water supply the faster the weathering.

What is mass wasting?

SOLUTION:

The movement of rock material downhill by the force of gravity is called mass wasting or movement. An overburden is formed from weathered rock materials on top of base rock. Since the material is loose, gravity can act upon it, pulling it downhill. Two types of mass wasting occur: fast mass wasting and slow mass wasting.

The most spectacular form of fast mass wasting is a landslide. Landslides are produced as large amounts of rock material move swiftly down a slope. Rain, earthquakes, and even the process of erosion can cause landslides.

Relatively slow movement downhill is a slump. A slump usually produces a curved depression due to its weight and speed. Mudflows occur when heavy rains or melted snow mixes with soil and rock. Since the soil is unstable due to its new weight and viscosity, it tends to react to gravity and move downhill.

Slow mass wasting is not as evident unless viewed over a long period of time. The rock and soil moved is usually a larger quantity than that moved by fast mass wasting. A creep takes place over years and moves more soil than a landslide. Soil flowing in cold climates is called solification. In the summer, surface ice melts, allowing movement of soil downhill with the flow of water.

● **PROBLEM 3-87**

What is soil and describe its formation.

Topsoil
Subsoil
Parent rock
Bedrock

SOLUTION:

Soil is weathered materials which cover an area of base rock. Two types of soil textures occur, sand and clay. Sand is usually made from gypsum, quartz, or calcite. Clay is usually produced by the chemical weathering of minerals forming very small particles. A combination of clay and sand produces loam.

Parent rock above the bedrock is broken down by weathering and erosion to produce a soil profile or horizons. The topsoil or A-horizon is the first layer of soil. Fertile topsoil contains humus and minerals necessary for the growth of plants. The B-horizon, or subsoil, has had minerals placed in it by water passing through the topsoil. With these minerals, living organisms and small amounts of humus will also be deposited. Parent rock found under the subsoil continues to produce new soil through weathering. Soil which does not move from on top of the parent rock is called residual soil.

● PROBLEM 3–88

What are the two types of soil texture?

SOLUTION:

Sand and clay are the two types of soil texture. Sand contains minerals such as gypsum, calcite, and quartz. These minerals are in large grains easily seen with the unaided eye. Clay has particles so small they are not usually visible without a magnifying glass. Clay is composed of minerals such as feldspar which produces a very hard soil. A combination of sand and clay produces loam. Loam is not usually classified as a separate soil texture and it is normally the best soil for cultivation.

● PROBLEM 3–89

What is exfoliation?

SOLUTION:

When rocks that have been buried under the pressure of the Earth's surface move to the surface, the pressure is lessened. Slab-like sheets of rock are then peeled from the large rock. This process is called exfoliation. The granite rock of Liberty Cap in Yosemite National Park is an example of the results of exfoliation.

Describe the formation of stalactites and stalagmites.

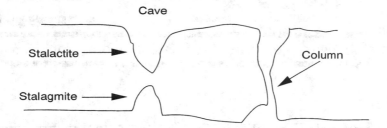

SOLUTION:

A stalactite forms as water drips carrying dissolved calcite. The water evaporates leaving the calcite on the roof of the cave. This forms an extension called a stalactite.

When water with dissolved calcite falls to the cave floor, a build-up of calcite is formed. This forms a stalagmite. As these processes continue the stalactite and stalagmite will join forming a column.

● **PROBLEM 3-91**

What is erosion?

SOLUTION:

Erosion is the actual wearing away and transport of rock by natural agents. There are two processes involved in erosion: transportation and abrasion.

Transportation occurs due to wind, water, and other agents picking up particles of rock and carrying them to another location. Abrasion occurs when these particles grind the rock over which they pass. Sand is the most common abrasive substance.

● **PROBLEM 3-92**

What is deposition?

SOLUTION:

Deposition is the process of settling of transported substances. When water and wind stop or slow their rate of movement particles are deposited. Glaciers deposit particles as the ice melts.

● PROBLEM 3–93

What are the two major forms of structural deformation?

SOLUTION:

Folding and faulting are the two forms of structural deformation. Folding occurs when pressure is exerted horizontally. As the rock is moved upward it buckles and folds. Faulting occurs where fractures occur in the crust. This causes movement of rock.

● PROBLEM 3–94

What is deflation?

SOLUTION:

Deflation is the transportation of particles by wind. Dry areas are usually the most susceptible to deflation. In the arid regions there is little or no plant life to hold the soil in place. The results of deflation occurring over many years is a surface called desert pavement.

Desert pavement is characterized by pebbles and small rocks.

● PROBLEM 3–95

Describe the deposits formed by deflation.

SOLUTION:

Light weight materials can be carried for long distances. When deposited this silt is called loess. Loess can cover large areas as in the midwestern United States.

Mounds of sand can build blocking more wind. As the wind is blocked, more sand is deposited forming a sand dune. Dunes form mostly along coastlines moving in the direction the wind blows.

What determines the size and shape of a sand dune?

SOLUTION:

There are four main factors which determine the size and shape of a sand dune. The consistency of the strength and direction of the wind is a major factor in determining the size and shape. Another determining factor is the speed and quantity of sedimentation. The amount and type of vegetation of the area is an influence over a sand dune. Finally, the type of surface on which the dune is built determines the shape and size of a dune.

What are the four major categories of sand dunes?

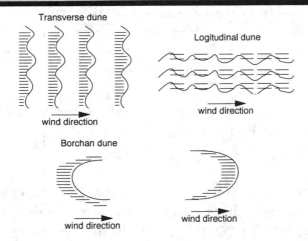

SOLUTION:

The four major categories of sand dunes are barchan dunes, transverse dunes, longitudinal dunes, and parabolic dunes. A barchan dune has a crescent shape with extensions pointing in the direction the wind is traveling. Transverse dunes are generally found in arid regions with winds traveling in a constant direction. They are characterized by wavelike patterns with sinuous crests. Longitudinal dunes are elongated sand deposits. These are found in arid regions with variable wind directions. Parabolic dunes are found in areas with some vegetation. Similar in shape to barchan dunes, parabolic dunes have extensions formed toward the wind direction.

SHORT ANSWER QUESTIONS FOR REVIEW

Choose the correct answer.

1. Of the following, which types of fracture are associated with faults and earthquakes? (a) Horsts (b) Oblique-slip (c) Grabens (d) All of the above.

2. Water can corrode and erode (a) any solid. (b) the most solid rock. (c) when distilled. (d) All of the above.

3. Erosion is a form of natural weathering that (a) led to the forming of mountain chains. (b) formed only a few mountains out west. (c) was proven false. (d) is caused by chemical, physical, and psychological means.

4. Earth swarms are (a) a long series of quakes with none being greater than the others. (b) a group of quakes which occur at the same time. (c) large tidal waves that occur because of an earthquake. (d) bees which form colonies along the fault line.

5. Eighty percent of the energy of earthquakes is released in areas bordering the (a) Pacific Ocean. (b) Indian Ocean. (c) Baltic Sea. (d) Atlantic Ocean.

6. Modern research of volcanoes was begun by Jean Etienne Guettard in the mid-eighteenth century as he analyzed volcanoes' role in (a) forming much of the Earth's crust. (b) forming the plates the Earth now rests on. (c) formation of Earth from atmospheric wastes. (d) rock formations.

7. A period of greater than normal volcanic action might (a) raise the ocean levels. (b) cool the Earth. (c) trigger hurricanes. (d) warm the Earth.

8. Mountains built by volcanic ash might expose large areas of new and unweathered rock to the air, causing (a) a warming of the Earth for an extended period. (b) an increase in the carbon dioxide levels, thus raising the temperature. (c) a decrease in the carbon dioxide levels,

thus lowering temperature. (d) a rise in carbon dioxide levels, thus lowering the temperature.

Items 9 to 12 refer to the following passage.

When an earthquake occurs, some of the energy released travels through the ground as waves. Two general types of waves are generated. One type, called the P wave, is a compression wave that alternately compresses and stretches the rock layers as it travels. A second type is a shear wave, called the S wave, which moves the rocks in an up and down manner.

A graph can be made of the travel times of these waves.

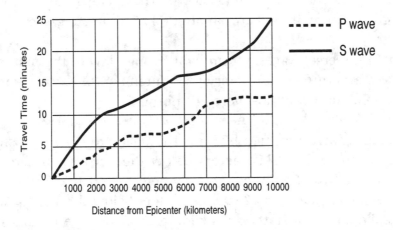

9. The main reason that a Travel Time graph can be used to determine distance to an earthquake's point of occurrence is that (a) S waves move up and down. (b) P waves are compressional. (c) P waves travel faster than S waves. (d) S waves travel faster than P waves.

10. It takes approximately 12 minutes for a P wave to travel (a) 1,000 km. (b) 8,000 km. (c) 25,000 km. (d) 10,000 km.

11. An earthquake occurs at noon, and the recording station receives the S wave at 12:05 pm. How far away is the earthquake? (a) 1,000 km (b) 2,000 km (c) 3,000 km (d) 4,000 km

12. If the difference in arrival time between P and S waves is seven minutes, the earthquake occurred (a) 4,000 km away. (b) 9,000 km away. (c) seven km away. (d) Cannot be determined from this data.

Items 13 to 15 refer to the following information.

Surface water waves are fundamentally different from sound waves in that the vibration of the former is perpendicular to the direction of motion, while that of sound is always parallel to the direction of motion. If a large disturbance in a material is created by a strong external blow, then it is possible for shear or transverse waves (like water waves) to propagate through the material. It is impossible, however, for these shear waves to travel through the inside of a liquid or gas; the attractive forces between the molecules are so weak that there is little restoring force to cause displaced sections of the liquid or gas to return to their original positions which is required for a continuous wave. These shear (or S-waves) are known to travel through the Earth at about 4.25 kilometers/sec.

13. Shear (transverse) waves, set up by a strong blow to the material, are able to travel through (a) water at room temperature. (b) the material if it is solid. (c) the atmosphere. (d) nothing.

14. Shear (or S-waves) created by an earthquake are known to stop at a depth of about 2,900 kilometers below the Earth's surface. This is evidence that the Earth has (a) a diameter of 2,900 kilometers. (b) a liquid portion that starts 2,900 kilometers below the Earth's surface. (c) a solid core that starts 2,900 kilometers below the Earth's surface. (d) a radius of 2,900 kilometers.

15. Earthquakes cause pressure-type waves (P-waves), which travel about twice as fast as the associated S-waves. If a seismographic station records an earthquake's P-waves arriving four minutes after the earthquake occurs, its distance away from the station must be about (a) 500 kilometers. (b) 1,000 kilometers. (c) 2,000 kilometers. (d) 3,000 kilometers.

Items 16 to 18 refer to the following passage.

The term "volcanic activity" can mean erupting volcanoes complete with lava and pyroclastic display, or it can mean a simple gaseous emission. It is believed that volcanic activity formed the early Earth's atmosphere. Volcanic gases typically include water vapor, carbon dioxide, hydrogen sulfide, sulfur dioxide, chlorine, and fluorine.

16. Which statement can be drawn in conclusion from the above information? (a) Volcanic gases can be more dangerous than lava. (b)

Erupting volcanoes always emit both lava and gas. (c) The term "volcanic activity" is always clear in its meaning. (d) Erupting volcanoes emit lava only.

17. Which statement is false? (a) The early Earth's atmosphere contained no free oxygen. (b) The early Earth's atmosphere was poisonous to present day life forms. (c) Current Earth's atmosphere be formed by factors other than volcanic activity. (d) Volcanic activity today emits oxygen to the atmosphere.

18. "Pyroclastic display" is best defined as (a) a fallout of ice and snow. (b) trees that fall near the volcano. (c) a mushroom-type cloud. (d) fire and rock particles.

19. The thickest layer of the Earth is called the (a) core. (b) ocean lining. (c) crust. (d) mantle.

20. In this diagram, which letter most likely represents the lithosphere?

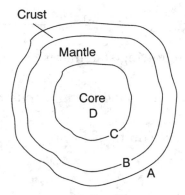

Fill in the blanks.

21. Two-thirds of all known active volcanoes have occurred in the _____.

22. The crust of the Earth is composed of a thin layer of rocks covering the surface. Rocks are defined as aggregates or collections of _____.

23. The center of the Earth acts as if it's a large _____.

24. Terracing, erosion, and sedimentation are responsible for forming the _____.

25. The natural wearing away of rock or soil due to chemical or physical actions is called _____.

26. Man can control erosion by _____.

27. Vibrations due to movements within and beneath the Earth's crust are called _____.

28. Earthquake intensity is measured on a scale called the _____.

29. Earthquakes are measured on a scale of 0 - _____.

30. The Richter Scale was introduced in _____.

31. There are about _____ known active volcanos.

32. Volcanoes discharge a large amount of _____.

Determine whether the following statements are true or false.

33. One layer of the Earth is called the lithosphere.

34. Minerals are the most common form of solid material found in the Earth's crust.

35. The shifting of the Earth's surface locations gives some proof to the Big Bang Theory.

36. A shelf that leads downward is called a continental slope.

37. Sediment is transported by lava and streams.

38. Sediment can be formed from water and snow.

39. Water can freeze at 100°C.

40. Rocks break down as oxygen, carbon dioxide, and water vapor due to chemical weathering.

41. Physical weathering occurs in dry, windy regions.

42. Erosion actually leads to forest growth.

43. Imperial Valley, California is known for having volcanic regions.

44. If vibrations are felt directly over the area affected, then one has experienced an Earth tremor.

ANSWER KEY

1. d
2. b
3. a
4. a
5. a
6. a
7. d
8. c
9. c
10. b
11. a
12. a
13. b
14. b
15. c
16. a
17. d
18. d
19. d
20. b
21. Pacific Ocean
22. minerals

23. magnet
24. continental shelf
25. weathering
26. rotating crops
27. earthquakes
28. Richter Scale
29. 9
30. 1935
31. 500
32. carbon dioxide
33. True
34. True
35. False
36. True
37. False
38. False
39. False
40. True
41. True
42. False
43. False
44. True

CHAPTER 4

HISTORY OF THE EARTH

Cenozoic Era — Quarternary Period	Holocene Epoch—.01 million years ago—Modern humans	
	Pleistocene Epoch—2.5 million years ago—Ice age	
Cenozoic Era — Tertiary Period	Pliocene Epoch—6 miilion years ago—Glaciers form	
	Miocene Epoch—25 million years ago—Herds of horses—Mastodons	
	Oligocene Epoch—38 million years ago—Cooler climate—Canines and felines	
	Eocene Epoch—55 million years ago—Large mammals	
	Paleocene Epoch—65 million years ago—Small mammals	

Mesozoic Era		
Creataceous Period — 140 million years ago — Extinction of dinosaurs — Flowering plants appear		
Jurassic Period — 195 million years ago — First birds		
Triassic Period — 230 million years ago — First dinosaurs — First mammals		

Paleozoic Era		
Permain Period—280 million years ago—Reptiles dominant—Most sea life disappears		
Carboniferous Period: Pennsylvanian Epoch — 325 million years ago — Reptiles Forests		
Carboniferous Period: Mississippian Epoch — 345 million years ago — Insects — Swamps		
Devonian Period—395 million years ago—Amphibians		
Silurian Period—435 million years ago—Land plants—First insects		
Ordovician Period—500 million years ago—First vertebrates—Fish		
Cambrian Period—600 million years ago—First plants—Marine invertebrates		

Precambrian Era	
4,600 million years ago — five times longer than any other era	
Life began—Bacteria—Algae	

Major Theories of Formation

● PROBLEM 4–1

Explain the formation of a protoplanet.

SOLUTION:

A protoplanet is formed from the shrinkage of large amounts of cold, spinning gases and dust. As the cloud spins, dust and gas collect, forming bulges. The central bulge is usually larger due to the inward gravitational force. This large bulge becomes a star; outer bulges become protoplanets. As the cloud contiues to spin, more material is added to form the planets.

● PROBLEM 4–2

What is the Earth's absolute age?

SOLUTION:

Many methods have been used to determine the absolute age of the Earth. Most have been unsuccessful according to most scientists. The earliest attempts were based on biblical accounts, the total thickness of the Earth's sediment, or the amount of salt content in the oceans.

The rate of sedimentation was once believed to be constant. This process of carrying materials through the air, by water, or by the movement of ice forms the thickness of sedimentary rock. This total thickness was used to determine the age of the Earth. Assuming no sedimentary rocks existed at the beginning of Earth's history, and assuming that the rate of sedimentation was constant, the thickness could be used to determine the age of the Earth. The absolute age of the Earth by this method was between 3 million and 1.5 billion years. The realization that the rate of sedimentation varies with climate and weather conditions caused scientists to disavow this method of determining the absolute age of the Earth.

Assuming that there was no salt in the oceans of the early Earth and that the only method of salination is through addition of salt by the process of decay of organisms within the ocean, the amount of present salt content could be used to determine the age of the Earth. The scientist must also assume that no salt is lost from the ocean. The estimated absolute age of the Earth through this method is between 9 million and 2.5 billion years.

Measuring the amount of heat lost by the Earth is a method used by Lord Kelvin of dating the age of the Earth. He measured the rate of cooling of the Earth, accounting for the heat within and the heat from solar radiation. He estimated the absolute age of the Earth to be between 20 million and 100 million years. Lord Kelvin did not know about radioactive elements, therefore, he did not realize the heat within the Earth was still being produced.

Once radioactive elements were discovered and understood, the process of radioactive decay was used to determine the absolute age of the Earth to be about 4.6 billion years. This method, called radiometric dating, uses the decay of uranium-238 to lead-206. Since the decay of a radioactive element is believed to be constant, the age of the oldest rocks would be the age of the Earth.

● **PROBLEM 4–3**

Explain the collision hypothesis.

SOLUTION:

As the sun was forming, another star traveled close to it, pulling matter from the sun. This matter separated as it was pulled out. The heavier materials were held close to the sun while the lighter materials were pulled closer to the approaching star. This hypothesis attempted to explain two fundamental questions about the solar system: 1) Why are the planets orbiting the sun in the same plane? and 2) Why are the outer planets larger? The hypothesis is not widely accepted because a near miss by a star is unlikely, and once the star passed, the gravity from the sun would pull the matter back.

● **PROBLEM 4–4**

Explain the modern nebular hypothesis.

SOLUTION:

The modern nebular hypothesis is based on the hypothesis that states that the Earth and the solar system formed from a spinning cloud of dust and gases. Most of the matter was pulled inward by gravity; however, some of the dust and gas formed whirlpools. The lighter gases were driven away from the sun due to the radiated energy from the sun; therefore, the heavier elements were held closer to the sun, forming the rocky inner planets such as the Earth. The outer planets were formed by the lighter gases.

● PROBLEM 4-5

How was water formed on the Earth?

SOLUTION:

Hydrogen and oxygen are predominate gases in the dust clouds of the universe. The dust cloud which produced the Earth and its solar system probably contained hydrogen and oxygen. As the Earth cooled, hydrogen and oxygen combined to produce water. The water was probably trapped within the Earth and later released into the atmosphere by volcanic activity.

● PROBLEM 4-6

Why do scientists believe the core of the Earth is predominately iron and nickel?

SOLUTION:

As the gaseous whirlpool which formed the Earth spun, the heavier elements were pulled to the center by gravity. Since most meteorites are composed of iron, scientists believe that the Earth was formed from a large quantity of iron. The magnetic nature of the Earth adds to the belief that the Earth has a great deal of iron and nickel, the only known elements to retain a magnetic property over time.

● PROBLEM 4-7

Georges L.L. de Buffon proposed a theory similar to the collision hypothesis. Describe his theory.

SOLUTION:

Georges L.L. de Buffon stated that a comet collied with the sun, forcing materials out. Lighter elements were thrown farther from the sun than the heavier ones. The Earth began as a liquid but solidified over time. As the Earth cooled, the rotational movement formed an equatorial bulge. As the liquid became a solid, wrinkles developed mountain ranges. Water vapor in the atmosphere formed the hydrosphere (the portion of the Earth that is is water, including liquid water, ice, and water vapor on the surface, underground, or in the atmosphere) through condensation. Some of the water cooled more land to produce the continents. This theory began a debate between scientists on the formation of the Earth.

The Geologic Time Scale

● PROBLEM 4-8

What organisms aid in determining the separation between the eras on the geological time scale?

One of the first multicellular organisms to exist was the jellyfish.

SOLUTION:

Each era has been associated with the introduction of distinct life forms. The Precambrian Era, which involved the beginning of life, had the first algae and bacteria. The Paleozoic Era followed, with the first fish and insects. During the Mesozoic Era the dinosaurs and birds developed. The era in which we live, the Cenozoic Era, has the first mammals and man.

● PROBLEM 4-9

What is the geologic time scale?

SOLUTION:

Divisions in the Earth's history based on changes in life forms and the Earth's crust form the geologic time scale. Life forms change in reaction to changes in environment. The Earth's crust changed over time causing a great many of the environmental changes which produced the evolution of life. The movement of the Earth's plates and the development of glaciers and their movement caused changes in the Earth's crust.

● PROBLEM 4–10

What are the main divisions on the geological time scale? Describe them.

SOLUTION:

There are three main divisions on the geological time scale. Era is the largest division. There are four eras on the geological time scale, the Precambrian, the Paleozoic, the Mesozoic, and the Cenozoic. These eras are based on the changes in life forms and in the Earth's crust which occurred during a specified time. The eras are divided into epochs. These smaller divisions of time are based on the extinction or appearance of major life forms. Only the Cenozoic Era has its epochs divided further. These divisions, called periods, are based on subtle changes in existing life forms or on glacier movements.

From the beginning of the Earth to about 1,500 million years ago, the Precambrian Era existed. During the Precambrian Era bacteria and algae formed. Toward the end of this era jellyfish developed.

Today, very little evidence of the Precambrian Era is visible. The rocks of the Precambrian Era are buried deep within the crust except in areas like the Grand Canyon and the Canadian Shield. These two land features give scientists access to Precambrian rocks and life.

The Paleozoic Era, or "ancient life," lasted from about 600 million years ago until about 290 million years ago. Called the Age of Invertebrates, the Paleozoic Era was a time when the sea was full of life. Towards the end of the era, reptiles and insects began to appear in swamps and forests. The life was not all seen at once, however. In order to understand the development of the different life forms, the Paleozoic Era is divided into six periods.

The first division is the Cambrian Period. During the Cambrian Period trilobites, brachiopods, and worms became abundant, all in the seas. Shelled organisms and jawless fish developed during the Ordovician Period. During the Silurian Period, the land began to develop life in the form of plants. The most abundant life was still in the sea, with jawed fish coming into existence. The first amphibians appeared during the Devonian Period. Fish, however, were the most abundant life. Land began having many diverse life forms during the Carboniferous Period. Forests and swamps had horsetails and club mosses with the first reptiles and insects. Finally, during the Permian Period at the end of the era, most of the sea life disappeared.

From 230 to about 140 million years ago, the Mesozoic Era existed. Mesozoic, or "middle life," is known as the Age of the Reptiles. Since the Mesozoic Era was the time of the dinosaurs, it is appropriately divided into periods according to the life of the dinosaurs. The first period, the Triassic, was when the first dinosaurs and the first mammals appeared. While dinosaurs dominated the Jurassic Period, birds took flight. Dinosaurs became extinct during the Cretaceous Period as flowering plants made their appearance.

The Age of Mammals, the Cenozoic Era, began about 65 million years ago and is continuing today. Meaning "recent life," Cenozoic is when the first Homo Sapiens made their appearance. Mankind has not dominated the entire Cenozoic Era, however. The first of two periods, the Tertiary Period, is divided into five epochs; each having the appearance or disappearance of specific life forms. During the Paleocene Epoch, small mammals began to become widespread. The Eocene Epoch had the development of larger mammals such as the whale and horse. A cooling climate during the Oligocene Epoch caused grasses to take the place of tropical plants. Land bridges between North America and Siberia are believed to have developed during the Miocene Epoch. This allowed mastodons and other large herd animals to come to North America. Glaciers formed during the Pliocene Epoch, causing ocean water levels to fall, forming land bridges where water once existed.

The shorter and more recent of the two periods, the Quaternary Period, is divided into two epochs. The Pleistocene Epoch is known as the Ice Age. Mankind and his civilizations developed during the Holocene Epoch, when the climate became warmer.

Fossils and the Theory of Uniformity

● **PROBLEM 4–11**

What is uniformitarianism?

SOLUTION:

Uniformitarianism is based on a hypothesis by James Hutton. His idea of "the present is the key to the past" utilizes the concept that the geological processes of the present were at work in the past. The hypothesis states that the rates these processes occur may vary with time and place but the actual events can be traced through history. Scientists, utilizing uniformitarianism, can explain the formation of the landforms known today.

● **PROBLEM 4–12**

What is a geologic column?

Geologic column with index fossils

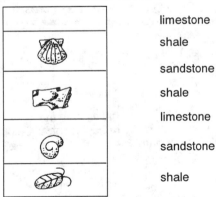

limestone

shale

sandstone

shale

limestone

sandstone

shale

SOLUTION:

While constructing a canal in the late 1970s, William Smith studied the fossils uncovered. He noted that the same kind of rocks had similar types of fossils. He then arranged the fossils in a sequence based on the depth where the rock was found, with earlier rocks being deeper in the ground. This process placed fossils according to their ages relative to each other. The result was the first geologic column. Today, scientists use the same process to date some fossils and rock layers in the field by using index fossils.

How is correlation used to date fossils?

Trilobites are used as index fossils.

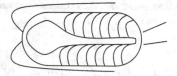

SOLUTION:

Fossils found only in specific rock layers are called index fossils. The index fossils are known to have existed during a specific time. Any rocks or fossils found in the same rock layer with the index fossil would have existed at the same geologic time. This process, called correlation, is used mostly in field work. On-site dating by the use of index fossils gives scientists an estimated time the organism lived on Earth.

● **PROBLEM 4–14**

Describe the difference between a facies fossil and a trace fossil.

Trace fossil

Animal steps in mud and makes an imprint.

Soil covers the dried imprint.

After pressure has been applied, the imprint remains as a fossil.

Cast fossil

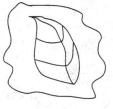

Leaf falls on mud.

Imprint of leaf remains after leaf decomposes. This is a mold.

Minerals fill the mold, harden, and become a cast fossil.

SOLUTION:

The fossil remains of organisms which lived only in certain environments are called facies fossils. These fossils allow scientists to make assumptions concerning the climate at specific areas during certain times. Facies fossils give an insight into the past environmental changes that occurred over history.

Evidence of the activity of organisms in the past are called trace fossils. Imprints such as footprints, trails, and burrows are examples of trace fossils. There are two types of trace fossils. Molds were formed when the organism left a hollow space such as a footprint in the mud. The hollow space is then hardened and is filled by sediment preserving the imprint. The other form of trace fossil is a cast. A cast is the result of a hollow being filled with mud or minerals which harden into a model of the part of the organism which caused the imprint. Both of these can give a scientist much information, such as the method the organism used for moving, the weight of the organism, and whether the organism moved in herds.

● PROBLEM 4–15

What are the types of fossil forms of an actual organism?

SOLUTION:

There are two main processes which form the fossils of actual organisms, carbonization and petrification. Carbonization is the process in which the organism dies and is buried. The sediment squeezes elements out of the organism, leaving behind a thin layer of carbon—one of the hardest elements. The carbon layer can have details of the organism such as the veins of a leaf.

Petrification is the other method of fossilizing the actual organism. During petrification, water dissolves the minerals of the organism by entering the hard parts of the organism, such as the bone. The minerals then harden forming a replica of the hard structure of the organism. Petrification produces fossils with microscopic detail of the organism.

● PROBLEM 4–16

What is the law of superposition?

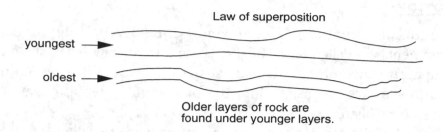

Law of superposition

youngest →

oldest →

Older layers of rock are
found under younger layers.

SOLUTION:

Sedimentary rock produces layers, with the younger layers of sediment building on top of the older layers. This process of sedimentation forms sedimentary rocks with older layers on the bottom. The law of superposition states that the older sedimentary rocks are formed beneath the younger sedimentary rocks. This knowledge allows scientists to give relative ages to the rock layers.

A break in the relative rock record is called an unconformity. This can be caused by part of the rock becoming exposed and weathered due to uplifting or faulting. New rock can then form in the place of older rock, forming a difference in the rock layers. This new layering cuts across the old. This process is an explanation of the law of cross-cutting relationships. The differences in the layers of the sedimentary rock involved are easily noticed by the presence of minerals, fossils, and other materials which are included in the rock layers.

● PROBLEM 4–17

What is the law of cross-cutting relationships?

SOLUTION:

Younger features cutting through older features in the rock formations is a statement of the law of cross-cutting relationships. Folds and faults are processes which occur after rock layers have been formed. An example of the process is when igneous rock intrudes into an older layer of sedimentary rock.

What determines the relative age of a rock layer?

SOLUTION:

The relative age of a rock layer is determined by using the law of superposition. Layers above and below a rock layer can be determined by fossil evidence. The approximate age or relative age of the middle layer can then be determined.

● PROBLEM 4-19

What is unconformity?

Unconformity due to tilting of the Earth's surface

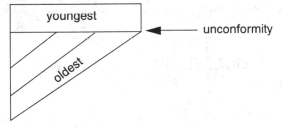

Unconformity due to folding of the Earth's surface

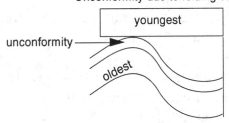

SOLUTION:

An unconformity is the result of erosion. When rock layers are eroded, new layers of soil and rock replace the old layers. This causes an unconformity.

● PROBLEM 4-20

What is the process of petrification?

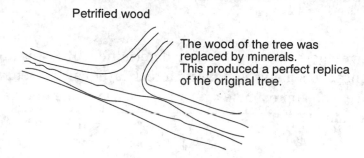

Petrified wood

The wood of the tree was replaced by minerals. This produced a perfect replica of the original tree.

SOLUTION:

Organisms are buried under mud, sand, or ash. The hard parts such as bones, shells, or wood, are replaced over time by minerals. The minerals harden producing rock. The rock has the same appearance, even the microscopic cells have their original structural appearance.

SHORT ANSWER QUESTIONS FOR REVIEW

Choose the correct answer.

1. Which is the best term to describe the remains of ancient plants and animals that have been preserved in solid rock? (a) Stratification (b) Fossils (c) Coproliths (d) None of the above.

2. "Planets move around the sun because of the gravitational force exerted by the sun" is part of which scientist's theory? (a) Aristotle (b) Newton (c) Einstein (d) Hipparchus

3. A planet chooses its shortest path through a four-dimensional world which is defined by the presence of the sun would be the theory of which scientist? (a) Aristotle (b) Newton (c) Einstein (d) Hipparchus

4. _____ developed the theory stating that the ocean covered the entire Earth. (a) Benjamin Warner (b) Joseph Copernicus (c) Abraham Werner (d) Alexander Bell

5. Hutton _____ before he was able to get his fellow scientists to accept his ideas. (a) left the scientific field (b) was institutionalized (c) died (d) disappeared

6. The major battle between theories is (a) which strategy is most correct. (b) which research is best developed. (c) which theory is best presented. (d) which strategy solves the problem.

Items 7 to 9 refer to the following table.

ERA	PERIOD	EVENTS	BEGAN MILLIONS OF YEARS AGO
CENOZOIC	Quaternary	Age of humans. Four major glacial advances.	2
	Tertiary	Increase in mammals. Appearance of primates. Mountain building in Europe and Asia.	65
MESOZOIC	Cretaceous	Extinction of dinosaurs. Increase in flowering plants and reptiles.	140
	Jurassic	Birds. Mammals. Dominance of dinosaurs. Mountain building in western North America.	195
	Triassic	Beginning of dinosaurs and primitive mammals.	230
PALEOZOIC	Permian	Reptiles spread and develop. Evaporate deposits. Glaciation in Southern Hemisphere.	280
	Carboniferous	Abundant amphibians. Reptiles appear.	345
	Devonian	Age of fishes. First amphibians. First abundant forests on land.	395
	Silurian	First land plants. Mountain building in Europe.	435
	Ordovician	First fishes and vertebrates.	500
	Cambrian	Age of marine invertebrates.	600
PRECAMBRIAN TIME		Beginning of life. At least five times longer than all geologic time following.	

from *Introduction to Oceanography*, fourth edition, 1988 by David A. Ross, Prentice Hall.

7. Which of the following statements is true? (a) Earth's history is divided into time blocks, determined by geologic events only. (b) Earth's history is divided into equal divisions of time. (c) Earth's history is divided into time blocks of differing amounts of time. (d) Each period of Earth's history is divided into time blocks called eras.

8. Which sequence of life is correct? (a) Invertebrates, Fish, Reptiles, Mammals (b) Fish, Invertebrates, Mammals, Birds (c) Plants, Invertebrates, Forests, Fish (d) Invertebrates, Mammals, Birds, Plants

9. According to the table, the Carboniferous period would have marked the appearance of the first relatives of the (a) sharks. (b) eagles. (c) Homo Sapiens. (d) common alligator.

10. In setting forth his Theory on Continental Drift, Alfred Wegener gave a series of proofs which supported his theory that the continents at one time were all connected. Which of the statements below would not support his idea? (a) The coasts of South America and Africa fit together like a jigsaw puzzle. (b) When continents are placed together, their mountain ranges connect. (c) The weather conditions on matching continents are similar. (d) Fossils of the same age and type are found on connecting continents.

Fill in the blanks.

11. According to the Big Bang Theory, the universe is thought to have been formed following an _____ that took place 10-15 billion years ago.

12. _____ formed the masses that were knocked loose at the time of the collision.

13. The theory that all life began with the settling of the water was formulated in the _____ .

14. The Creation Theory is based on the first chapter of _____ .

15. According to the Creation Theory, the beginning of the Earth occurred in the year _____ .

Determine whether the following statements are true or false.

16. The factors that dispel the Big Bang Theory are the escape of dust and gases.

17. One accepted theory for the formation of our solar system from a rotating cloud of gas and dust was proposed by Immanuel Kant.

18. Hutton's theory stated how the Earth was gradually changing and would continue to change in the same ways.

19. Various attempts have been made to establish the correct order of beginnings based on data and dates in the Koran.

20. When considering evolution and change, survival and prosperity of the Universe is the basis for all theories.

ANSWER KEY

1. b
2. b
3. c
4. c
5. c
6. d
7. c
8. a
9. d
10. c

11. explosion
12. Planets
13. 1700s
14. Genesis
15. 3760 BC
16. False
17. True
18. True
19. False
20. True

CHAPTER 5

GEOLOGY

Mineral Chart
This is only using examples
It is NOT a complete chart

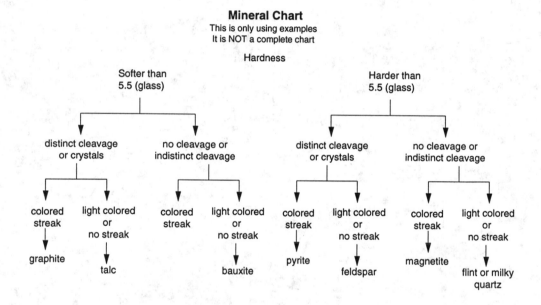

Hardness

Softer than 5.5 (glass) — Harder than 5.5 (glass)

Softer than 5.5 (glass): distinct cleavage or crystals / no cleavage or indistinct cleavage

distinct cleavage or crystals: colored streak → graphite; light colored or no streak → talc

no cleavage or indistinct cleavage: colored streak; light colored or no streak → bauxite

Harder than 5.5 (glass): distinct cleavage or crystals / no cleavage or indistinct cleavage

distinct cleavage or crystals: colored streak → pyrite; light colored or no streak → feldspar

no cleavage or indistinct cleavage: colored streak → magnetite; light colored or no streak → flint or milky quartz

Atomic Structure and Bonding

● **PROBLEM 5–1**

Explain basic atomic structure.

Basic atomic structure using Bohr's atom.

nucleus: protons and neutrons

electrons orbiting in shells

Atoms are the smallest part of an element that retains the properties of the element. They are not the smallest particles in existence. Atoms can be broken down to electrons, protons, and neutrons, as well as many even smaller particles.

Protons and neutrons are located in the center or the nucleus of the atom. Surrounding the nucleus are orbiting electrons.

Each electron maintains its own location which cannot be definitely determined. The wave nature of the electron only allows for a prediction of position in the orbit in which it is found. Electrons maintain the lowest energy state possible, but no two electrons in an atom can maintain the same energy state. When two atoms approach each other, the electrons at the outer energy levels can transfer to the other atom or be shared between both the atoms. This transfer or sharing forms chemical bonds, and a molecule results.

Crystal Types and Formation

● PROBLEM 5–2

What type of bonding is common in the formation of crystals?

SOLUTION:

Ionic bonding, or the transfer of one or more electrons from one atom to another, is common in the formation of crystals. This type of bonding allows the atoms to form an orderly pattern because the charges produced by the gain and loss of electrons holds the atoms together. The orderly pattern formed is called a crystal.

● PROBLEM 5–3

What are the two main types of bonding?

SOLUTION:

The two main types of bonding are called ionic bonding and covalent bonding.

```
A •  ◄────── • B          C   :   D
  −1          +1
ionic bond               covalent bond
```

As you look at the diagram of the ionic bond, you can see that atom "A" took an electron from atom "B." This is because atom "A" is more powerful than is atom "B." This power is called electronegativity.

As you look at the diagram of the covalent bond, you can see that atom "C" and atom "D" shared the electrons that were between them. You could conclude that "C" and "D" must have electronegativities (power) that were very similar, which allowed neither to gain control of the electrons between them.

The bond between "C" and "D" is called a non-polar, covalent bond. The covalent term means that the electrons are shared (rather than transferred from one atom to another), while the non-polar term means that this sharing is one in which neither atom ("C" or "D") has more power to pull the electrons.

Suppose that two atoms in a bond were not sufficiently different in their power to cause an ionic bond to form, but also were not so similar in power to cause a non-polar covalent bond. This situation is called a polar-covalent bond and can be pictured as follows:

```
        E •• F
```

The shared pair of electrons has been pulled toward "E," but that pull was not enough to make the bond ionic. You could conclude that the "E" had the higher electronegativity. The "E" end of this molecule will be a little more negative than the "F" end of the molecule because the negative electrons in the bond lie closer to that end.

An ionic compound is held together by the attraction of its opposite charges (see diagram of ionic bond, above), while a covalently bonded compound is held together by the sharing of electrons.

● PROBLEM 5–4

What is the difference between a mixture and a compound?

SOLUTION:

A pure substance is one in which the chemical composition is the same throughout. When two substances combine forming a mixture, they can be separated by physical means. Usually a mixture is a blend of one pure substance with another or one substance dissolved in another. An example of a mixture is coffee. Some of the coffee is dissolved in the water forming a mixture. The water can be evaporated, which separates the grounds from the water.

A compound cannot be separated into its components by physical means. Only a chemical reaction can separate a compound. Two or more substances combined by chemical bonding form a compound. The hydrogen and oxygen molecules in water cannot be separated except by a chemical reaction with another substance, such as calcium carbonate. This releases the hydrogen and allows the oxygen to combine with the calcium to produce calcium oxide.

● **PROBLEM 5–5**

Define the six basic crystalline structures and explain what determines a crystalline structure.

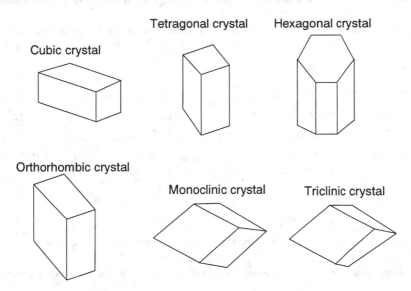

Cubic crystal

Tetragonal crystal

Hexagonal crystal

Orthorhombic crystal

Monoclinic crystal

Triclinic crystal

SOLUTION:

Each crystalline structure is identified by the position of the atoms along imaginary lines within the crystal, called axes. The simplest crystal shape is cubic. In a cubic crystal the atoms at the end of the axes are equally spaced from each other. The axes are at right angles to each other. A

111

tetrahedral crystal shape has a single long axis with two side axes of equal length. These axes are also right angles to each other. An eight-sided crystal has a hexagonal shape. A crystal with a shape similar to a rectangular box is called an orthorhombic crystalline shape. Each of the three axes are of different lengths but they are at right angles to each other. A monoclinic-shaped crystal has three varying length axes, two of which are at right angles. The sixth crystal shape is a triclinic shape. The triclinic-shaped crystal is similar to the tetragonal shape, but the axes are not at unequal angles to each other.

The composition of a crystal determines the internal arrangement of the atom or molecules of the crystal. The size, shape, and the amount of electrostatic forces determine the arrangement of the unit cell of the crystal. The unit cell is the smallest part of the crystal with the same shape of the main crystal. The geometric shape of the unit cell determines the shape of the crystal lattice. The crystal lattice becomes a three-dimensional pattern of the repeating crystal unit cell.

● PROBLEM 5–6

How are crystals formed?

SOLUTION:

Magma needs to be a fluid with time to cool to produce crystals. In order for crystals to be produced, the ions within the magma must have time to join in the lattice form of a crystal. If ions are not allowed proper cooling time, only the embryonic crystal can be shaped. This does not allow a lattice of crystals to be formed.

● PROBLEM 5–7

What causes the varying size of crystals in rocks?

SOLUTION:

The speed at which rock cools produces different sizes of crystals. Small crystals are formed from the slow cooling of molten rock, usually deep within the earth. Fast cooling on the surface or in the air usually produces large crystalline shapes. These are usually coarse-grained crystals.

Embryonic crystals are cooled almost immediately, usually producing a glass-like crystalline appearance.

What is the characteristic called parting?

SOLUTION:

Parting is a physical property similar to cleavage. Caused by structural imperfections, parting surfaces are due to strains within the mineral structures. Parting is not a characteristic of the mineral crystal but only of an individual crystal.

Categories of Minerals

What is a mineral?

Silicate molecule forms a tetrahedron

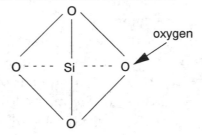

SOLUTION:

A mineral is a substance with a specific composition forming a crystalline pattern. The mineral can be composed of a single element but usually it is formed by ionically bonded compounds. Minerals combine in different ratios and combinations to produce different types of rock.

Distinguish between silicates and nonsilicates.

SOLUTION:

Silicates and nonsilicates are divisions of minerals. Silicates form more than 92 percent of the minerals in the crust. They are composed of silicon and oxygen in tetrahedron shapes with other elements attached to the tetrahedron. Feldspars, quartz, and micas are three divisions of silicates.

Nonsilicates are minerals composed of elements other than silicon. Nonsilicates include sulfides, sulfates, carbonates, oxides, and halides.

What are the families of silicates and nonsilicates?

SOLUTION:

Silicates are minerals that contain silicon. There are three main families of silicates. Fifty percent of the crust of the Earth consists of feldspars. Feldspars are silicates which have a hardness of about six on the Mohs' scale. Other than SiO tetrahedrons, feldspars can contain aluminum, sodium, potassium, and calcium.

The second family of silicates is quartz. Quartz contains only tetrahedrons of silicon and oxygen. Most sands are particles of quartz. Colorful combinations can be found in samples of quartz.

A very soft family of silicates are the micas. They rate about 2.5 on the Mohs' hardness scale. Micas are usually layered and easily separated into sheets.

Nonsilicates do not contain silicon. Sulfides are nonsilicates which contain sulfur plus at least one other metal. Sulfides do not contain oxygen. Sulfates are nonsilicates which contain the polyatomic ion SO_4. The most common sulfate is gypsum, or calcium sulfate. The most important component of oxides is oxygen. In oxides, metals such as iron combine with oxygen to form such minerals as magnetite and hematite. The fourth family of nonsilicates contains halogens. The halides will usually contain either chlorine or fluorine with sodium, potassium, or calcium.

• PROBLEM 5–12

What is a gem?

SOLUTION:

A mineral is a gem if it is colorful and reflects light easily. The more pure and colorful the mineral the more value it has. Gems can be precious or semiprecious. A precious stone is one which is rare and has desirable characteristics such as durability. A semiprecious stone is more abundant and less valuable.

• PROBLEM 5–13

What is a rock?

SOLUTION:

Rocks are combinations of one or more types of minerals. They are composed of essential minerals with accessory minerals. Rocks are classified into three categories: sedimentary, metamorphic, and igneous.

• PROBLEM 5–14

What is an ore?

SOLUTION:

An ore is a mineral deposit which can be mined for profit. Metallic ores contain valuable metals. Nonmetallic ores contain substances such as limestone and sulfur. The main qualification for an ore is that it is valuable for use in some industry.

• PROBLEM 5–15

What is a geode?

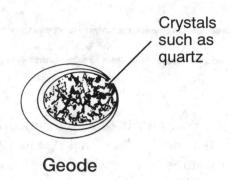

Geode

SOLUTION:

A geode is a hollow, ball-shaped rock up to 30 centimeters in diameter. Mineral crystals are found inside the geode. Quartz is a common crystal lining for a geode.

● **PROBLEM 5-16**

What is a vein environment?

A vein of ore may be at a few centimeters depth or several kilometers

vein of ore

SOLUTION:

A vein is a sheetlike mass of mineral found in fractures of the earth's crust. Veins can spread in any direction just as a fracture. Generally, veins are separated by small areas of rock.

● **PROBLEM 5-17**

Describe a hypothermal vein.

SOLUTION:

Deep underground where temperatures range between 300°C and 500°C, hypothermal veins contain coarse grained minerals. These veins are pushed up toward the surface where they are mined. Ranging from one centimeter to several meters in thickness, hypothermal veins can be as long as a few kilometers. Metal ores are commonly found in hypothermal veins.

● PROBLEM 5–18

Describe a mesothermal vein.

SOLUTION:

Mesothermal veins are produced between 200°C and 300°C at moderate pressure. Small veins of one centimeter to about three meters can be mined for distances up to three meters.

● PROBLEM 5–19

Describe an epithermal vein.

SOLUTION:

Epithermal veins are produced at low temperatures between 100°C and 200°C. These are shallow veins, no deeper than a kilometer. Since they are close to the surface, many epithermal veins have been exhausted. Both metals and nonmetals can be mined from the near-surface veins.

● PROBLEM 5–20

What are placers?

SOLUTION:

Placers are deposits of minerals found on the surface of the Earth. Most placers are produced by the weathering from streams and waves. Most precious metals such as gold and platinum, are associated with placers.

What are malleability and ductility?

SOLUTION:

Metals have two distinct characteristics: malleability and ductility. Malleability is the ability to hammer a metal into sheets. The ability to be pulled into a wire strand is called ductility. These properties make metals easy to work with and very valuable minerals.

What is radioactivity?

Radioactive decay of $^{235}_{92}U$ to produce heat.

$$^{235}_{92}U + ^{1}_{0}n \rightarrow ^{144}_{56}Ba + ^{90}_{36}Kr + 2\ ^{1}_{0}n + heat$$

SOLUTION:

Radioactivity is the property of some minerals to break down. The nucleus of the atom breaks down to produce a lighter nucleus. This breakdown produces energy, generally in the form of heat.

Identification of Minerals

What two tests use color to identify minerals?

SOLUTION:

The color of the mineral is an important method of identifying a mineral; however, the color of a mineral can be misleading. Some minerals have the same color characteristics. In order to further identify minerals, the streak test is used.

The streak test uses the color of the mineral on an unglazed white porcelain tile. The mineral is struck on the tile to produce a color streak. This streak can distinguish between minerals which appear to be identical. The streak test can, however, only give a limited amount of information.

A white or transparent streak usually identifies only that the mineral is nonmetal in composition.

● **PROBLEM 5-24**

What is the Mohs scale?

SOLUTION:

A scientist compares the hardness of one mineral to another by testing resistance to scratching. The Mohs scale is a scale used to determine the hardness of a mineral based on the comparison between specific minerals. The scale is based on the following: 1-talc, 2-gypsum, 3-calcite, 4-flourite, 5-apatite, 6-orthoclase, 7-quartz, 8-topaz, 9-corundum, and 10-diamond (the softest is one and the hardest is 10). These minerals are used to scratch an unknown mineral. If the mineral is scratched by the known mineral it is softer than the known mineral. If it scratches the known mineral, the unknown mineral is harder.

● **PROBLEM 5-25**

What is luster?

SOLUTION:

The reflection of light by the mineral is luster. A metallic luster reflects light easily. It is considered shiny and mirror-like. A nonmetallic luster varies in the amount of light reflected. A glassy luster means the mineral reflects some light similar to the way glass reflects light. The other types of nonmetallic lusters are also identified by substances which reflect small amounts of light. These are pearly, waxy, or dull.

● **PROBLEM 5-26**

What is the difference between cleavage and fracture?

SOLUTION:

When a mineral splits with a smooth surface, the split is called cleavage. If the split forms a rough, uneven surface a fracture is formed. One

119

unusual type of fracture is the conchoidal fracture. This type of fracture produces a curved surface at the break.

● PROBLEM 5–27

What tests are used to compare the heaviness of minerals?

SOLUTION:

There are two tests used to determine the density, or heaviness, of a mineral. Specific gravity compares the mass of a mineral with the mass of an equal volume of water. Another comparison is done by using the relative weights of the minerals. Two minerals are held, one in each hand. The weight of each is compared. This method determines the heft of one mineral to another.

● PROBLEM 5–28

Define the term "physical property."

SOLUTION:

A physical property is an observed characteristic of a substance. The characteristic does not change the substance. Examples of physical properties are color, taste, odor, and density. Generally, physical properties can be "sensed."

● PROBLEM 5–29

Define the term "chemical property."

SOLUTION:

A property which describes the reaction between the substance and another substance is a chemical property. Chemical properties are basically descriptions of changes which occur due to a chemical reaction.

What is double refraction?

SOLUTION:

Double refraction is when light hits a material and is split into two separate beams. A double image of objects is seen when viewed through a substance with the property of double refraction.

Describe the property of fluorescence.

SOLUTION:

Named after the mineral fluorite, fluorescence is the ability of a mineral to glow under ultraviolet light. Many minerals with this property actually have different colors under ultraviolet light.

Describe the property of phosphorescence.

SOLUTION:

When a mineral continues to emit visible light after the source of ultraviolet light is removed, the mineral phosphoresces. A mineral can phosphoresce for several minutes.

What is the difference between essential minerals and accessory minerals?

SOLUTION:

Essential minerals are those which always occur in a particular rock. For example, quartz and feldspar are always present in granite. Mica is an accessory mineral in granite. It occasionally appears.

Describe the three phases of matter.

Solid phase

Particles are close together.
They are held by cohesive forces.

Liquid phase

Particles are not as close together.
They take the shape of the container.

Gas phase

Particles are far apart, filling the container
in both volume and shape.

SOLUTION:

The three main phases of matter are solid, liquid, and gas. In a solid the atoms and molecules are tightly packed. This causes a solid to have definite shape and volume. A liquid has atoms or molecules which are not as tightly packed. This allows a liquid to have an indefinite shape. A gas has atoms or molecules spread at distances producing no definite shape or volume.

Metamorphic Rocks

● **PROBLEM 5–35**

Distinguish between the main categories of metamorphic rock.

SOLUTION:

Foliated and nonfoliated are the two main categories of metamorphic rock. Foliated rocks are banded with different alternating bands of color. These different colors are due to different minerals which are found in the bands.

Nonfoliated rocks are not banded. These rocks are formed from a single mineral with crystals of similar sizes and shapes.

How are metamorphic rocks formed?

Formation of metamorphic rock by heat

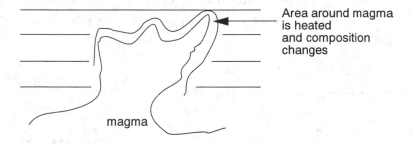

Area around magma
is heated
and composition
changes

magma

Formation of metamorphic rock by pressure

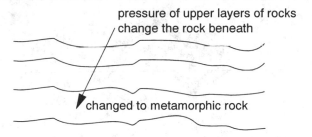

pressure of upper layers of rocks
change the rock beneath

changed to metamorphic rock

SOLUTION:

Metamorphic means "changed in form," so metamorphic rock is rock which has been changed. The changes occur due to extreme heat and pressure under the Earth's surface. The weight of the sediments above the rock and the extreme heat of the magma below the rock force the rock to undergo changes. Uplifting of mountains is another method that causes changes to occur in rock due to heat and pressure. In order for metamorphic rock to be produced, a change must occur in the rock. The change is usually compositional in nature.

● **PROBLEM 5–37**

Define regional metamorphism and contact metamorphism.

SOLUTION:

When large areas of rock undergo changes, regional metamorphism occurs. Heat and pressure caused by uplifting of mountains is an example of regional metamorphism.

When magma pushes into solid rock, the heat from the magma causes reactions within the rock to occur. This, combined with the pressure exerted on the rock by magma and gravity, force new rock to be produced. This direct contact with magma in a usually small area is called contact metamorphism.

Sedimentary Rocks

How are sedimentary rocks classified?

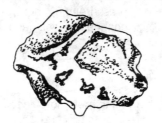

Clastic Rock
Appearance

SOLUTION:

Sedimentary rocks are classified into two groups according to the size of the particles with which they are composed. Clastic rocks are sedimentary rocks formed from sediments of different sizes. Clastic rocks are divided into three groups. When pebbles are embedded in the rock, the rock is either a conglomerate or a breccia. If the particles are the size of sand, the rocks are called sandstone. Siltstone rocks are formed from particles which cannot be seen with the unaided eye. Shale is another clastic rock type. Shale contains particles which are extremely small and compressed tightly together.

Nonclastic sedimentary rocks are characterized by the remains of past life forms or dissolved minerals. These rocks contain quartz, halite, gypsum, and calcite.

What is the most common method in which sedimentary rocks are formed?

SOLUTION:

Igneous and metamorphic rock become exposed to the surface of the Earth. Weathering breaks down these rocks into smaller pieces which can be carried away by wind, water, or ice. Over time the sediments build on top of each other, producing pressure. The sediments become compact under this pressure, forming rocks called sedimentary rocks.

● **PROBLEM 5-40**

What are the differences between chemical sedimentary rocks and organic sedimentary rocks?

SOLUTION:

Rocks made of chemical sediments which have been dissolved from minerals are chemical sedimentary rocks. The precipitating of solid minerals from their solution in water causes the sediments to layer, producing pressure on the sediments beneath (when entire bodies of water evaporate leaving behind these sediments they are called evaporites). An example of chemical sedimentary rocks are concretions. Concretions are ball-shaped rocks formed when ground water is lowered, leaving behind sediment. The most common material found in concretions is silica.

Organic sedimentary rocks are composed of organic sediments from once-living organisms. These sediments are the result of dissolving the harder portions of the organism. The minerals then precipitate, producing rocks. Fossils are usually found in organic sedimentary rocks.

● **PROBLEM 5-41**

What is the most common rock found on the earth's surface? Why?

SOLUTION:

Sedimentary rocks are the most common rocks found on the earth's surface. They are produced by the effects of weathering. Igneous rocks and metamorphic rocks are produced by heat and/or pressure. They are exposed to the earth's surface where weathering occurs. Changes are produced in them causing sedimentary rocks to be produced.

● **PROBLEM 5–42**

What is the most common agent which produces sedimentary rocks?

SOLUTION:

Water comes in contact with nearly all rocks. Water can change a rock by erosion or reaction. Water is the most common agent which produces sedimentary rocks.

● **PROBLEM 5–43**

Describe the process of compaction.

SOLUTION:

Compaction occurs when sediments build, producing pressure on the lower levels. This pressure squeezes the particles of sediment together producing rock. The rock is held together due to the compaction of the particles.

● **PROBLEM 5–44**

Describe the process of cementation.

SOLUTION:

Quartz and calcite are examples of substances which act as cementing agents for particles of sediment. These minerals fill the spaces between the sediments and harden. The rock which is produced is held together by cementation.

Describe the process of precipitation.

SOLUTION:

When dissolved minerals in water settle out, precipitation occurs. These sediments harden which produces rocks.

What is an evaporite?

SOLUTION:

An evaporite is a chemical rock which has been left behind by an evaporating body of water. Rock gypsum is an example of an evaporite. Usually rock gypsum is left behind by water deposits. An example of rock gypsum is the white cliffs of Dover in England.

What produces ripple marks?

SOLUTION:

Ripple marks are produced by the movement of particles by wind or water. Ripple marks are found in sedimentary rocks. Generally, the sedimentary rocks are in areas which were covered by water or which are very arid.

What is a concretion?

SOLUTION:

A concretion is a ball-shaped rock. It can range in size from a few centimeters to several meters in diameter. Concretions are formed as minerals precipitate around a fossil. As the fossil decays, the concretion is left behind.

Igneous Rocks

● PROBLEM 5–49

How are igneous rocks formed?

SOLUTION:

Igneous means "from fire." The formation of igneous rocks occurs when hot molten rock cools and solidifies. Igneous rock can be produced deep in the Earth from magma or on the surface of the Earth from lava.

● PROBLEM 5–50

How much of the Earth's surface is made of igneous rocks?

SOLUTION:

Ninety percent by weight of the Earth is composed of igneous rocks. Most igneous rocks are silicates. This makes silicate rocks the most common type on Earth.

● PROBLEM 5–51

How do geologists classify igneous rocks?

SOLUTION:

Igneous rocks are classified by the minerals found within the rock as well as by the texture of the rock. Mineral composition divides igneous rocks into a high silicate group and a low silicate group. The amount of silica can be seen easily; the more silica, the lighter the color of the rock.

Texture is caused by the speed at which cooling takes place. Slower cooling produces larger crystals. This allows for two categories of texture: smooth and glass-like such as obsidian, and rough and coarse-grained such as granite.

What are the classifications of igneous rock?

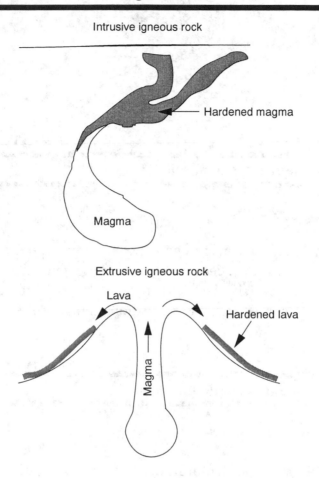

Intrusive igneous rock

Hardened magma

Magma

Extrusive igneous rock

Lava

Hardened lava

Magma

SOLUTION:

Igneous rocks are classified into three categories. Formed deep in the Earth from cooled magma, intrusive rocks have large crystals due to the slow cooling. Coarse-grained rocks such as granite are classified as intrusive. Extrusive igneous rocks are formed on the surface of the Earth by fast-cooling lava; small crystals or no crystals are formed. When magma begins cooling and then is suddenly pushed to the surface to complete the cooling process, a combination of crystal sizes will be produced. Rocks with this combination of small and large crystals are called a porphyry.

Porphyry

What is hydrothermal metamorphism?

SOLUTION:

Hydrothermal metamorphism occurs when large amounts of fluids are moved over igneous rock. These fluids carry dissolved sodium, potassium, and similar metals, which react with the rock to produce changes. This chemical reaction causes actual composition changes in the rock.

What are volcanic rocks and plutonic rocks?

SOLUTION:

Both volcanic rocks and plutonic rocks are types of igneous rocks. Volcanic rocks are extrusive and formed from lava. Plutonic rocks are intrusive and formed from magma.

Intrusive and Extrusive Rocks

Distinguish between intrusive and extrusive rocks.

SOLUTION:

An intrusive rock is formed by the cooling of molten rock within the Earth. Intrusive rocks, such as granite, usually cool slowly, producing very large crystals. Small crystals of extrusive rock, such as basalt, are usually produced by rapid cooling on the crust of the Earth.

How are extrusive and intrusive rocks identified?

SOLUTION:

Usually microscopic crystals such as those in basalt or the absence of crystals indicate an extrusive rock. Non-crystalline obsidian is an example of a glassy extrusive rock. These are usually cooled so rapidly that crystals do not have time to form. Vesicular extrusive rock such as scoria is usually cooled quickly from lava. The gases do not have an opportunity to escape. This forms pockets of gases in the rock. Pumice, a very lightweight rock, is an example of a pyroclastic rock. These types of extrusive rock are thrown out of a volcano in an explosive manner. The gases escape, forming holes in the rock and causing the rock to be so lightweight it can usually float on water.

All intrusive rocks have large crystals which can be seen with the unaided eye. Coarse-grained crystals such as granite are larger than 2 mm. Medium-grained crystals are between 1 mm and 2 mm. Fine-grained crystals are between 0.062 mm and 1 mm. These rocks are called phaneritic if the grain size is larger than 0.062 mm.

Does an igneous rock which is intrusive differ in composition from an extrusive igneous rock?

SOLUTION:

Composition of igneous rock occurs from the type of rock melted to produce the magma. As the magma is pushed upward, some cools below the surface but the rest may cool above the surface. The composition will be the same, but the crystals composing the rocks will be different. Since the melting point is dictated by the composition, however, the speed at which the rock cools is determined by its composition.

The Rock Cycle

Explain the rock cycle.

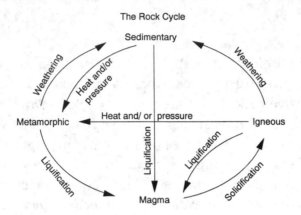

The Rock Cycle

SOLUTION:

The rock cycle is a simplified diagram of rock formation. Each type of rock is shown with the processes needed for the formation of the type of rock indicated. Magma cools to produce igneous rock which can undergo more heat and pressure to become metamorphic rock. On the surface of the Earth, igneous rock which undergoes weathering can become sedimentary rock. Sedimentary rock can be buried which can cause heat and pressure. This will produce metamorphic rock. Exposed metamorphic rock can be weathered to produce sedimentary rock. Either metamorphic or sedimentary rock which is buried and then melted can then become magma. This process is a continuous cycle of changes.

Describe the method which produces each type of rock.

SOLUTION:

Igneous rock can only be produced from liquid rock which is magma or lava. The liquid rock hardens, forming crystals which identify the type of igneous rock. Sedimentary rocks form from weathered material produced from exposed metamorphic, sedimentary, or igneous rock. These sediments are carried by wind, water, or ice, and then layered. The layering produces pressure which causes compaction and the formation of rock. Metamorphic rock is produced when any type of rock undergoes the combination of heat and pressure. This combination changes the shape and composition of the rock.

● PROBLEM 5-60

What conditions must be available in order for each part of the rock cycle to occur?

SOLUTION:

For igneous rock to be produced, magma must be cooled. It can cool deep under the surface of the Earth or it can cool on the surface. For the rocks to be produced, the minerals from which they are formed must be stable at high temperatures. They cannot break down to their elemental components.

Sedimentary rocks are formed from the weathering of other rocks. These sediments are carried to a new location and piled on top of each other, producing pressure. This causes compaction of the particles which form the rocks.

Metamorphic rocks are changed deep within the Earth. In order to be formed metamorphic rocks must be near enough to the magma to be heated but not melted. The heat from the magma causes a rearrangement of the elements. The pressure of the layers of rock above cause the formation of a different rock.

SHORT ANSWER QUESTIONS FOR REVIEW

Choose the correct answer.

1. To be considered a mineral, the substance must never have been a part of a living organism and must be found in (a) rock. (b) ore. (c) nature. (d) sand.

2. Sedimentary rocks are formed from the accumulation of silt, rock, and soil particles on the surface of the Earth. Of the following, which is

NOT identified as a sedimentary rock type? (a) Limestone (b) Diorite (c) Shale (d) Both (b) and (c)

3. Rocks are classified into three main groups. Which major rock classification consists of rock that forms from molten material that has solidified? (a) Igneous (b) Sedimentary (c) Volcanic (d) Metamorphic

4. Which of the following are characteristic of metamorphic rocks? (a) Shows evidence or recrystallization (b) Evidence of fossils of animals and plants (c) Reorientation of crystals within rock (d) Both (a) and (c)

5. Minerals can be found in two or more forms while still maintaining the same chemical composition. This property is called polymorphism. Examples of this property include (a) quartz. (b) conchoidal. (c) carbon. (d) both (a) and (c).

6. A geologist is a person who studies (a) geography. (b) rocks only. (c) chemical composition. (d) soil.

7. Rock formed by the cooling and hardening of molten material is called (a) igneous. (b) crystal. (c) metamorphic. (d) sedimentary.

8. Sedimentary rocks include samples that include non-clastic and clastic properties. Which of the following properties WILL NOT be found in sedimentary rocks? (a) Graded bedding (b) Stratification (c) Recrystallization (d) Ripple marks

9. Minerals can be categorized by (a) lustre. (b) color. (c) hardness. (d) all of the above.

10. Which of the following statements about minerals is true? (a) They occur naturally in nature. (b) A few minerals are man-made. (c) Feldspar is a category of minerals. (d) (a) and (c) only

11. Which of the rocks below are metamorphic rocks? (a) Gneiss (b) Marble (c) Slate (d) All of the above

Fill in the blanks.

12. The sedimentary rock forms are commonly called _____.

13. If there are eight (8) electrons in the outermost shell of an atom, the atom is considered to be very _____.

14. The combination of elements is called a(n) _____.

15. Azurite got its name because of its _____ color.

16. Although most diamonds are colorless, some can be _____.

17. Igneous rocks are solid forms of _____.

18. The layers found in sedimentary rock are known as _____.

Determine whether the following statements are true or false.

19. Igneous rock forms are commonly called granite.

20. Cleavage is a type of fracture that is associated with mineral identification.

21. The solid part of the Earth is called ore.

22. Metamorphic rock forms are commonly called limestone.

23. Minerals are found in the Earth's crust.

24. The symbol for gold is Gd.

25. Electrons in an atom give a random appearance.

26. Iron is made up of minerals, but is not a mineral itself.

ANSWER KEY

1. c
2. b
3. a
4. d
5. d
6. c
7. a
8. c
9. d
10. d
11. d
12. limestone
13. stable

14. compound
15. blue
16. green, black, and blue
17. magma
18. strata
19. true
20. false
21. false
22. true
23. true
24. false
25. false
26. false

CHAPTER 6

NATURAL RESOURCES

Gems

● PROBLEM 6-1

What could make one mineral more valuable than another?

SOLUTION:

Gems are prized minerals because of their beauty, and because the supply of gems is limited. These stones are colorful and pretty as well as bright and durable. They can be cut and polished to increase the effects of their physical properties. Because of these properties they are highly prized possessions for investors, collectors, and consumers.

● PROBLEM 6-2

From an economic perspective describe the importance of gems and gemstones. Explain the same from a historical perspective.

SOLUTION:

In the past, as is today, rare stones and precious gems bring a premium price in the marketplace. The country that can dominate and monopolize any given market can in effect solidify its political position and economic strength. Besides their value, gems also offer beauty and a sense of lasting permanence.

The intrinsic value of gems and gemstones have been understood throughout the history of humankind. One driving force for early earth scientists was locating and acquiring precious stones and metals for the rulers of their country or residence. The more efficient the search and searcher, the greater the personal, professional, and economic gain. Seeking these resources became a rush for riches between competing world powers, just as we can see in today's global economy.

● PROBLEM 6–3

List several gems and describe the reasons that they are considered valuable.

SOLUTION:

The first gems that come to mind for most people are diamonds, rubies, and emeralds. These along with many other precious minerals are valuable for several reasons. First, they have a natural beauty that make them desirable to own and display. Secondly, they are rare and their scarce nature puts them at a premium in the competitive marketplace. These gems have durability, and beauty that make them sought after as investments as well as objects to wear and show.

● PROBLEM 6–4

Explain why a type of quartz called amethyst is considered a gemstone while other types of quartz are not.

SOLUTION:

Quartz is a very common mineral and can be found in many different forms. Amethyst is considered a gemstone. First, it is found in crystalline form. Second, its deep purple color is pleasing to the eye and thus makes it a desirable gem. Other forms of quartz may be considered to be gems such as smoky or crystalline quartz, but most forms of quartz silica are considered to be just minerals and not gemstones.

Fossil Fuels

● **PROBLEM 6-5**

What is a fossil fuel and describe the various types of fossil fuels.

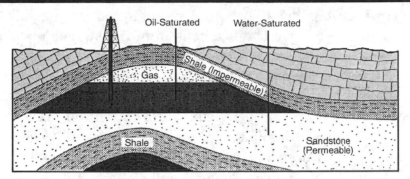

Coal Fields in the United States

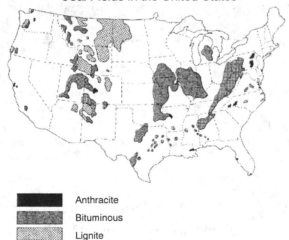

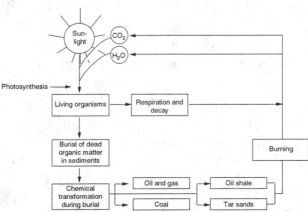

Photosynthesis produces organic matter that is buried, transformed, and so becomes a "fossilized" product of photosynthesis—a fossil fuel.

SOLUTION:

A fossil fuel is a general term used to describe any hydrocarbon compound such as coal, natural gas, or petroleum. These resources generally form in marine sediments in basins with poor water circulation. In environments void of oxygen, decay stops and the organic material can be preserved as it is covered by subsequent sediments. Additional pressures then squeeze the hydrocarbons from the organic material and the fossil fuel migrate to areas where they are trapped.

Coal is the first of the natural energy resources to be used by humans. It is a sedimentary rock comprised of compacted organic material that has not decayed. Natural gas and petroleum seem to form in marine type of sediments from the accumulation of organic materials. Petroleum is a liquid containing hydrogen and carbon compounds. This liquid oil can be distilled into many different products. Natural gas is a gaseous form of hydrocarbon compounds and is found within many of the same areas as oil.

● PROBLEM 6-6

Explain how an understanding of earth sciences will help in location and extraction of fossil fuels.

SOLUTION:

Fossil fuels are sought because modern civilization depends on them to run the machinery of technology. Without fossil fuels, the world as we know it would be a far different place than it is today. The quest of the geologist is to locate these resources in a scientific and efficient manner. The task is simple: search out, locate, and extract these precious fuels. The job can only be accomplished with a thorough understanding of the rock units beneath the surface of the Earth. The nature of the rocks as well as the layers, types, and contacts need to be studied and compared to past successes as well as past failures. Earth scientists learn, as do all scientists, from trial and error. The secret is to combine all data and hypothesize based on the best evidence available.

Describe the environmental concerns associated with the continued use of fossil fuels and present some possible alternatives to the consumption of fossil fuels.

SOLUTION:

The mode used to release the energy in fossil fuels is combustion. This releases soot, particulate matter, and heat into the environment. Greenhouse gases and acid rain are both hot topics of debate and continued research will provide insight into these issues. Also, these energy sources are considered to be nonrenewable and thus will eventually run into short supply.

The best possible route for energy consumption seems to be the combination of many different types of energy resources. The effect of this strategy is to decrease dependence on any one type of energy source as other energy technologies are increased. The supply of nonrenewable sources will eventually be depleted and then total dependence on other sources will be the only option. An increase in the other types of energy resources is logical for the future of society.

Renewable Resources

● **PROBLEM 6–8**

Define the term renewable resources, and list some.

SOLUTION:

A renewable resource is one that can be reused, regrown, recycled, or is not consumed with use. These are resources that can be conserved. It can be argued that most geological resources are nonrenewable as they are used at a far greater rate than they form in nature. Wood, foods, and ground water are renewable in that they can in most cases be produced as fast as they are consumed. Other resources that are considered renewable are those that can be recycled or reused in some shape or form without being consumed in the process. At the present time, though, few resources are being recycled at a high enough percentage to make a major impact.

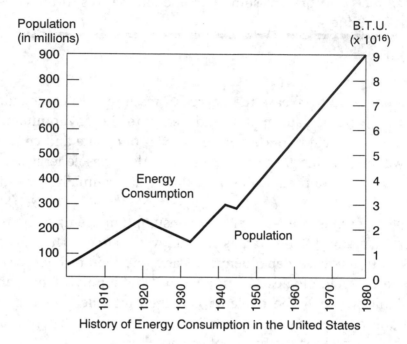

History of Energy Consumption in the United States

The renewable energy source that first comes to mind for most people is solar power in the direct form of sunlight. Solar energy can be a passive source used to heat our homes and help grow biomass sources. Some types of biomass (organic matter) can be used to generate electricity as could the generation of power by burning trash and organic waste that would end up in landfills. Solar energy can also be connected with wind and water power. The energy from the sun powers the water cycle and weather systems. Hydroelectric and wind power are renewable energy sources. One other type of energy that falls into this category is heat from the interior of the Earth. Geothermal energy could also be used to help ease the dependence of society on nonrenewable energy sources.

● PROBLEM 6-9

Describe the importance of the three "R's" of resources and how they may shape the economic structure of spaceship earth.

SOLUTION:

The three R's of resources are reduce, reuse, and recycle. To reduce is to cut back on the purchase of items that cannot be cycled back into the economic marketplace. This may require that items not be bought if they cannot be reused or recycled in some form. The term reuse is simple to understand. Any item should be used as many times as possible before it is discarded to a landfill.

● PROBLEM 6–10

What suggestions would apply to products that are difficult to recycle?

SOLUTION:

If a product cannot be reused in some form, then a hard look should be made before the purchase of that item. Recycle is to take items that are to be discarded into landfills and instead reintroduce them into an economic market. A recycled product can take on a new shape or form. The material used to create a first item will later be used to create a second item. Paper can be recycled as well as aluminum, plastic, glass, and many other market items. The intelligent consumer can make an impact on the conservation and environmental issues that face our populations. Wise selections can help to reduce landfill space, save energy sources, and conserve natural resources.

● PROBLEM 6–11

Consider our renewable energy resources. What changes can be expected in the future?

SOLUTION:

In the United States, less than three percent of all energy used today comes from renewable sources. The majority of energy comes from nonrenewables such as coal, oil, natural gas, and uranium. Considering the inherent problems associated with these nonrenewables other options need to be evaluated. The power needs of future generations will eventually exhaust the reserves of known energy sources and alternatives will have to take on an expanded role in power production.

Define the "new" conservation term: precycle.

SOLUTION:

As the prefix pre- suggests, a hard look may be taken with any resource before it is introduced into the marketplace mainstream. It may be more efficient or economical to adjust, adapt, or remove the resource before it is used or has the opportunity to become an environmental liability. The old saying about an ounce of prevention..., could for some products, be a safer environmental bet for the future.

● PROBLEM 6-13

Generalize information regarding the following natural energy resources: geothermal, wind, wave, tidal, river, coal reserves, and syncrude power.

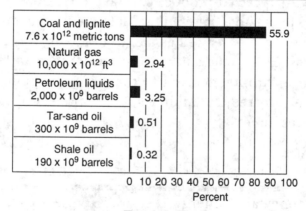

Fossil Fuel	Total Amount in Ground (billions of barrels)	Amount Possibly Recoverable (billions of barrels)
Coal	About 100,000	62,730*
Oil and gas (flowing)	1,500-3,000	1,500-3,000
Trapped oil in pumped-out pools	1,500-3,000	0-?
Viscous oil (tar sands)	3,000-6,000	500-?
Oil shale	Total unknown; much greater than coal	1,000-?

* 0.22 ton of coal = 1 barrel of oil

144

SOLUTION:

a) Geothermal Power—In the interior of planet Earth radioactive elements release large amounts of heat, which in turn heat rock layers close to the crust. This leakage of heat from the mantle below is much more evident in some locations as it is closer to the surface there. These areas appear most frequently in areas of recent volcanism where hot fractured rock is abundant along with natural water reserves. The combination of heat and water creates steam, which can be used to generate electricity. The energy in the geothermal field can be used directly to heat homes. If the source is hot enough (above 180 degrees C) then electric generation is possible.

b) Wind Power—The sun creates winds over the surface of the Earth due to uneven heating of the crustal and oceanic surfaces. It is possible to use this solar power to turn windmills and generate energy. Some experts suggest that within the next two decades between 20 and 50 percent of our total oil consumption could be replaced by wind power. Presently, less than one half of one percent of our total energy consumption comes from wind. Since it is safe to say that the winds will always blow, enthusiasts insist for more development of this technology. It seems that this style of energy production may be suited to provide energy on a small scale for local factories and communities rather then to expect large windmill fields generating power for the masses.

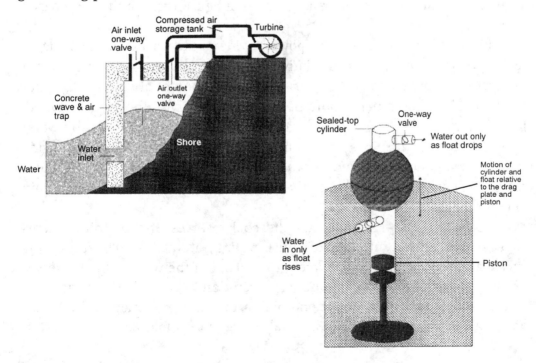

c) Wave Power—Power generated from the tides would provide a needed alternative energy source for coastal communities. The combined power estimated from global wave output is about three thousand times greater than the output of the Hoover dam; however, the energy though is widely spread about the ocean surface and is not constant at all times. Still, efforts are being made to tap this solar energy through the use of several different methods. First is using the rise and fall of an object, as the waves lift and lower a "bobber" to generate energy through the use of potential energy. A second alternative is to use the orbital motion of an object as the waves rock it back and forth. These techniques may not provide energy for large cities, but they could work on a smaller scale to provide energy for local communities in coastal areas.

d) Tidal Power—The twice daily rise and fall of ocean levels provides opportunities for energy production in many coastal areas. One concept is that of a tidal dam operating on the same principles as a hydroelectric dam. As sea water rises, it will fill a natural or artificial bay. As the sea level lowers, the water behind the dam is released and turns turbines to generate power. Another form of tidal power production uses the rise of the ocean to trap air in very large artificial storage tanks. The trapped air is then forced out of the tanks as water levels rise. The resultant air flow (windmill style) turns a turbine to make electricity. These technologies may not produce enough energy to be considered for large scale production. They may be able to produce energy for small local communities in coastal areas.

e) River Power—Hydroelectric power is one of the least expensive energy technologies. The concept is relatively simple, slow the flow of a stream or river and convert the energy of the water to potential energy. As water levels build behind a dam, more potential for energy production is gained. By releasing some of the water at a controlled rate gravity pulls the water downhill through turbines. In this manner, areas with large or fast flowing streams can generate power. Because the water cycle is endless, the water supply will continue to fall from the sky and fill the reservoirs through rain and runoff.

f) Coal Reserves—Estimates for the coal reserves of the United States suggest that at current rates of consumption, a 300- to 400-year supply exists. The U.S. holds approximately 15 percent of the world's total reserves of all types of coal, Russia about 50 percent, and China about 20 percent. Current consumption is about one billion tons a year, which accounts for about 25 percent of the nations' total energy use. Most coal is burned in

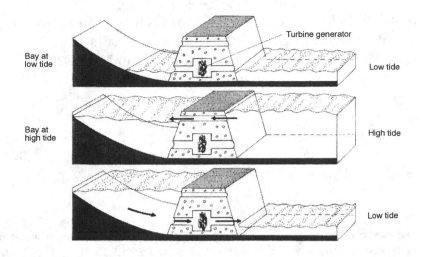

Bay at low tide

Turbine generator

Low tide

Bay at high tide

High tide

Low tide

factories and power plants to produce electricity. Newer technologies also can convert coal into other usable forms of energy called syncrude.

g) Syncrude Power—New technologies have produced synthetic variations of well-known fuels. In the case of coal, it can be converted to gaseous or liquid fuels similar to petroleum. Experiments with syncrude picked up during the oil shortages of the mid 1970s. These experiments were cut back as supplies increased and prices decreased in the U.S. Experts suggest that syncrude prices will come in line with those of crude oil as crude reserves dwindle and prices continue to rise. Should this energy source become cost competitive they believe that several million barrels per day of syncrude could be extracted from coal reserves.

● **PROBLEM 6-14**

Analyze some of the problems associated with the use of alternative natural energy sources.

SOLUTION:

First of all, people are slow to accept change. This is true of consumers, producers, as well as political leaders. The hopes that science and technology will solve the energy crunch of the next few centuries are perhaps too optimistic. Perhaps some of the solutions are with us today in the forms of natural energy in waves, rivers, and the winds. These solar energies are renewable, basically non polluting, and free as a result of the influx of solar radiation into the atmosphere of Earth. Problems arise because at this time, other more convenient sources are available for consumption. The alternative energy sources available also may not meet the large scale demands of a state or country. These sources are at this time as cost effective as the use of "fossil fuels" and therefore sit on the back burners of technological importance. With the prospects of oil and gas shortages in the next few decades, alternatives may well be a long-term solution.

Non-Renewable Resources

● **PROBLEM 6–15**

List the types of nonrenewable energy resources used in society today and explain some of the problems with using them.

SOLUTION:

The resources that we consume faster than nature can replace them are considered to be nonrenewable. The major energy sources that run the economies of the world are all generally considered to be nonrenewable. These sources include natural gas, coal, and oil. These energy sources are collectively known as fossil fuels and are the remains of plants and animals that have been stored for millions of years beneath the surface of the Earth.

The escalation of the use of these fossil fuels is a concern to modern economies due to their dependence on these limited major energy sources. Technology depends on these fuel supplies, yet they are being consumed at a far greater rate than they are produced in nature. The United States, with six percent of the world's population, uses 26 percent of the world's oil production and must import 50 percent of the oil it uses. This heavy dependence on imports could prove to be disastrous should the supply be cut off. There are also major environmental concerns associated with the heavy use of fossil fuels.

● **PROBLEM 6–16**

What is the expected future of a civilization heavily dependent on nonrenewable resources?

SOLUTION:

There are three main groups of geologic resources. They include: energy sources, metals, and nonmetallic resources. Although many of these resources can be recycled and reused, only a very small percentage are. Since this is the case and these are considered to be nonrenewable, then it must be expected that the supply will eventually be depleted. The society dependent on these resources will need to switch to alternatives, or do without.

● **PROBLEM 6-17**

Describe the differences between reserves and resources and how resources could become reserves.

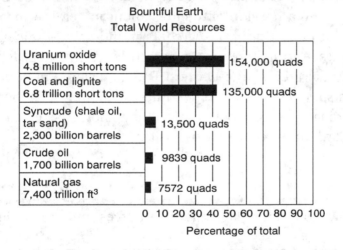

Bountiful Earth
Total World Resources

Uranium oxide 4.8 million short tons	154,000 quads
Coal and lignite 6.8 trillion short tons	135,000 quads
Syncrude (shale oil, tar sand) 2,300 billion barrels	13,500 quads
Crude oil 1,700 billion barrels	9839 quads
Natural gas 7,400 trillion ft^3	7572 quads

0 10 20 30 40 50 60 70 80 90 100
Percentage of total

SOLUTION:

Reserves are a small part of total resources. They are discovered deposits that can be used under present conditions. Resources are defined as the sum total of all deposits discovered and undiscovered. The total of all resources is but an estimate of reserves sizes and possible locations. These resources may not be extractable using current technology.

The extraction and use of a resource subtracts from reserves. New technologies and discoveries add to reserves. As new inventions and theories make the location and extraction of resources possible, the quantity that can be added to reserves increases. As prices for resources increase, so does the profit and thus the possibility that previous resources will be tapped. Regulations, laws, and governmental agreements can also change and allow for the extraction of a resource to become profitable.

149

Where will we find mineral reserves sources should known reserves be fully consumed?

SOLUTION:

In the past three decades some startling discoveries about mineral resources have been made. In the early 1960s exploratory drilling for oil and gas in California struck a super hot water solution at a depth of about one mile. In this hydrothermal solution were copper and silver in a rich mineral deposit. This area provided the first evidence that metallic resources could concentrate from sediments. Just a few years later a second such discovery was made at the bottom of the Red Sea. The combination of discoveries and the active tectonic connection between the two localities led to a revision of theories about mineral formation. In late 1978 on the Pacific sea floor, researchers found sulfide mineral deposits near hot springs. And in 1989 in the search for more such deposits, they located a tectonic area in the western Pacific called a subduction zone. Now, geologists no longer need to hypothesize about how mineral deposits form, and through new geologic theory they know specifically where on the crust of Earth to look for new deposits.

Where will we look for solar system resources and what will we find there?

SOLUTION:

Our solar system is a vast "warehouse" of resources. Of course, the problem lies in developing the technology to tap into those resources. As supplies diminish and prices continue to rise, they will call on the planetary storehouse. The terrestrial planets Mercury, Venus, and Mars are so named because of their similarity to the terrestrial Earth. Their crusts are composed of many of the same materials as Earth and look to be future sites of resource development. The Moon, due to its proximity with Earth, would be a first step and its resources could be used for colonization of the lunar surface. This would serve as a stepping stone for resource shipments back to Earth, as well as a sort of lunar airport to the rest of our solar system. The rusted surface of Mars would provide needed iron and oxygen as well as the hidden possibility of water in the regolith and polar caps. Mars could serve as a stepping stone to the asteroid belt, which is an orbiting supermarket of natural resources that could be mined in orbit or returned to Earth's orbit for recovery. Beyond the asteroids are the Jovian gas giants. Their hydrogen, helium, ammonia, water, and methane atmospheres could provide fuels to propel space ships even further into the cosmos. These, of course, are visions of resource recovery in the future.

● PROBLEM 6-20

What is resource conservation and why is it important?

SOLUTION:

Using resources wisely is just as important as discovering new resources. According to some experts, the industrial nations of the world could cut their consumption of energy of all types in half through conservation efforts. In the US alone, this would cut production and consumer costs enough to make products competitive in world markets. The savings may start small, such as turning off unneeded power, more efficient heating units, using less air conditioning, and more efficient transportation. As savings grow, so can the scope of efforts to continue the reductions. Industry, government, and the public can all take steps to contribute to the changes. If the effort includes education of future generations of consumers, then the cycle may grow stronger.

Energy Use

The United States consumes huge amounts of energy. By 1990 the United States was consuming ten times the amount of energy that it used in 1900. In 1973 and 1978 came steep price rises for petroleum. The need for conservation and fuel-efficient buildings and transportation became more and more apparent. From 1979 to 1985 total United States energy use declined and so did its dependence on petroleum (particularly imported oil). Since a precipitous drop in oil prices at the beginning of 1986, however, there has been a sharp increase in both United States energy use and its reliance on imported oil.

The sources of United States energy have been changing in recent years in response to changing prices.

	1975	1980	1985	1900
Oil	46%	46%	42%	41%
Natural gas	28	26	24	24
Coal	18	20	24	23
Nuclear	3	4	5.5	8
Hydroelectric	5	4	4.5	4

Note that oil and gas account for almost two-thirds of the nation's energy supply; fossil fuels (coal, oil, and gas) provide almost 90% of our energy.

Gas is not only used to cool and heat homes.
It has a thousand and one other uses.
Here are just a few of them.

● PROBLEM 6–21

How much energy does the United States get from each of the types of energy sources it uses? Where does that energy go once it is produced?

SOLUTION:

Petroleum provides 40 percent of the total energy used; natural gas covers 28 percent; coal, 22 percent; water power, 5 percent; nuclear, 5 percent; and all others, 0.2 percent. Of that amount, 37 percent is used by

Per Capita Consumption, 1990

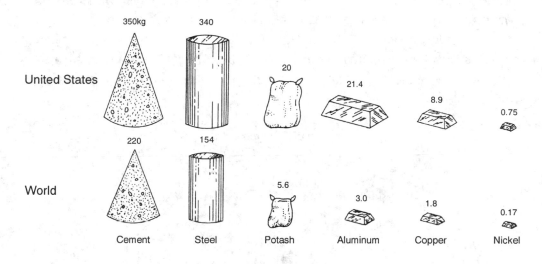

industry, 36 percent in homes and businesses, and 27 percent for transportation.

Experts say, however, that 49 percent of the energy produced by all sources is wasted. Many claim that value can be greatly reduced through simple conservation, with a subsequent savings to consumers amounting to billions of dollars.

● PROBLEM 6–22

What does NIMBY mean and what environmental problems does it face?

SOLUTION:

The issues of energy, resources, conservation, and pollution are complex in nature and very difficult to fully understand. Almost everyone wants to have a cleaner environment. Almost everyone wants to conserve energy. Almost everyone who reads the newspaper or listens to the news agrees that steps have to be taken to protect Earth. The problems arise when the issues themselves start to affect us personally. NIMBY, "not in my backyard" can be looked at as a selfish symbol of how much we want done but how little we want it to directly affect us. Cleaner air is great if I don't have to walk or take the bus. Let someone else give up their polluting car, or backyard grill. Cleaner air is a good thing as long as the factory that pays wages and taxes in my town can still operate. Cleaner landfills are great as long as I don't have to work to separate the recyclables and then store them for pick up at a later date. They might take up too much space or even leave an odor in the garage. NIMBY in itself may be the biggest environmental hazard civilization has to face because solving the many problems we face will take all of us together and perhaps just a bit of IMBY as well.

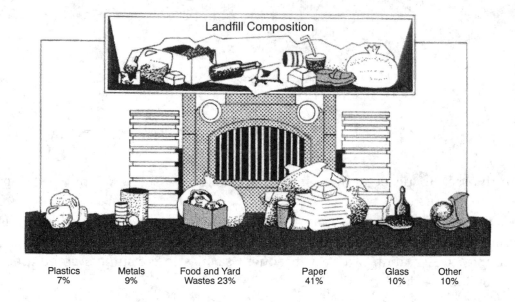

| Plastics 7% | Metals 9% | Food and Yard Wastes 23% | Paper 41% | Glass 10% | Other 10% |

SHORT ANSWER QUESTIONS FOR REVIEW

Choose the correct answer.

1. An alternate energy source is (a) crude oil. (b) ethanol. (c) coal. (d) methanol.

2. Presently, oil and gas are energy sources being derived from (a) the oceans. (b) space. (c) nuclear reactions. (d) none of the above.

3. Conservation is (a) protection and wise use of animals. (b) protection and wise use of Earth's resources. (c) protection and wise use of some of Earth's resources. (d) management of natural resources only.

4. The cost of living will be lower for everyone and more ideal surroundings will be present (a) with legislation to get better conservation laws. (b) with or without conservation enforcement. (c) after forgetting the conservation laws. (d) with conservation enforcement.

Items 5 and 6 refer to the following information.

The average home use of electricity in the United States as compared to a developing country like Brazil is shown in the table below. The amount of electrical energy used is given in kilowatt-hours (KWH) per household per year. (October 1990, *Scientific American*, p. 113)

Use	United States	Brazil
Lighting	1,000	350
Cooking	635	15
Water Heating	1,540	380
Air Conditioning	1,180	45
Refrigeration	1,810	470
Other	1,180	200

5. Which of the statements below is the best conclusion based on the data provided? (a) Because it is warmer in Brazil, the percentage of electricity used in air conditioning is greater than that used in the United States. (b) The greatest amount of electricity use in both countries is for lighting. (c) United States households use more electricity for water heating than lighting, while Brazilian households use more electricity for lighting than water heating. (d) Both countries have a somewhat similar pattern of electricity consumption.

6. The average household in the United States consumes more electrical energy then the average household in Brazil by a rate of _____ times. (a) 20 (b) 10 (c) 5 (d) 2

Fill in the blanks.

7. Crude oil, natural gas, and coal are called _____ sources.

8. A geyser is considered _____ energy.

9. _____ benefits all living things, including man.

Determine whether the following statements are true or false.

10. When salt water is distilled, it is a very good conductor of electricity.

11. Fossil fuels are considered to be nonrenewable because they can never be replaced.

12. Conservation of nonrenewable energy sources means recycling fossil fuels.

ANSWER KEY

1. b
2. a
3. b
4. a
5. d
6. c

7. fossil fuel
8. geothermal
9. Conservation
10. false
11. true
12. false

CHAPTER 7

METEOROLOGY

The Layers of the Atmosphere

● PROBLEM 7–1

What would be the correct order of the following atmospheric layers with respect to the distance from the Earth's surface?

Mesosphere   Stratosphere   Thermosphere   Troposphere

SOLUTION:

The following order is correct:

Troposphere   Stratosphere   Mesosphere   Thermosphere

The troposphere is the lowest layer (0 to 12 km) in the atmosphere. Most of the Earth's weather occurs in this layer. The stratosphere is the next layer (12 to approximately 49 km). In this layer, ozone absorbs harmful ultraviolet light, thus protecting life at the surface of the Earth. The third layer is the mesosphere (49 to 88 km). In the mesosphere, the atmosphere reaches its lowest average temperature (–130°F). The highest layer is the thermosphere (88 to 500 km). Typical temperatures of 2200°F are reached here. The high temperatures in this region occur partially because of the sparse number of ionized oxygen atoms (created by strong solar radiation) that exchange electrons with neutral oxygen molecules, creating heat.

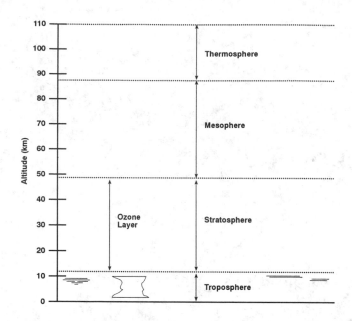

Which region of the atmosphere contains large concentrations of ions and free electrons?

SOLUTION:

The ionosphere is the region which contains large concentrations of ions and free electrons. The ionosphere is not a true layer of the atmosphere but it is an ionized region (above 70 km) found primarily in the mesosphere and the thermosphere. Ions and free electrons are created in the ionosphere in several ways:

1. Ultraviolet radiation interacting with atmospheric molecules.

2. Particles from the Earth's magnetic field colliding with air molecules.

3. Cosmic energy (high energy atomic particles from space) colliding with atmospheric molecules.

These collisions force molecules to gain or lose electrons. This results in many free electrons and ionized molecules in the upper atmosphere and forms the ionosphere.

● PROBLEM 7-3

Explain why molecules may leave the Earth's atmosphere and escape into space. At what layer in the atmosphere does this occur?

SOLUTION:

This phenomena occurs in the exosphere. This layer begins above the thermosphere and defines the boundary of the Earth's atmosphere. The concentration of molecules at this altitude is extremely low and molecular collisions occur less frequently than at lower layers. Thus, lighter and faster molecules exist. These molecules sometimes escape the gravitational force of the Earth and depart into space.

● **PROBLEM 7–4**

Of the various groups of gases listed below, what is the most likely composition of the Earth's atmosphere at an altitude of 750 km?

N_2, O_2, and Ar
N_2, O_2, and O
He, H, and O

where: N_2 is nitrogen
O_2 is oxygen
Ar is argon
He is helium
H is atomic hydrogen
O is atomic oxygen

SOLUTION:

He, H, and O are the gases which most likely compose the Earth's atmosphere at an altitude of 750 km. Above approximately 85 km, collisions between molecules are infrequent. Subsequently, less mixing occurs above this altitude. Heavier molecules such as N_2, O_2, and Ar descend to lower altitudes while lighter atoms such as H, O, and He ascend to higher altitudes.

● **PROBLEM 7–5**

What is the term used to describe the boundary between the troposphere and stratosphere?

The tropopause is the term used to describe the boundary between the troposphere and stratosphere. This boundary separates the troposphere and stratosphere. The altitude of the tropopause varies with latitude and season, but it is usually between 8 and 18 km.

There are two significant aspects of the tropopause of interest to the operational meteorologist:

(1) The tropopause is isothermal; the temperature remains constant as altitude increases, which indicates a stable atmosphere. Below the tropopause, however, the atmosphere is usually unstable, and thunderstorms often develop. As a result of its stability, the tropopause often establishes the upper limit of growth of a thunderstorm. The intensity of a thunderstorm can be determined by its height (a thunderstorm reaching 56,000 feet, for example, is much stronger than one at 23,000 feet). Thus, the height of the tropopause can help the meteorologist to determine thunderstorm intensity.

(2) The position of the tropopause can assist the meteorologist in locating the jet stream (a narrow current of high speed winds in the atmosphere).

The Necessity of the Ozone Layer

● PROBLEM 7–6

Explain how the ozone layer protects life on Earth.

SOLUTION:

Most of the ozone in the atmosphere is found in the stratosphere (12 to 49 km). Ozone is initially formed when sunlight acts on oxygen molecules. Although the concentration of ozone is small (10 to 20 parts per billion), it protects life on Earth by absorbing ultraviolet (UV) radiation (solar radiation with wavelengths between 0.2 and 0.3μm). The reaction of ozone and UV is shown below.

$$O_3 + UV \rightarrow O_2 + O$$

As the UV radiation is absorbed by the ozone, both atomic and molecular oxygen are formed. This reaction protects life on Earth in several ways. UV radiation destroys DNA, an essential building block of life. If excessive UV radiation reached the Earth's surface, there would be an increase in both skin cancer and genetic defects. Also, without the ozone layer, the Earth's climate would change due to an increase of radiation reaching the surface. The ultimate impact on the global climate is unclear.

● **PROBLEM 7-7**

Which item listed below contributes to the destruction of ozone in the atmosphere?

Carbon dioxide

Carbon monoxide

Argon

Chlorofluorocarbons (CFCs)

SOLUTION:

Chlorofluorocarbons contribute to the destruction of ozone in the atmosphere. CFCs are used as propellants in aerosol cans, refrigerators, and air conditioners. CFCs escape from these products and slowly propagate into the stratosphere (the atmospheric layer where the ozone layer exists). Ultraviolet (UV) radiation decomposes the CFC molecule, releasing chlorine (Cl). Chlorine combines with ozone, forming the molecule chlorite (ClO). This reaction reduces the amount of ozone in the stratosphere, destroying the ozone layer.

● **PROBLEM 7-8**

Explain how the destruction of the ozone layer would cause temperatures at the Earth's surface to increase.

SOLUTION:

Ozone not only absorbs ultraviolet (UV) radiation, but also infrared (IR) radiation (heat) in the stratosphere. A decrease of ozone would cause more IR radiation to reach the Earth's surface, causing temperatures to rise.

Which naturally occurring event listed below contributes to the destruction of the ozone layer?

    Lightning
    Release of solar particles
    Earthquakes
    Tornadoes

SOLUTION:

Solar particles contribute to the destruction of the ozone layer. Solar particles decompose molecular nitrogen (N_2) into atomic nitrogen (N). Atomic nitrogen combines with atomic oxygen (O) to form nitric oxide in the reaction:

$$N + O \rightarrow NO$$

Nitric oxide then combines with ozone in the reaction:

$$NO + O_3 \rightarrow NO_2 + O_2$$

This series of reactions reduces the amount of ozone in the atmosphere and contributes to the destruction of the ozone layer.

● **PROBLEM 7–10**

Explain why ozone (O_3) is considered a pollutant when found in the troposphere.

SOLUTION:

Ozone is formed in the troposphere due to a reaction between pollutants emitted from the burning of petroleum fuels (hydrocarbons and nitrogen oxides). In a stable atmosphere, ozone and other pollutants are not dispersed. As a result, ozone accumulates and can become a component of smog.

The Different Air Movements in the Atmosphere

● PROBLEM 7-11

Describe how a sea breeze most likely develops in the summer on a warm, clear day.

SOLUTION:

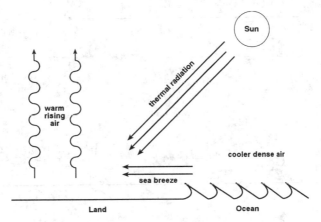

Intense thermal radiation and heating by the sun causes the air over the land to warm. As the air warms, it becomes buoyant and rises. To replace the rising air, cooler and less buoyant air over the ocean moves inland. The movement of this air is called a sea breeze.

● PROBLEM 7-12

Which of the figures shown on the following page illustrates a mountain breeze?

SOLUTION:

Mountain 3 illustrates a mountain breeze. A mountain breeze occurs when air near the top of a mountain cools, usually by radiational cooling (cooling due to a loss of heat) during the night. As it cools, the air sinks into the valleys, creating winds. Mountain 1 is an example of a valley breeze. During the day, the sun heats the surface of the Earth. The air warms, rises, and displaces the cooler air near the mountain. Mountain 2 shows the interaction between a mountain range and low level winds. If the air is not buoyant enough to glide over the surface of the mountain,

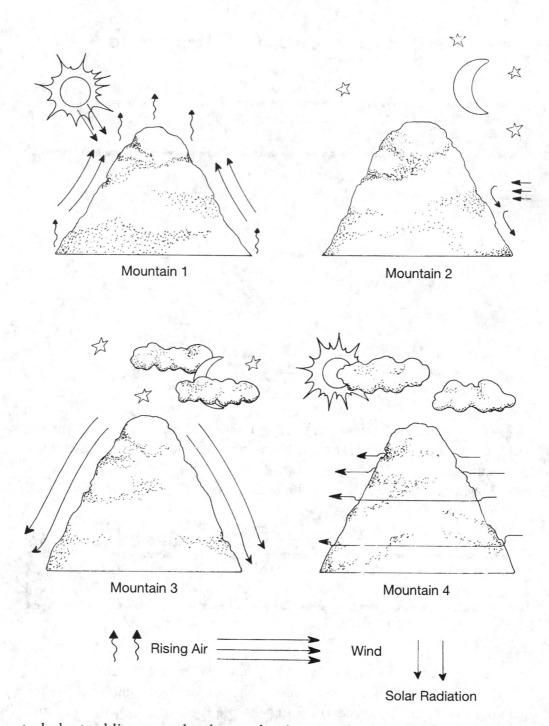

Mountain 1

Mountain 2

Mountain 3

Mountain 4

Rising Air ⟶ Wind ⟶ Solar Radiation

turbulent eddies may develop and spin near the base of the mountain. Mountain 4 is an example of how wind may flow around a single mountain. A single mountain would not be as large of a barrier as a mountain range. If the air was not buoyant enough to glide over the mountain, it would flow around it.

Describe a Chinook wind and how it is formed.

SOLUTION:

A Chinook wind is a dry, warm wind found east of the Rocky Mountains. A Chinook wind forms when strong westerly winds rise over the mountain range. As the air rises, it cools and loses moisture. On moving down the easterly side of the mountains, the air warms as it sinks into the valley. Since the air is less moist, it will warm more quickly than it cooled. As it reaches the eastern valleys of the Rocky Mountains, the air may be 10 to 50°F warmer than on the western side. See the figure.

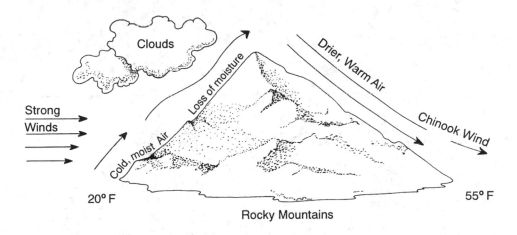

● PROBLEM 7–14

It is a hot, sunny, and humid day in Florida on July 27. During the afternoon, cumulus clouds begin to develop overhead. Which process listed below would cause the formation of the cumulus clouds?

Convection   Radiation   Conduction

SOLUTION:

All three energy processes contribute to the formation of cumulus clouds, although convection is the most important. Intense solar radiation (electromagnetic waves) heats the surface of the Earth. Air contacting the surface begins to warm through conduction (transfer of energy through contact with an energy source). Rising air currents lift an air parcel higher into the atmosphere. As the parcel continues to rise, it cools and eventually condenses to form a cloud. This process is called convection. (See figure.)

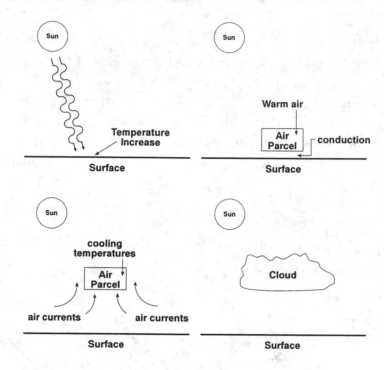

Explain why wind speeds tend to be greater over open, level land than in a big city.

SOLUTION:

Although cities seem to be windier than open areas, urban areas are actually less windy because energy dissipation due to friction is greater. When air flows over or around buildings and other structures, frictional forces develop at the building surfaces, tending to diminish wind speeds. In open country, there are fewer structures and therefore fewer objects to impede the wind.

The Coriolis Effect

Give the four factors that affect the strength of the Coriolis force acting upon an object moving in the atmosphere.

SOLUTION:

Using the equation:

Coriolis force = $2m\Omega V\sin\phi$

where m = the mass of the object

Ω = the rate of the Earth's rotation, a constant value

V = the velocity of the object

ϕ = the latitude of the object

The mass of the object, the velocity of the object, the latitude of the object, and the rate of the Earth's rotation all affect the strength of the Coriolis force acting upon the object. These factors are directly proportional to the force, i.e., the force increases correspondingly as any factor increases.

● PROBLEM 7–17

An airplane pilot plots a course from Point A to Point B. Point A is 1,000 miles directly north of Point B. The pilot decides to fly due north to save fuel. An observer standing on the ground sees the plane fly overhead. In what direction does the observer see the plane flying?

SOLUTION:

An observer would see the plane flying northeast, due to the Coriolis effect. The airplane is moving north, in a straight line; however, the observer sees the path of the airplane deflect to the right. The course of the airplane does not change but the observer's position moves because the Earth is rotating. Thus, it appears to the observer that the airplane is moving northeast (see figure below).

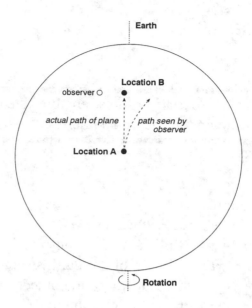

Earth

Location B

observer O

actual path of plane

path seen by
observer

Location A

Rotation

At what latitude is the Coriolis effect always equal to zero?

SOLUTION:

At the equator, 0 degrees latitude, the Coriolis effect equals zero. Using the equation:

Coriolis force = $2m\Omega V \sin\phi$

where m = the mass of the object

Ω = the rate of the Earth's rotation, a constant value

V = the velocity of the object

ϕ = the latitude of the object

Since the sin (0) = 0, the Coriolis effect will also be equal to 0.

Two dirt particles are moving in the atmosphere above New York City. The Coriolis force acting upon Particle A is stronger than Particle B. If both particles have the same velocity, which particle has the greater mass?

SOLUTION:

Particle A has the greater mass. Given the equation:

Coriolis force = $2m\Omega V \sin\phi$

where m = object's mass
            Ω = the Earth's angular rate of spin
            V = object's velocity
            ϕ = latitude

If the velocity and the latitude of the objects are equal, the only parameter which is variable is the mass. The Coriolis force acting upon Particle A is larger than that of Particle B. Thus, Particle A must have the larger mass.

● PROBLEM 7–20

A parcel of air is subject to the Coriolis force and the pressure gradient force (PGF). Both applied forces are equal. Is the parcel flow governed by geostrophic conditions?

SOLUTION:

Yes, the parcel flow is goverened by geostrophic conditions. Geostrophic flow is an idealized condition often assumed in practice, in which the PGF and Coriolis force are the only forces acting upon the parcel, and where the forces are equal. In geostrophic flow, the wind follows the contours of isobars (equal lines of pressure) at a constant velocity. Thus, the meteorologist can easily estimate the wind direction, because it is parallel to the isobars.

Weather Instruments

● PROBLEM 7–21

Two barometers are hanging on a wall. The barometric pressure indicated by Barometer A is 1030 millibars (mb). Barometer B indicates that the barometric pressure is 29.95 inches (in). Which barometer displays the higher value?

SOLUTION:

Use the conversion:
         1 in = 33.865 mb

Converting Barometer B's value into millibars, we get:

$$29.95 \text{ in} \times \frac{33.865 \text{ mb}}{1 \text{ in}} = 1014.26 \text{ mb}$$

Since the barometric pressure of Barometer A is 1030 mb and the barometric pressure of Barometer B is 1014.26 mb, Barometer A displays the higher value.

● PROBLEM 7-22

Two meteorologists are recording air temperatures for their city (see chart). Meteorologist A works in Flagstaff, Arizona and Meteorologist B works in Paris, France. Which meteorologist recorded a higher temperature?

Time (Local)	Meteorologist A Temp °F	Meteorologist B Temp °C
1 pm	55	15
2 pm	57	15
3 pm	63	16
4 pm	59	13
5 pm	52	12

SOLUTION:

Meteorologist A recorded the higher temperature. The first step is to convert the highest temperature recorded by Meteorologist B (16°C) into Fahrenheit. The equation is:

Temp °F = (Temp °C × 1.8) + 32

Using the equation, 16°C is equal to 60.8°F. The highest temperature recorded by Meteorologist A was 63°F. Since 63°F is greater than 60.8°F, Meteorologist A recorded the higher temperature.

● PROBLEM 7-23

Explain why Doppler radar is more beneficial to a meteorologist than conventional radar.

SOLUTION:

Both Doppler and conventional radars help meteorologists detect the presence and intensity of precipitation for a given location. Both types of radars emit an electromagnetic signal. When this signal encounters precipitation, it is reflected back to the radar. The strength of the reflection determines the intensity of the precipitation; however, Doppler radars have an additional capability: they can detect frequency changes in the reflected signal. As a result, this radar can determine wind velocities in the region of precipitation. Doppler radars utilize the principle of the Doppler shift. When an object is moving, there will be an apparent change in its emitted frequency. For example, a police car siren will have a higher frequency as it approaches a fixed point, because the number of waves per second as measured at that point will be greater than the actual emitted frequency. Conversely, the measured frequency will be lower after it passes. Similarly, Doppler radar can detect if precipitation is moving toward or away from the radar site. This is useful because the wind patterns of a storm can be observed and analyzed for the presence of more severe weather such as tornadoes or microbursts (strong downdrafts in thunderstorms often hazardous to aircraft).

● **PROBLEM 7-24**

A weather balloon is launched from a weather station in Dallas, Texas on a cloudy night. A radiosonde (weather instruments enclosed in a box) is connected to the end of a cord and is attached to the weather balloon. As the balloon rises into the atmosphere, it records the air temperature, dew point temperature, air pressure, wind speed, and wind direction. This information is modulated or placed on radio waves, which are then transmitted back to the weather station, where it is demodulated, or recovered. Based on the information recorded in the chart, at what altitude in the atmosphere are clouds most likely to develop?

Altitude (meters)	Air Temperature (°C)	Dew Point Temperature (°C)	Pressure (mb)	Wind Speed (knots)	Wind Direction
500	17	11	1,000	5	Southeast
1,470	10	10	850	20	Southeast
3,120	0	0	700	35	South
5,700	−19	−20	500	55	Southwest

SOLUTION:

The altitude that clouds will most likely develop is 1,470 meters. Condensation occurs when the air temperature reaches the dew point temperature. At 1,470 meters the air temperature is equal to the dew point temperature, thus condensation is occurring at this altitude.

● **PROBLEM 7–25**

Which of the instruments listed below does not measure wind speed?

Anemometer   Aneroid barometer   Wind profiler   Aerovane

SOLUTION:

The aneroid barometer does not measure wind speed. The aneroid barometer measures atmospheric pressure.

The anemometer is a device that measures wind speed. It is usually made from a series of cups mounted on a vertical rod. The cups spin in response to air movements (wind) in the atmosphere. A voltage is produced from the spinning cups and is converted into a speed on a display.

A wind profiler uses the same technique used by Doppler radar to determine wind velocity.

The aerovane is a type of anemometer that also measures the wind direction. It usually consists of a propeller blade mounted on a metal body (the aerovane looks similar to an airplane without wings).

Reading Weather Maps and Symbols

● PROBLEM 7–26

Based on the reported temperatures shown on the map, give the approximate location of the cold front.

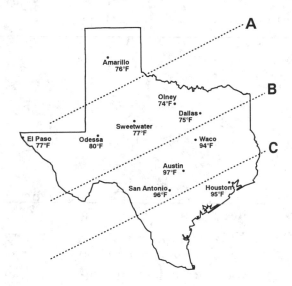

SOLUTION:

The cold front position can be approximated by the temperatures shown on the map. A cold front is the transition zone between a cold air mass and a warm air mass. Area B would be the most likely location of the cold front because it separates the cold temperatures from the warm temperatures.

● PROBLEM 7–27

Given the temperature ranges below, which most accurately represents a valid temperature range in Region A (see figure below).

15 to 20°F   20 to 25°F   25 to 30°F   30 to 35°F   35 to 40°F

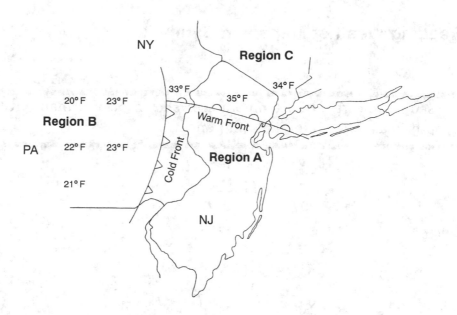

SOLUTION:

The temperature range of 35 to 40°F would be the most accurate. Temperatures rise after a warm frontal passage. In the figure, the warm front has already passed through Region A; therefore, temperatures in Region A would be higher than in Region B or C. Behind a cold front (Region B), temperatures are colder than in Region A. Thus, the answer must be a temperature range greater than those observed in Region B. Ahead of a warm front (Region C), temperatures are warmer than Region B, but colder than Region A. Thus, the answer must also be a temperature range greater than those observed in Region C. The only temperature range that fills both criteria is the temperature range of 35 to 40°F.

● **PROBLEM 7–28**

Using the weather symbols in Chart A as a guide, what is the correct order of weather events as observed in Casper, Wyoming.
1. freezing rain, light rain, light snow, moderate snow, fog
2. freezing drizzle, light snow, moderate snow, heavy snow, hail
3. sleet, rain showers, light snow, heavy snow, fog
4. freezing drizzle, sleet, light snow, heavy snow, freezing rain
5. rain showers, sleet, light snow, moderate snow, freezing rain

TIME	OBSERVED WEATHER
12 noon	⌢•⌣
3 pm	• •
6 pm	❄ ❄
9 pm	❄❄❄
12 midnight	═══

SOLUTION:

The correct order of weather events is:

1. freezing rain, light rain, light snow, moderate snow, fog

See the symbol guide below for more information.

Weather Event	Weather Symbol
Fog	═══
Freezing Drizzle	⌢⌣
Freezing Rain	⌢•⌣
Hail	△
Light Rain	• •
Moderate Rain	•• •
Heavy Rain	•• • •
Rain Showers	▽
Light Snow	❄ ❄
Moderate Snow	❄❄❄
Heavy Snow	❄❄❄
Sleet	⬙

Correctly label all fronts and pressure systems on the surface weather map in the figure below.

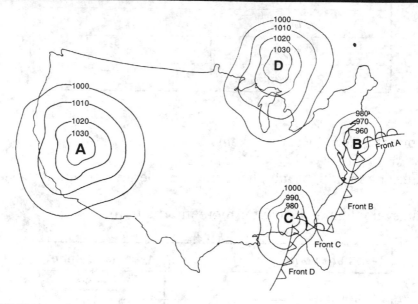

SOLUTION:

Air Masses A and D are high pressure systems because the pressure decreases away from the air mass. Air Masses B and C are low pressure systems because the pressure increases away from the air mass.

All fronts can be identified by the following symbols:

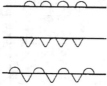

Thus, Front A = Warm Front
      Front B = Cold Front
      Front C = Stationary Front
      Front D = Cold Front

A meteorologist uses her psychrometer to calculate the wet-bulb depression for Sea City. The measured dry-bulb temperature is 78 degrees F. The measured wet-bulb temperature is 75 degrees F. Another meteorologist calculates the wet-bulb depression for Jay City. The dry-bulb temperature is measured at 80 degrees F. The wet-bulb temperature is measured at 68 degrees F. Which city has a lower relative humidity?

SOLUTION:

Jay City has a lower relative humidity. The first step is to calculate the wet-bulb depression for each city. Using the equation:

$$Td - Tw = WBD \quad \text{where:} \quad \begin{aligned} Td &= \text{dry-bulb temperature} \\ Tw &= \text{wet-bulb temperature} \\ WBD &= \text{wet-bulb depression} \end{aligned}$$

thus,

Sea City: $78 - 75 = 3$
Jay City: $80 - 68 = 12$

The wet-bulb depression is an indicator of the amount of moisture in the air. A larger wet-bulb depression reflects a lower relative humidity.

● **PROBLEM 7-31**

Some weather maps that meteorologists use contain symbols that represent various types of clouds. What types of clouds do the following symbols represent?

SOLUTION:

Cumulonimbus, cirrus, altocumulus, and stratus. See the figure below for a more complete listing of cloud symbols.

Cumulus	⌒⌐	Stratocumulus	⌣
Stratus	──	Fractostratus	─ ─ ─
Cumulonimbus	⊠	Altostratus	∠
Altocumulus	⌄		
Cirrostratus	⌁⌁	Cirrus	⌒⌒⌒⊃
Nimbostratus	⊖	Cirrocumulus	⌒ι

Meteorological forecasts are often incorrect. Give three factors that limit the accuracy of any forecast.

SOLUTION:

There are many factors. Listed below are several limitations on meterological forecasting.

(1) Data errors: Weather data from local observations are placed into many computer algorithms. Even slight errors in initial data can be multiplied by several factors, resulting in large forecasting errors.

(2) Coverage: There are large gaps in local observation data across the country. This data is essential to forecasting algorithms and less accurate forecasts. Also, the national radar network has gaps in its coverage that result in less accurate real-time weather forecasting.

(3) Knowledge: Our knowledge of many atmospheric processes is limited. These critical processes go unaccounted for in computer algorithms. This too results in less accurate forecasts.

(4) Rounding errors: Computer data is often "rounded" or truncated to save time and computer memory. The loss of data can be multiplied by several factors, resulting in large forecasting errors.

(5) Interpretation: Weather forecasting is a science, skill, and somewhat of an art. Meteorologists use their own knowledge, experience, and intuition when interpreting weather maps and data; therefore, forecasts will differ among meteorologists.

Fronts' Effect on the Weather

Two surface station models are shown below. Model 1 represents the weather in Las Vegas, Nevada. Model 2 represents the weather in Gallop, New Mexico. Which location has just recently experienced a cold front passage?

50\	100	67	80
22	+90*	65	11\

Model 1	Model 2

SOLUTION:

Las Vegas just experienced a cold front passage. A station model provides a meteorologist with important information about weather conditions at the surface of the Earth. The example model below is used to explain the weather conditions at both locations.

```
      A      C
        (E)
      B      D
```
Example Model

The first step is to consider which meteorological conditions would suggest that a cold front passed through a given location. These conditions often are:

1. Falling pressure, followed by rising pressure
2. A wind direction from the west or northwest
3. The presence of dry air

The air temperature (A) and air pressure (C) would not assist a meteorologist in this example because prior conditions are not known. An initial indication of a cold front passage would be pressure tendency (D). Model 1 indicates that the pressure during the last three hours has fallen and then risen (*). It also shows a total air pressure change of 9.0 millibars has occurred during the last three hours. Model 2 indicates that the air pressure during the last three hours has fallen (\) 1.1 millibars. The next indication of a cold front passage is the wind direction (E). The wind direction from Model 1 is northwest and from Model 2 is southeast.

Finally, the presence of dry air (E and B) also may suggest the passage of a cold front. At Las Vegas, the amount of cloud cover (E) is 25% and the dew point temperature (B) is 22°F. These conditions suggest that dry air is present. At Gallop, however, the amount of cloud cover is 75% and the dew point temperature is 65°F, suggesting moist air is present. Thus, based on the three conditions described above, Las Vegas has experienced the cold front passage.

● **PROBLEM 7–34**

The meteorological data were recorded in a chart for Memphis, Tennessee for two time periods: Observation 1 (noon) and Observation 2 (1 pm). The following conditions were recorded: wind direction, temperature, barometric pressure, and relative humidity. Based on these observations, what type of front moved through Memphis?

Meteorological Condition	Observation 1	Observation 2
wind direction	Southeast	Southwest
temperature	55°F	73°F
barometric pressure	30.10 in.	30.15 in.
relative humidity	70%	85%

SOLUTION:

A warm front just moved through Memphis. After a typical warm front passage, the winds shift from the southeast to the southwest, and warm air replaces cooler air. Thus, the temperature increases. Barometric pressure usually will not change significantly but usually a slight rise occurs. The relative humidity will increase because the warmer air mass contains more moisture than the cooler air mass.

● **PROBLEM 7–35**

Meteorological data were recorded in Chart A for Springfield, Illinois. The air temperature, dew point temperature, barometric pressure, wind speed, and wind direction were recorded for five hours. After which hour did the cold front pass through Springfield?

180

CHART A

HOUR	AIR TEMP (°F)	DEW POINT TEMP (°F)	BAROMETRIC PRESS (mb)	WIND SPEED (mi/hr)	WIND DIRECTION
1	82	77	1,010	5	South
2	79	75	1,011	4	South
3	78	75	1,007	4	South
4	78	74	998	6	Southwest
5	65	48	1,022	11	Northwest

SOLUTION:

The cold front passed through after the fourth hour. When using surface weather data as in Chart A, the following criteria are collectively used to determine if a cold front has passed through a given location:

1. A drop in the air temperature
2. A drop in the dew point temperature
3. Falling (followed by rapidly rising) barometric pressure
4. A change of wind direction from the south to the west or northwest

Although there was a drop in both the air temperature and dew point temperature between the first and fourth hours, the drop was not significant enough to indicate the passage of a cold front. After the fourth hour, however, there was a large drop in air temperature and dew point temperature. Perhaps the most important observation is the falling pressure at the fourth hour, followed by a sharp rise in pressure at the fifth hour. Finally, the winds shifted direction from the southwest to the northwest between the fourth and fifth hour. Wind speed was also recorded, but is not in itself a reliable or primary indicator of a frontal passage.

● PROBLEM 7–36

Explain why the presence of a cold front near a given location increases the chance of precipitation.

SOLUTION:

There are two primary reasons:

1. There is an increase of instability, caused by two processes. An elongated area of low pressure, which encompasses the cold front, causes air to rise. Also, cold fronts wedge their way under warm air as they

181

advance, forcing the warm air to rise. In both processes, air rises, cools, and condenses to form clouds.

2. There is an increase of moisture above and beyond that normally created by rising air. Warm, moist air is advected ahead (usually east) of the cold front. The moist air contributes to greater condensation.

These two factors will begin the condensation process leading to precipitation; however, both processes must continue long enough for precipitation to commence.

● **PROBLEM 7–37**

A meteorologist in Chicago issues a weather report over the radio. He tells the listening audience that "...the current temperature is 33 degrees Fahrenheit, winds are southeast at 5 miles per hour, barometric pressure is 30.02 inches and falling slowly, and the dew point temperature is 32 degrees Fahrenheit. Right now at our weather station, it is raining due to the frontal system to our west." An hour later, he issues a second weather report: "...the current temperature is 30 degrees Fahrenheit, winds are northwest at 7 miles per hour, barometric pressure is 30.08 inches and rising slightly, and the dew point temperature is 29 degrees Fahrenheit. The frontal system has just passed and the precipitation will be ending within the hour followed by clearing skies."

What type of frontal system passes through Chicago?

SOLUTION:

An occluded front passes through Chicago. An occluded front develops when a cold front "catches up" to a warm front. An occluded front is defined as a frontal system where a cold air mass is replaced by a colder air mass, with warmer air aloft. In contrast, a cold front is defined as a frontal system where warm air is replaced by a cold air mass.

The best indicator of the occluded frontal passage is the drop in air temperature. The observed temperatures show that a cold air mass is replaced by a colder air mass. The possibility of a warm front can be eliminated because the temperatures did not rise. The change in the dew point temperature is a good differentiator between the passage of a cold front and an occluded front. In this example, the dew point dropped slightly. A cold front passage would have caused a much sharper drop in the dew point temperature. The slight drop in barometric pressure also suggests that the front was an occluded front. Again, a cold front would have caused the pressure to drop sharply then rise rapidly. Wind direction and speed is usually not a reliable factor in differentiating between occluded and cold fronts.

● **PROBLEM 7-38**

Explain why a pressure system that stalls over a region can cause severe air pollution.

SOLUTION:

In an area of static high pressure, air higher in the atmosphere sinks to intermediate levels and warms, causing an inversion. An inversion defines a condition where the temperature increases with altitude. With cooler air at the surface and warmer air aloft, a stable atmosphere develops. In a stable atmosphere, winds remain weak and little vertical mixing occurs. Consequently, air pollutants cannot be readily dispersed, causing a large concentration of pollutants.

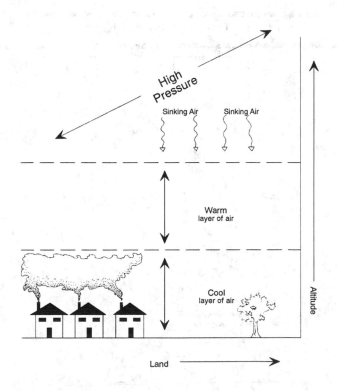

Explain why fog may form ahead of an approaching warm front.

SOLUTION:

When the air from a warm front moves over a relatively cold surface, rain associated with the front falls through the colder air mass, increasing its moisture content. As this process continues, the cold air will become saturated, and low clouds and fog will form.

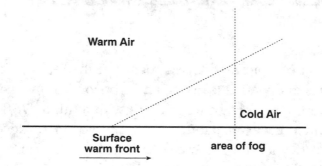

What type of frontal boundary is Line A in the diagram below?

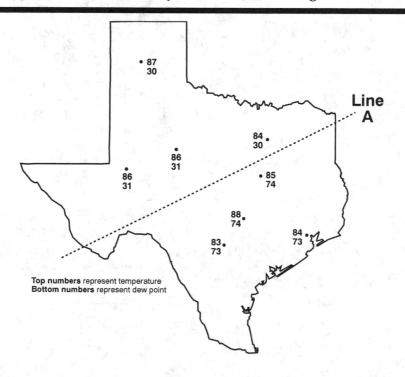

SOLUTION:

Line A is known as a dry-line. A dry-line is the boundary between warm, dry air and warm, moist air. Thunderstorms often form along the dry-line. This is due to increased lifting in the atmosphere caused by convergence in the two air masses.

● PROBLEM 7–41

Two cities, City A and City B, are 20 miles apart. Daily observations are made at 5 a.m. at both cities. No frontal systems are near the area. Using the information provided in the chart, which city is more likely to have a lower temperature at 5 a.m.?

Observation	City A	City B
Dew Point	20 degrees F	20 degrees F
Wind Speed	8 miles per hour	Calm
Wind Direction	South	N/A
Cloud Cover	80%	Clear

SOLUTION:

City B will have a lower temperature at 5 a.m., because of greater radiational cooling at night. Radiational cooling, a process that occurs when the Earth's surface radiates (loses) infrared radiation (heat), is generally greatest when the atmosphere is dry, winds are calm, and there is little or no cloud cover. A dry atmosphere cools faster than one containing significant water vapor, because water vapor helps retain heat due to water's large heat capacity. A clear atmosphere cools faster because clouds absorb heat that is radiated by the surface and re-emit a portion of the infrared energy back to Earth. Windless conditions ensure that there will be no mixing of atmospheric layers; mixing tends to reduce the temperature differences between surface and air aloft, therefore diminishing ground radiation. On a clear night with calm winds, the surface will radiate more heat into the middle and upper atmosphere.

Major Weather Systems

● PROBLEM 7–42

A specially designed aircraft flew into the eye wall of Hurricane X. A meteorologist onboard recorded the following observations:

> Temperature: 74°F
> Barometric Pressure: 952 millibars
> Wind Direction: Northeast
> Wind Speed: 121 mph

Using the Saffir-Simpson scale, what category hurricane is Hurricane X?

SOLUTION:

Hurricane X is a Category 3 hurricane. The criteria for a Category 3 hurricane (see chart below) is a pressure between 945-964 mb and a wind speed between 111-130 mph. The temperature and wind direction are not used as criteria.

Saffir-Simpson Scale

Category	Barometric Pressure (mb)	Wind Speed (mph)
1	980+	74 to 85
2	965 to 979	96 to 110
3	945 to 964	111 to 130
4	920 to 944	131 to 155
5	below 920	155+

● PROBLEM 7–43

A tornado struck a town in Texas. In the newspaper the next day, a preliminary report stated that cars have been overturned, large trees leveled, and many houses destroyed. On television, a meteorologist covering the tornado story stated that the tornado was a F1 category tornado on the Fujita Tornado Scale. Assuming that the meteorologist is correct, was the newspaper story accurate?

SOLUTION:

No, according to the Fujita Tornado Scale (see below), an F1 level tornado would only cause light damage.

Scale	Description	Wind Speed	Damage
F0	Weak	40-72 mph	Light. Tree branches broken.
F1	Weak	73-112 mph	Moderate. Small trees and windows broken.
F2	Strong	113-157 mph	Considerable. Big trees are uprooted. Mobile homes destroyed.
F3	Strong	158-206 mph	Severe. Trees leveled. Cars overturned. Moderate damage to large houses.
F4	Violent	207-260 mph	Devastating. Large houses destroyed.
F5	Violent	261-318 mph	Incredible. Complete devastation.

● PROBLEM 7-44

Weather conditions for Portland, Oregon were observed for a three-day period. During this time the weather was cool and rainy. What type of air mass was controlling the weather in Portland?

SOLUTION:

A maritime polar air mass (mT) was controlling the weather in Portland. The characteristics of a maritime polar air mass are cool, moist, and unstable weather conditions (see chart below).

Symbol	Air Mass	Source Region	Core Characteristics
cP	Continental Polar	Land	Cold, dry, stable
cT	Continental Tropic	Land	Warm, dry, stable or unstable
mP	Maritime Polar	Water	Cool, moist, unstable
mT	Maritime Tropic	Water	Warm, moist, unstable

During which condition listed below would it be unlikely that a low pressure system would strengthen?
- warm air rising over a mountain range
- cold air moving over a large body of warm water
- cold, dense air sinking over land
- warm, moist air rising over a cold air mass

SOLUTION:

A low pressure system (cyclones) would not be likely to strengthen in areas of cold, dense, sinking air over land. Cold, dense sinking air generally occurs in a stable atmosphere. A low pressure system is unlikely to strengthen in a stable atmosphere.

The development and strengthening of a low pressure system is called cyclogenesis. Two major factors that contribute to cyclogenesis are instability and the presence of warm air in the atmosphere.

Warm air rising over a mountain range and warm, moist air rising over a cold air mass will both cause instability. During both conditions, condensation is likely to occur, providing additional heat to the atmosphere.

Cold air moving over a large body of warm water will amplify the contrast of warm and cold air in the upper atmosphere (warm advection). Heat from the warm water will rise, condense, and release energy. This energy will add heat to the upper atmosphere.

Location A is a major city with a population of 3 million people. It is an extremely urbanized area with many large buildings and industrial structures. Location B is a small rural town, 35 miles away from Location A. Location B is mostly residential and farming is its major industry. Both locations are at the same elevation and not near any bodies of water.

The average daily temperature is 3°F higher in Location A. Explain why Location A has a warmer climate.

SOLUTION:

The heat island effect is the reason Location A has a warmer climate. In major cities and urban areas, most solar energy is absorbed by concrete structures and asphalt. Thus, most of the sun's energy is converted into heat, which allows temperatures to rise. At night, heat is retained in the concrete and asphalt, which keeps temperatures warmer. In rural areas, a large percentage of solar energy is used to evaporate moisture from soil and vegetation; this is a cooling process. Thus, less solar energy is available to be converted in heat, which keeps temperatures cooler than in the city.

● PROBLEM 7–47

What does Figure 1 and Figure 2 represent?

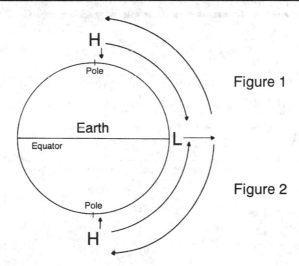

SOLUTION:

Figures 1 and 2 represent Hadley cells. Heating at the equator produces a broad area of low pressure due to a general area of rising air. At the poles, cold air sinks to create a large area of high pressure. A large circulation pattern develops to move the warm air pole-ward and the cold air toward the equator. This is a simplified wind pattern of the Earth's circulation system and does not actually exist.

...depth of water that results from melting a sample of snow is called ... liquid equivalent.

The following observations were made in Town A and Town B for the same 24-hour period:

Observation	Town A	Town B
Liquid Equivalent	1 inch	1 inch
High Temperature	32 degrees F	14 degrees F
Snowfall	6 inches	15 inches

If the storm only produced snow (no rain, sleet, or freezing rain), why did Town B receive more snow?

SOLUTION:

Various forms of ice crystals fall as snow. The type of snow crystal is dependent on the air temperature. See the chart below.

Temperature (degrees F)	Type of Ice Crystal
32-25	moist thin plates
24-14	columns
13-10	plates
9-3	dendrites
<3	dry plates

Crystals that form in warmer air may only produce 6 inches of snow for every 1 inch of liquid equivalent. Drier air may produce 15 inches of snow per inch of liquid equivalent. Thus, the ratio of snow/liquid equivalent at Town A was less than the ratio at Town B. This smaller ratio represents why less snow fell at Town A.

● **PROBLEM 7-49**

Explain why cities leeward of the Great Lakes receive much more snow than cities on the windward side.

Moist, relatively warm air over the Great Lakes generally rises (convection). In the presence of an advancing cold air mass, the rising (warm) air quickly reaches its dew point. Condensation then occurs and low (stratocumulus) clouds form. These clouds carry great amounts of moisture that is released when the cold airstream reaches elevated land on the lake shores, forcing the air to rise.

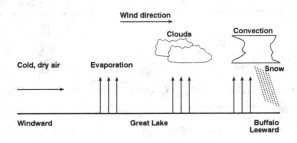

● **PROBLEM 7–50**

Why is a microburst dangerous to aircraft?

SOLUTION:

A microburst is a strong downdraft from a thunderstorm that induces sudden changes in wind speed and direction (wind shear) near the ground. The width of a microburst ranges between 40 meters to 4 kilometers, although most are between 1 and 4 km. Intense microbursts have produced winds as high as 168 mph.

A microburst is dangerous to an aircraft because it can cause an immediate loss of altitude. The pilot's attempt to compensate for this condition often is futile, for strong changes in wind speed and direction limit his ability to gain enough lift for the craft to remain airborne, increasing the chances for a crash.

● **PROBLEM 7–51**

Using the figure below, where do the most tornadoes occur annually? Why?

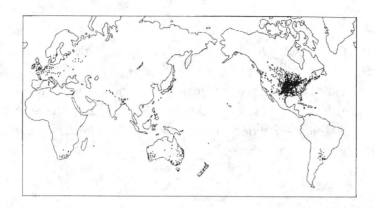

SOLUTION:

The most tornadoes occur annually in the United States. Tornadoes occur in many areas of the world; however, the United States, specifically the Midwest, encounters the most every year. This is due to the unique climatology of the Midwest, which is not found in other parts of the world. Warm, moist air from the southern United States often converges with dry, cold air from the North. This contrast of air masses can occur during any month; however, it is most common and strongest in the spring. When this contrast of air masses occurs, a very unstable atmosphere results and thunderstorms often form. Tornadoes are produced in the severest of thunderstorms. Although thunderstorms are found in most places in the world, severe thunderstorms are most commonly found in climates that experience a sharp contrast of air masses, as described above.

● **PROBLEM 7–52**

Name the parts of the thunderstorm in the diagram below. In which area is a tornado most likely to form? In which area is a microburst most likely to form?

SOLUTION:

(A)—The anvil. The anvil forms in a mature thunderstorm and demarcates the limit of growth. It is formed when rising air encounters the tropopause (an area of stability in the upper atmosphere).

(B)—The updraft. A tornado is most likely to form here. It is a local area of intense low pressure. The updraft develops when warm air quickly rises to replace air lost in the downdraft.

(C)—The downdraft. The downdraft is an area of higher pressure formed

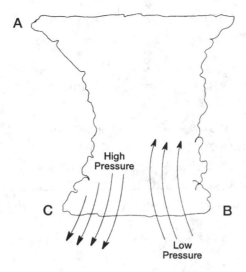

by cooling air and drag created by precipitation. A microburst is most likely to develop at this location.

Use the diagram and the conversion factors below to demonstrate why thunder "rumbles."

Speed of sound = 1,100 feet/second
1 mile = 5,280 feet

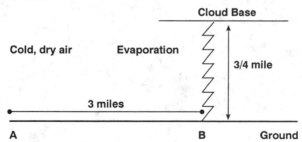

SOLUTION:

The first step is to convert 3 miles to feet. Using the conversion factor:
$$3 \text{ miles} \times (5{,}280 \text{ feet/mile}) = 15{,}840 \text{ feet}$$
Next, determine how long it takes the thunder to travel from Point B to Point A.
$$15{,}840 \text{ feet} \times (1 \text{ second}/1{,}100 \text{ feet}) = 14.4 \text{ seconds}$$
Now, using the geometric equation $H^2 = X^2 + Y^2$, we find the distance from Point A to Point C is:

$$H^2 = (.75)\ (.75) + (3)\ (3) = 9.5625$$

$$\text{taking } \sqrt{9.5625},\ H = 3.092$$

Thus, the distance from Point A to Point C is 3.092 miles or 16,325.76 feet.

Calculating the time it takes for the thunder to travel front Point C to Point A:

$$16{,}325.76 \text{ feet} \times (1 \text{ second}/1{,}100 \text{ feet}) = 14.84 \text{ seconds}$$

Hence, it takes the sound waves longer to travel from Point C to Point A than from Point B to Point A. So, an observer would hear thunder from the part of the lightning strike which was closest to the surface and hear the thunder near the base of the cloud last. This time delay produces the "rumble" of thunder.

● PROBLEM 7–54

What type of precipitation is formed during the process represented in the diagram below?

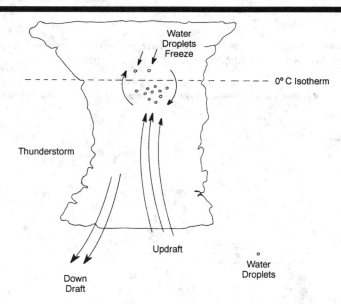

SOLUTION:

Hail is formed. Water droplets below the 0 degree Celsius isotherm (the freezing level) get caught in strong updrafts produced by the thunderstorm. The water droplets freeze, then sink again below the 0 degree Celsius isotherm, but remain frozen. Next, water droplets condense on the frozen precipitation. Usually, for hail to form, this cycle is repeated many times until the updraft can no longer support the hail stone. At this point, the hail falls to the ground.

The Major Climate Zones of the Earth

Which item listed below would best explain why the winter climate is milder in San Francisco, California than in St. Louis, Missouri?
- Latitude
- Prevailing winds
- Altitude
- Mountain barriers

SOLUTION:

Prevailing winds cause the winter climate to be milder in San Francisco. The prevailing winds in San Francisco are westerly. This west wind flowing over relatively warm ocean water keeps surface temperatures in San Francisco mild. In St. Louis, where the prevailing winds are from the northwest, cold arctic air keeps the surface temperatures much colder. The latitude for St. Louis (38°) and San Francisco (37°) is approximately the same. This slight difference would not cause a milder climate. Although the altitude in San Francisco is lower than in St. Louis, the difference in elevation is only 500 feet, which would not be large enough to contribute to a substantial difference in winter temperatures. Mountains do not provide a barrier from weather systems for either city. Thus, this factor would not account for a difference in climate.

Using the Koppen climate classification system, match the major climate type (A, B, C, D, or E) with the locations listed below.
Tucson, Arizona
Key West, Florida
Barrow, Alaska
Atlanta, Georgia
Burlington, Vermont

Location	Climate Classification
Tucson, Arizona	B
Key West, Florida	A
Barrow, Arkansas	E
Atlanta, Georgia	C
Burlington, Vermont	D

The major climate zones defined under the Koppen classification system are:

(A)—Tropical moist climate. Every month is considered warm (average temperature is greater than 64°F), moist (average rainfall is greater than 2.4 inches), and no winter season exists. The climate in Key West, Florida is classified as a tropical, moist climate with a winter dry season.

(B)—Dry climate. Every month is considered dry (average precipitation is less than average evaporation). The climate in Tucson, Arizona is classified as an arid, desert climate with hot temperatures (average temperature is greater than 64°F).

(C)—Moist, mid-latitude (with mild winters) climate. The summer season is warm (average temperatures are above 72°F) and the winter season is mild (between 27°F and 64°F). The climate in Atlanta, Georgia is classified as a humid, subtropical climate with long, warm summers.

(D)—Moist, mid-latitude (with severe winters) climate. The summer season is warm (average temperatures are above 50°F) and the winter season is cold (average temperatures are below 27°F). The climate in Burlington, Vermont is classified as a humid, continental climate with a short summer season, a long winter season, and moist during all seasons.

(E)—Polar climate. Every month is considered cold (warmest monthly average is below 50°F), and no summer season exists. The climate in Barrow, Alaska is classified as a polar tundra climate (the average temperatures are between 32°F and 50°F).

What is the major Koppen climate classification for the location whose climate is described by only the data provided in Chart A?

CHART A

	Jan	Feb	Mar	Apr	May	Jun	Jul	Aug	Sept	Oct	Nov	Dec
Avg High Temp	74°F	75°F	77°F	80°F	83°F	88°F	92°F	90°F	87°F	80°F	78°F	75°F
Avg Low Temp	59°F	60°F	63°F	66°F	68°F	71°F	74°F	72°F	70°F	65°F	60°F	58°F

SOLUTION:

Major climate A is described in Chart A. The first step is to calculate the average monthly temperature. The results of this calculation are:

Jan 66.5°F	Jul 83.0°F
Feb 67.5°F	Aug 81.0°F
Mar 70.0°F	Sept 78.5°F
Apr 73.0°F	Oct 72.5°F
May 75.5°F	Nov 69.0°F
Jun 79.5°F	Dec 66.5°F

Major climate types A, C, D, and E can be determined only by average monthly temperatures. Major climate type B is determined by precipitation and evaporation. Since each month has an average temperature above 64°F, the climate of the example location is defined as humid, tropical (major Koppen climate type A).

● PROBLEM 7–58

Explain why Atlantic City, New Jersey has a continental climate and not a marine climate.

SOLUTION:

Although Atlantic City is on the Atlantic coast, its climate is continental. Since the prevailing winds in Atlantic City are westerly (NW to SW), the climate is influenced by air masses that form over land.

In a marine climate, such as exists in San Francisco, the prevailing winds are also westerly (NW to SW); however, the air masses that influence the climate in San Francisco form over the ocean.

● **PROBLEM 7–59**

In Barrow, Alaska the average daily temperature is below freezing each day of the year. Why does Barrow receive less snow each year than Syracuse, New York?

SOLUTION:

Although the air is extremely cold in Barrow, it is also very dry (the air, on average, contains relatively small amounts of water vapor). Thus, the average annual precipitation in Barrow is approximately four inches. In a climate such as exists in Syracuse, however, the amount of water vapor in the air on average is significantly higher, and as a result the average annual precipitation is more than 40 inches.

SHORT ANSWER QUESTIONS FOR REVIEW

Choose the correct answer.

1. The cause of the Earth's magnetic field is (a) enormous currents. (b) space satellites. (c) unknown. (d) in the Earth's crust.

2. Warmer air has molecules of air that are far apart; therefore, it produces (a) a low pressure cell. (b) a high pressure cell. (c) rainy weather. (d) dry conditions.

3. Why is stratospheric ozone depletion (destruction of the ozone layer) a serious concern? (a) It is a major cause of the "greenhouse effect." (b) It will increase the amount of ultraviolet radiation reaching the ground. (c) It causes acid rain. (d) It is really nothing to worry about.

4. Land and sea (or lake) breezes form because of (a) uneven heating of coastal environments. (b) the pressure gradient force. (c) the

difference in temperature between land and water surfaces. (d) All of the above.

5. How is the relative strength of a thunderstorm updraft estimated? (a) By the intensity of the lightning (b) By the height of the cloud base (c) By the speed of the wind gusts measured at the surface (d) By the size of the precipitation particles (raindrops or hailstones)

6. Why does saturation of a rising parcel lead to a slower adiabatic lapse rate? (a) Because of the release of latent heat by condensing water vapor (b) Because of the release of latent heat by evaporating water droplets (c) Because cloud droplets add frictional drag to the rising parcel and slow it down (d) Because temperature decreases with height

7. Mt. Adiabatic, a 3,000 foot mountain, separates Towns A and B. Air is being forced up on the side facing Town A, and it flows down the slope on the side facing Town B. Town A has launched a weather balloon and found that the rising air will be 100% saturated at 1,000 ft. (the lifting condensation level). Assuming Town A has an air temperature of 70°F, what will be the temperature of the air when it reaches Town B? (a) 70.0°F (b) 67.8°F, (c) 74.4°F, (d) 70.2°F

8. Why do we see lightning before we hear thunder? (a) Because the lightning occurred closer than the thunder (b) Because lightning is composed of multiple strokes (c) Because thunder occurs higher in the cloud (d) Because of the difference between the speeds of light and sound

9. Why is radiation the only method of heat transfer capable of bringing the sun's energy to the Earth? (a) Because space is a vacuum (b) Because other methods are too slow and lose too much energy by the time they reach Earth (c) Because blockage by stellar debris inhibits other methods (d) Because solar convection is propelled away from the Earth

10. Why does evaporation lead to cooling? (a) Because of the change in state involved as water evaporates (b) Because of the absorption of latent heat by water droplets (c) Because of the release of latent heat by water droplets (d) (a) and (b) only

11. The warmest summer temperatures in the Northern Hemisphere occur on the summer solstice because (a) the sun is at its closest to the Northern Hemisphere. (b) the sun reaches its maximum azimuth. (c) the Northern Hemisphere is tilted toward the sun. (d) maximum summer temperatures aren't reached on the solstice.

12. It can rain when the temperature is (a) 32°F. (b) 25°F. (c) 33°F. (d) All of the above.

13. Water can remain a liquid at (a) 60°F. (b) 40°F. (c) 0°F. (d) All of the above.

14. Why does your body perspire when you get hot? (a) Water vapor condenses on your skin. (b) It is your body's biological method to cool itself. (c) Your body temperature slowly increases and approaches the dew point of the surrounding air. (d) None of the above.

15. It is possible for snow to fall in tropical regions because (a) hurricanes can be very cold. (b) of elevation considerations. (c) the land cools significantly at night. (d) All of the above.

16. Water displays a blue color because of (a) scattered sunlight. (b) heavy plant growth. (c) organic material in water. (d) the lack of organic material in water and the presence of inorganics.

17. A control of the color of water is the (a) population present. (b) amount of oxygen. (c) types of minerals present. (d) lack of water movement.

18. Temperature is controlled by (a) weather. (b) position of the axis. (c) pressure. (d) the sun.

19. Air temperature, movement of air, and weather changes are all affected by (a) air pressure. (b) low pressure only. (c) high pressure cells. (d) clouds.

20. Colder air is more dense (air molecules are relatively close) and tends to form a (a) low pressure cell. (b) high pressure cell. (c) flooding condition. (d) dry condition.

21. Low pressure cells form because the molecules in the cell are (a) blown upward. (b) relatively close together. (c) relatively far apart. (d) bouncing up and down.

22. Climate affects all of the following except (a) number of human chromosomes. (b) transportation. (c) organisms. (d) outdoor activities.

23. Hurricanes occur when (a) atmospheric conditions change slowly. (b) severe climate changes occur at the poles. (c) the sky changes color. (d) atmosphere and pressure change is severe.

24. Hurricanes occur over (a) land. (b) water. (c) water and land. (d) the polar caps only.

25. August, September, and October normally have more hurricanes documented than any other months with (a) September having the greatest number of hurricanes. (b) August having the greatest number of hurricanes. (c) October having the greatest number of hurricanes. (d) August and October having the greatest number of hurricanes.

26. A typhoon is a severe storm that occurs over (a) bodies of water making up rivers. (b) bodies of land and water. (c) bodies of land. (d) bodies of water making up oceans.

27. A decrease in temperature will cause the density of water to (a) be cut in half. (b) decrease. (c) weaken. (d) increase.

28. Fog will primarily interfere with one's ability to (a) see over a small area. (b) see at a distance. (c) see large moving objects. (d) see anything.

29. Fog is also called a (a) geyser. (b) hydrotherapy. (c) fallen cloud. (d) hydrometer.

Items 30 to 32 refer to the following diagram:

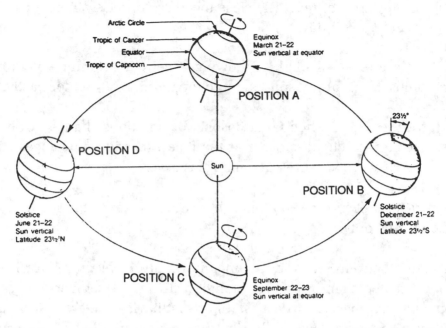

30. Which position(s) in the above diagram results(s) in the north Polar regions being referred to as the Land of the Midnight Sun? (a) Position A (b) Position B (c) Position C (d) Position D

31. Which position results in equal day and night? (a) Position A (b) Position B (c) Position D (d) Positions A and C

32. The Earth's seasons are caused by the (a) tilt of the Earth's axis. (b) distance from the sun to the planet. (c) rotation of the sun. (d) rotation of the Earth.

33. Two main factors of climate are temperature and rainfall, and these factors depend on a whole set of conditions called climatic controls. Which of the following would not be a climatic control? (a) Latitude (b) Prevailing winds (c) Population density (d) Topography

34. On the centigrade temperature scale, water freezes at ____°C and boils at ____°C. (a) 32; 100 (b) 0; 212 (c) 32; 212 (d) 0; 100

35. Life is most abundant in which atmospheric layer? (a) Ionosphere (b) Thermosphere (c) Stratosphere (d) Troposphere

Items 36 to 38 refer to the following graph.

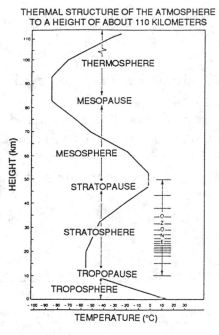

THERMAL STRUCTURE OF THE ATMOSPHERE
TO A HEIGHT OF ABOUT 110 KILOMETERS

36. The warmest place in the atmosphere is near the ground because (a) the ground is under the ozone layer. (b) the ground can store heat. (c) the ground is covered by ice in some regions. (d) the Earth is both land and water.

37. The coolest layer of the atmosphere is the (a) mesopause. (b) thermosphere. (c) stratopause. (d) stratosphere.

38. Which would be a reason for temperature changes as you travel up through the atmosphere? (a) Distance from the sun decreases (b) Weather disruptions cause mixing of the temperatures. (c) Presence of ozone (d) Changes in composition

Fill in the blanks.

39. An odorless, colorless gas that surrounds the Earth is commonly called _____.

40. The source of evaporation is the _____.

41. _____ is a collection of minute water droplets.

203

42. The atmosphere is made up of 78% _____.

43. Cloud formations float in the lowest portion of the atmosphere called the _____.

44. A belt of radiation surrounding the Earth is called the _____.

45. One of the few substances that can exist in all three states, at temperatures naturally encountered on Earth, is _____.

46. The characteristic weather representative of a given region is called _____.

47. Air is warmest at the _____.

48. The study of climate is called _____.

Determine whether the following statements are true or false.

49. Hurricanes occur over land only.

50. Mountain and valley breezes form because of gravity and heating.

51. When air descends, it becomes more humid.

52. An inversion is stable.

53. The sky appears blue because sunlight is scattered by the atmosphere before it reaches the Earth.

54. It cannot rain when the temperature is 25°F.

55. Longitude lines curve from north to south.

56. Aurora Borealis, the beautiful display of colored streamers, is commonly called the Southern Lights.

57. Aurora Australis is seen in the Antarctic region.

58. One of the factors that causes a change in temperature is changing air currents.

ANSWER KEY

1. c	30. d
2. a	31. d
3. b	32. a
4. d	33. c
5. d	34. d
6. a	35. d
7. c	36. b
8. d	37. b
9. a	38. d
10. d	39. air
11. d	40. sunlight
12. d	41. Fog
13. d	42. nitrogen
14. b	43. troposphere
15. b	44. ionosphere
16. a	45. water
17. a	46. climate
18. b	47. equator
19. a	48. climatology
20. a	49. false
21. c	50. true
22. a	51. false
23. d	52. true
24. c	53. true
25. a	54. false
26. d	55. true
27. d	56. false
28. b	57. true
29. c	58. true

CHAPTER 8

THE HYDROSPHERE

The Structures of the Ocean Floor

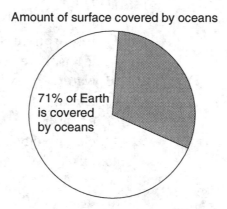

Amount of surface covered by oceans

71% of Earth is covered by oceans

● **PROBLEM 8–1**

Describe the three main features of the ocean basin.

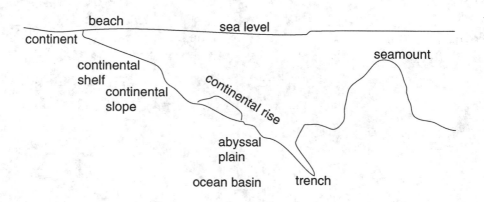

The ocean basin has similar physical features to the Earth's continents. Trenches are long, narrow valleys that extend more than 11 kilometers below sea level at the deepest part of the ocean basin. Abyssal plains are level areas formed from sediment covering the ocean floor. Seamounts are volcanic mountains rising above the ocean floor. Hawaii is a good example of a seamount which rises above sea level. All of these features combine to give the ocean floor its characteristics.

● **PROBLEM 8-2**

What are the sources of ocean floor sediment?

SOLUTION:

Ocean floor sediments form in four ways. The weathering and erosion of land causes sediments to build in rivers. These sediments travel down the river and become deposited in the ocean. Sediment can also be carried to the ocean by the wind where it slowly sinks to the floor. Ooze from the hard parts of aquatic plants and animals is another primary source of ocean floor sediment. Finally, dissolved minerals which precipitate out of the water are eventually deposited as sediment on the ocean floor.

● **PROBLEM 8-3**

What are the types of coral reefs?

SOLUTION:

Coral reefs are colorful deposits of coral. Coral is an oceanic animal which lives in the shallow waters of tropical climates. These animals form three types of reefs. A fringing reef occurs around an island or along a coastline and is the most common. A barrier reef is separated from the coastline by water. The largest barrier reef is the Great Barrier Reef off the coast of Australia. An atoll is a ring-shaped coral reef around a lagoon. Atolls usually surround a seamount that was once an island.

Describe the continental margin.

SOLUTION:

There are three parts to the continental margin: the continental shelf, the continental slope, and the continental rise. The shelf is a gently sloping area which begins at the shoreline. The slope falls about 1.7 meters for every kilometer from shore. The size of the continental shelf varies with the type of shoreline present; mountainous regions will have a very small shelf. The continental shelf supports a large variety of sealife. When the slope changes to a drop of 70 meters for every kilometer, the continental slope has been reached. At the end of the continental slope the decline becomes gentle again with a drop of 6 meters for every kilometer. This marks the continental rise. Thick accumulations of sediment are found at the continental rise.

● PROBLEM 8-5

What are submarine canyons?

SOLUTION:

Deep canyons running through the continental shelf and slope are called submarine canyons. These V-shaped trenches have winding paths that can have a width of up to 37 kilometers and a depth of up to 5 kilometers. The submarine canyons are formed from underwater landslides caused by turbidity currents.

● PROBLEM 8-6

What are manganese nodules?

SOLUTION:

Lumps of matter from the ocean floor which contain a large amount of manganese are called manganese nodules. Manganese nodules apparently form from shark teeth and bone fragments. Since manganese and iron have electrical properties, they attract other metals. These metals collect on the teeth and bone fragments to form the nodules. Manganese nodules can contain iron, copper, nickel, and cobalt.

● PROBLEM 8-7

What contributions were made by the explorers of the HMS *Challenger*?

SOLUTION:

The explorers on board the HMS *Challenger* traveled the oceans beginning in 1872. One of the most important discoveries was that of manganese nodules. John Murray and Charles Thomson wished to discover everything possible about the oceans. During their four-year expedition thousands of samples and measurements were taken.

The Layers of the Ocean

● PROBLEM 8-8

What are the layers of the ocean which correspond to the life found in the layers?

SOLUTION:

There are three zones given to the areas of life forms found in the ocean. The one most familiar to everyone is the shore zone. This area extends from the high tide line to the low tide line. In the shore zone are found clams, crabs, and seaweed. Due to the changes in tides, this area has extreme changes in environment, causing multiple hazards for the life forms.

Beyond the shore zone following the continental shelf down are ocean dwellers such as coral and octopus. This area is the neritic zone which has a good supply of sunlight with very little temperature change.

Beyond the continents is the oceanic zone. Three regions are formed in the oceanic zone due to the amount of sunlight reaching the depth. The light region is on the surface where many types of plankton and nekton are found. From 200 meters to about 2,000 meters is the bathyal, or deep-sea, region. Many life forms survive in this region such as whale, tuna, and swordfish. No sunlight reaches the deepest region of the ocean. The abyssal region sustains only a few life forms, such as the angular fish and the sea cucumber, specifically adapted to life at these great depths.

● PROBLEM 8-9

What are the three groups of living things in the ocean?

SOLUTION:

Plants and animals which survive on the ocean floor are called benthos. Corals and crabs are examples of the few organisms which can survive on the floor of the ocean. Nekton are the living things which swim through the ocean. Fish, whale, and squid are examples of nekton. Plankton make up the final category of organism. Plankton are microscopic organisms that float at or near the surface of the ocean. They feed on the nutrients brought up by upwellings from the lower areas of the ocean.

● PROBLEM 8-10

What is upwelling?

SOLUTION:

Water rising from deep in the ocean is called upwelling. Upwellings occur along coastlines. Nutrients which support plant and animal life are brought to the surface by upwellings.

● PROBLEM 8-11

What is salinity of the ocean?

SOLUTION:

Salinity refers to the amount of dissolved salt found in the ocean. The salinity is measured in grams of dissolved salt in one kilogram of water. The average salinity is 35 g/kg. The salinity tends to be lower near the mouth of a river due to the flow of fresh water into the saltwater. In areas of high temperatures, such as at the equator, or low temperatures such as in the Arctic and Antarctic Oceans, the salinity tends to be higher due to a loss of water through evaporation and ice formation, respectively. Salinity rarely drops below 33 g/kg or rises above 38 g/kg.

The ocean dissolves many types of salts from sediments and the atmosphere. The most common is sodium chloride. Magnesium salts and sulfur salts, as well as small amounts of others, are also found in the oceans.

Currents of the Ocean

● PROBLEM 8–12

What causes ocean currents?

SOLUTION:

There are two types of ocean currents, each produced by different means. The surface currents are produced by the wind moving over the ocean. Continents block the path of the currents, causing them to change direction. The Coriolis effect from the Earth's rotation causes the surface currents in the Northern Hemisphere to flow in a clockwise circular pattern. The Southern Hemisphere surface currents move in a counterclockwise pattern.

Deep ocean currents flow vertically perpendicular to the ocean's surface. Density differences in ocean water cause the more dense water to sink, forcing less dense, cooler water to the surface. This produces a circulation of water beginning approximately 100 meters below the ocean's surface and continuing to the ocean floor. The circulation formed may continue for hundreds of years.

● PROBLEM 8–13

Describe the parts of a wave.

SOLUTION:

A wave consists of a crest, or top, and a trough, or bottom. The distance between the crest and trough is called the wave height. The amplitude is equal to the distance between the crest and the rest position of the wave. The wave height is equal to two times the amplitude. The distance between

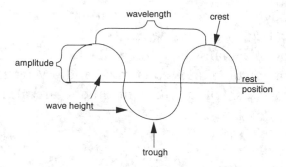

two consecutive crests is called a wavelength. The wave amplitude can vary from 3 meters on a calm day to 30 meters during a storm. Wind speed, the length of time the wind has blown, and the length of ocean the wind has blown over all determine the amplitude of the wave.

● **PROBLEM 8-14**

What is a breaker?

SOLUTION:

When the crest of a wave moves forward faster than the rest of the wave, the wave begins to fall forward. At this point, the wave is said to be breaking and can be called a breaker. Breakers form the familiar foamy surf found at most beaches.

● **PROBLEM 8-15**

Define longshore currents and turbidity currents.

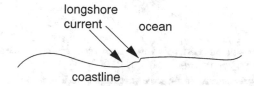

SOLUTION:

Ocean currents close to the shore which travel along, not toward, the shore are called longshore currents. These currents carry large amounts of sand which is not readily deposited. It is only when the current reaches an area forcing it to slow that the sand is deposited. Sand deposited around islands by longshore currents can eventually connect islands with each other or a large landmass nearby. These connections are called tombolos.

Landslides down the continental slope cause turbidity currents. These currents can travel at speeds up to 80 km/h. Telephone cables have been snapped by turbidity currents. Turbidity currents can erode the sediments of the continental slope forming submarine canyons.

● PROBLEM 8–16

What are the major ocean currents?

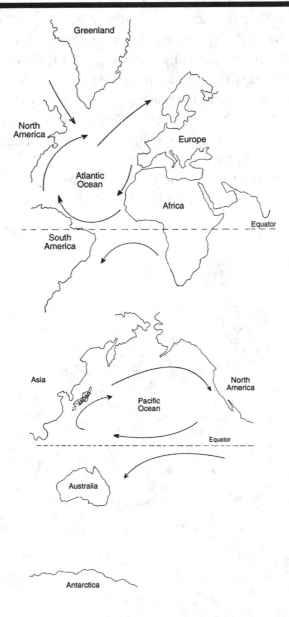

SOLUTION:

In each of the oceans there are one or more major currents. These ocean currents are also called "gyres" and travel in a circular direction. Interestingly enough, these huge patterns of moving water move clockwise in the Northern Hemisphere and counterclockwise in the Southern Hemisphere (see diagram).

Ocean currents influence weather, both on the ocean and on the land that is relatively close to the ocean, as currents usually follow the coastlines of the continents.

In the Southern Hemisphere of the Atlantic Ocean, there is only one major current, called the southern equatorial current. In the Northern Hemisphere of the Atlantic Ocean there are five major currents: 1) the north equatorial current traveling east to west along the equator, 2) the Gulf Stream traveling from the equator north along the North American coast, 3) the Labrador current travelling southeast between Greenland and North America, 4) the North Atlantic drift traveling northeast between Greenland and Europe, and 5) the Canary current traveling south along the European and African coasts.

Using these descriptions of the currents, label the following map with the correct name of each Atlantic current.

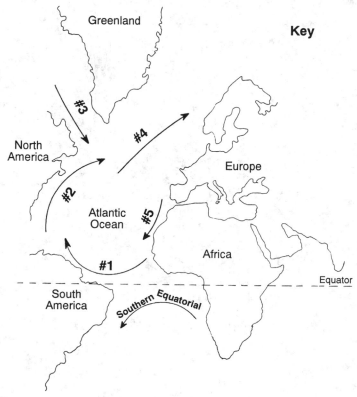

In the Pacific Ocean there are four gyres (also called currents): 1) the south equatorial current in the Southern Hemisphere, 2) the north equatorial current moving west along the equator in the Northern Hemisphere, 3) the Japan current moving north from the equator past Japan, and 4) the north Pacific current moving east then south along the western coast of North America.

Using these description of the Pacific currents, label the following map with the correct name of each current.

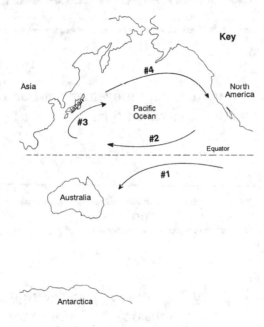

The Antarctic Ocean also has a major gyre. This is the only current which encircles the Earth. It is the Antarctic current.

● PROBLEM 8–17

What is a tidal range?

SOLUTION:

A tidal range is the difference between high tide and low tide. The tidal range of an area can show the average height of the tides. This information is valuable in determining the amount of shoreline exposed to wind and water.

● **PROBLEM 8–18**

What are tidal bores?

SOLUTION:

A tidal bore is caused by the rapid movement of tide toward land. This movement produces large waves called tidal bores. Surfers take advantage of tidal bores.

● **PROBLEM 8–19**

Define the shoreline, a barrier island, and a spit.

SOLUTION:

The boundary between the land and sea is called the shoreline. A rocky shoreline does not allow much erosion, therefore there is little sediment produced. Beaches form where erosion has occurred along a shoreline.

Deposits of sand running parallel with the shoreline are called barrier islands. These deposits may be formed by sediments which are deposited by the ocean current or they could be remnants of sand dunes where beaches existed at one time.

When sand is deposited in an extension from the mouth of a bay, a spit is formed Usually a spit occurs where currents slow, allowing sediments in the water to settle. Over time these sediments build, forming a barrier of sand.

● **PROBLEM 8–20**

What is a baymouth bar?

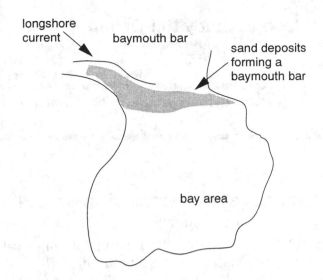

longshore current

baymouth bar

sand deposits forming a baymouth bar

bay area

SOLUTION:

A baymouth bar is a sand deposit stretching across the mouth of a bay. Longshore currents deposit sand, slowly closing the mouth of a bay. Once the sand reaches across, a baymouth bar is formed.

● PROBLEM 8–21

What are tombolos?

SOLUTION:

Tombolos are deposits of sand around an island which connect the island to the mainland.

● PROBLEM 8–22

What are groins and jetties?

SOLUTION:

Groins and jetties are structures which are built along shores to capture sand. The walls built are called groins. Jetties are piles of rock. As these structures collect sand, areas down shore erode. Beaches need a continual supply of new sand to be maintained.

Instruments Used to Study the Ocean

● PROBLEM 8–23

Who were the first scientists to view the ocean at a depth of one kilometer?

SOLUTION:

In the early 1930s, Otis Barton and William Beebe descended to about one kilometer below the ocean surface. They used a steel sphere of less than two meters in diameter. The sphere withstood approximately seven tons of pressure, allowing Barton and Beebe to view an area of the ocean that had never been seen by anyone.

● PROBLEM 8–24

What is a Nansen bottle?

SOLUTION:

Nansen bottles are designed to collect water from different depths in the ocean. They are attached to a cable with devices used to trigger subsequent Nansen bottles on the line to invert collecting water samples. The sample is checked for temperature and pressure at the depth the sample is taken. When the readings are set the Nansen bottles close, sealing the sample of water inside. It can then be brought to the surface for further testing.

● PROBLEM 8–25

What is a bathyscaphe?

SOLUTION:

A bathyscaphe is a deep-sea diving apparatus that can be maneuvered without a cable. It has a submarine-shaped float and a steel observation cabin. The bathyscaphe allows scientists to venture to the deepest parts of the ocean. Special lights and high-speed film allow pictures to be taken for recording findings that cannot be brought to the surface.

What does scuba stand for and what is its function?

SOLUTION:

Self-contained underwater breathing apparatus, or scuba, allows scientists and others to dive to depths of about 100 meters. This allows first hand study of areas of the ocean. Pressure-controlled diving suits can be used for depths below 100 meters to about 600 meters.

What is sonar?

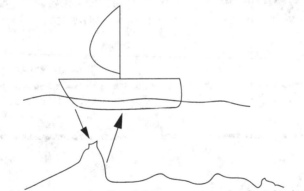

Sound waves are sent to the floor of the ocean and reflect back to the ship.

SOLUTION:

Sonar, sound navigation and ranging, is an instrument which uses sound waves to take measurements of objects below the surface of the ocean. The ocean floor has been mapped by the use of sonar. Organisms and submarines have been tracked using sonar. Sound waves are emitted downward toward the bottom of the ocean. They bounce off objects on the ocean floor and are received on board a ship by the sonar detector. This translates the sound into a shape, giving scientists an idea of what is beneath them.

Glaciers' Impact on the Earth

● PROBLEM 8-28

What causes glaciers to move?

SOLUTION:

Glaciers are large blocks of ice which can cover a continent. Snow falls and does not melt, producing a large accumulation. Over time, compaction of the snow turns to ice. Friction caused by the force of gravity on the glacier causes some of the ice to melt. This gives the glacier something on which it can float, producing a moving glacier. The glacier slides over the rocks that are under it. Another type of glacier movement is produced by internal pressure, which allows gravity to pull some layers of the glacier over the other layers: the top layers slide over the lower layers.

● PROBLEM 8-29

What are the main types of glaciers and what are the erosional features they produce?

SOLUTION:

Valley glaciers are formed in mountains. Gravity forces them to move down-hill, collecting debris as they move. Valley glaciers are usually very dirty due to the debris. Crevices are formed when the glacier is forced to move around curves or uneven surfaces. This usually causes part of the glacier to move faster, leaving gaps in the glacier. These gaps are called crevices.

Continental glaciers are sheets of ice covering large areas of land. Today Antarctica and Greenland have continental glaciers. The ice forms a dome shape, forcing the ice sheet to move until it eventually reaches the sea. At the sea, pieces of the glacier break off, producing icebergs.

Valley glaciers can form cirques. A cirque is formed when a glacier hollows out an area of land forming a bowl-shaped basin. When several cirques are formed close together, the ridges between them form a horn.

Large glaciers can combine with small glaciers to form hanging valleys. These valleys are usually U-shaped and above the floor of the main valley.

Waterfalls are formed from these hanging valleys as water melts, moving down the hanging valley until it falls to reach the lower main valley.

Rocks carried by the glacier can cause erosional features. Striations are long parallel scratches formed as pieces of rock are pulled along by the glacier. When the bedrock is soft, deeper cuts, called grooves, can be formed. Grooves usually have a polished appearance.

● PROBLEM 8-30

What are the depositional features from the glacier?

SOLUTION:

Drifts from a glacier can form two main features. A till is rock which has been directly deposited by the glacier. It consists of all sizes of rock. Moraines are a type of till left by the melting glacier that is in the form of a ridge. When left at the end of the glacier's advance, the moraine is called a terminal moraine. An outwash is rock deposited by the water melted from the glacier. An outwash plain is an area where sand, silt, and gravel have been deposited. A kettle can be found in an outwash plain. It is a depression left by a piece of the glacier having been lodged in a till and subsequently melted. Also in outwashes are eskers, which are long, narrow hills formed from the drift deposited by streams from the glacier. Kames are cone-shaped hills at the openings of glaciers along steep-sided hills.

● PROBLEM 8-31

What is an ice age?

SOLUTION:

An ice age is a cool period in the history of the Earth. During these periods, ice sheets and glaciers can advance toward the equator. There have been at least ten ice ages in the last two million years. There are many possible causes. Dust from volcanoes covering the sun and the sun not producing as much energy are two hypotheses accepted by some scientists. The most commonly accepted hypothesis is that the Earth's tilt changed, causing the area around the equator to cool.

Formation of River Systems

What are three stages in the life of a river?

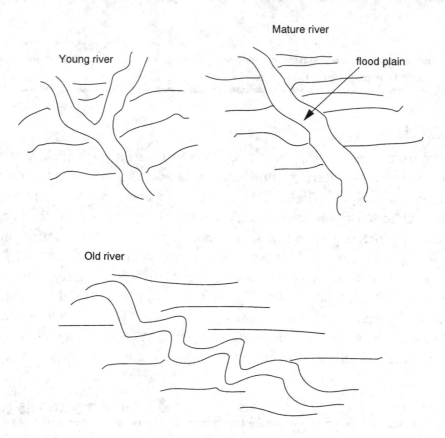

SOLUTION:

A river in its youth is a rapidly flowing stream of water. The water erodes the land to the base level where the river can go no deeper. Since the depth is established, the river begins to erode land surrounding it. As the river widens, it forms the winding appearance characteristic of a mature river. This meandering appearance continues into the river's old age. As the river creates new meanders and sediments accumulate, the oxbow lakes and large flood plains are formed which are characteristic of an old river.

Define the features of a river system, a flood plain, a delta, and a divide.

SOLUTION:

A river system is composed of the river and its tributaries. The watershed which feeds the river is also considered part of the river system. Areas of flooding, such as flood plains and the delta, can also be parts of the river system.

A flood plain is an area surrounding a river that is normally inundated when the river overflows its banks. Silt is deposited in the flood plain producing fertile soil. There can also be a great deal of devastation in the flood plain area. The rich soil of the flood plain entices farmers to settle in the area, but flood waters can devastate crops and property.

A river delta is an area at the mouth of the river. The river drains into the ocean through the delta. Accumulation of sediment may cause the delta to move from one area to another. The rich soil can then be farmed until the river moves the delta back again.

A divide is an area of high elevation which separates watersheds of rivers. The divide is generally a large mountain range which does not allow water to flow from one watershed to another.

Formation of Lakes

● **PROBLEM 8–34**

What are the characteristics of a lake?

SOLUTION:

Lakes are generally large, natural or man-made depressions filled with fresh water. The water can come from rain, rivers, and springs. Some lakes are filled with salt water, such as the Great Salt Lake in Utah.

Other than by glaciers, how are lakes formed?

SOLUTION:

Lakes can be formed when a dam is built, stopping the flow of water in a river. A natural dam can also form a lake. A landslide can stop the flow of water to produce a lake. Large sinkholes, called karsts, can be filled with water to produce a lake. Any large depression which fills with water will form a lake. Some lakes are remnants of ancient oceans which have since disappeared. The water in these lakes is usually salty.

How were the Great Lakes formed?

SOLUTION:

During a period of advancing glaciers from the Arctic, the Great Lakes were gouged from a river system. The glaciers pushed sediments into the river, stopping much of the river's flow. As the glaciers melted and receded, water filled the newly formed Great Lakes.

What is the life cycle of a lake?

SOLUTION:

In its youth a lake has very little life. It is rich in oxygen and the water is clear. As more nutrients are added to the water, plant and animal life increase. Middle age is reached when the fish are large and the bottom has a good quantity of nutrients. Old age arrives as the nutrients begin to cause an overabundance of bacteria which rob the fish of their oxygen. Eutrophication usually occurs in an older lake, and completes the life cycle.

What is eutrophication?

SOLUTION:

The slow process in which a lake disappears is called eutrophication. Nutrients are added to a lake by natural plant life or by man. These nutrients feed the bacteria which consume the oxygen in the water. The lack of oxygen causes the death of fish resulting in organic waste covering the bottom of the lake. The water depth slowly decreases, and the lake is filled in over time.

Other Fresh Water Sources

● PROBLEM 8–39

Describe the water cycle.

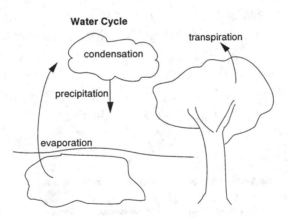

Water Cycle

SOLUTION:

The process by which water is transported from the Earth to the atmosphere and back is called the water cycle. It consists of evaporation from the surface water and transpiration from plants which sends water to the atmosphere. In the atmosphere, water condenses around tiny particles in the air, forming clouds. Clouds precipitate in some form—rain, sleet, snow, or hail—sending the water back to the Earth.

What is ground water?

SOLUTION:

Ground water is accumulated water found below the Earth's surface in the zone of saturation. The water is kept in this area due to an impermeable rock layer below the zone. The water table is the upper boundary of the ground water which gives ponds and lakes their water level. The average temperature of ground water is between 5°C and 15°C. Warmer and cooler temperatures can be found near areas of volcanic activity and glaciers, respectively.

What is a water budget?

SOLUTION:

A water budget is a record of the evaporation and precipitation in a specific area. The precipitation is considered to be the water "income" and the evaporation is the water "outgo." Together these measurements give information concerning the water supply. When more precipitation has occurred than evaporation, there is a water surplus. When more evaporation has occurred, there is a water deficit.

What is the water table?

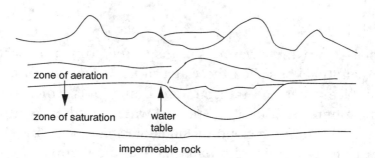

SOLUTION:

The boundary between the zone of aeration and the zone of saturation is the water table. The zone of aeration is the area through which water readily flows. Water stops at the zone of saturation. The slope of the land usually dictates the slope of the water table. Rainfall and climate cause the water table to vary from place to place and season to season.

● PROBLEM 8–43

What are aquifers?

SOLUTION:

A rock layer which holds water is called an aquifer. Generally, the water in an aquifer will flow downhill due to the pull of gravity. Pores in the rock layer allow the water to pass through so the flow is slow but usually constant. When the rock layer is exposed to the surface of the Earth, the water comes to the surface. At this time an aquifer is called a spring. The water in a spring is usually very clear and clean since it has passed through rocks which filter out impurities.

● PROBLEM 8–44

What is an artesian well?

artesian well

impermeable

permeable

impermeable

SOLUTION:

Ground water which rises to the surface naturally is called an artesian well. It usually comes to the surface due to a force pushing it upward into the air. Heated water from an artesian well produces a greater force, causing a spectacular occurrence called a geyser. Geysers usually only erupt as the water is heated enough to push it up out of the ground.

● PROBLEM 8-45

What are the differences between soft water and hard water?

SOLUTION:

Hard water is what most of us use everyday. What causes it to be called "hard water" is the presence of calcium, magnesium, and/or iron ions. These ions come from rocks encountered by the water as it flows through streams, rivers, lakes, and underground strata. "Soft water" is water which has no calcium, magnesium, or iron. It may, however, contain other elements or minerals. For example, water may contain sulfur which certainly causes the water to have a disagreeable odor, but it would be described as "soft water."

The hardness of water is a consumer issue for several reasons. It does not lather as well as soft water and hard water produces a salty type of deposit which creates problems for water use appliances such as hot water heaters and steam irons. Mineral water sold for drinking purposes is a form of hard water, while distilled water is soft water.

● PROBLEM 8-46

Describe the process of desalination.

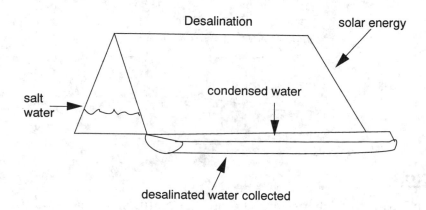

Desalination

solar energy

salt water

condensed water

desalinated water collected

SOLUTION:

Desalination is the process of removing salts from seawater. Seawater is collected in covered containers and heated. The heated water evaporates, and the water vapor condenses on the top of the container. This water trickles down to a trough where it is collected. The salt is left in the original container, and the water collected in the trough is now virtually salt-free.

● PROBLEM 8–47

Explain the theory which describes how minerals were first collected in the oceans.

SOLUTION:

Volcanic activity of the Earth threw large amounts of water, gas, and minerals into the atmosphere. As the Earth cooled, the water vapor in the atmosphere condensed to form water drops which fell to the Earth as rain, carrying airborne gases and minerals with it. This process probably produced oceans similar to today's oceans in salt and mineral content.

● PROBLEM 8–48

What is degassing?

SOLUTION:

Degassing is the process by which gases are released through volcanic activity. These gases cool, condense, and fall to Earth in liquid form. These gases contain salts, so as they fall they add salt to the waters of the oceans.

● PROBLEM 8–49

Describe the process of sublimation.

SOLUTION:

Sublimation is the process of changing a solid directly to a gas or a gas into a solid. This occurs in the water cycle during the formation of snow. Water vapor sublimates to a solid to produce snow.

What is the porosity of a material?

SOLUTION:

Porosity is the comparison of the number of pores or openings in a material to its volume. The greater the porosity the easier water is transported through the substance.

● PROBLEM 8–51

Describe a geyser.

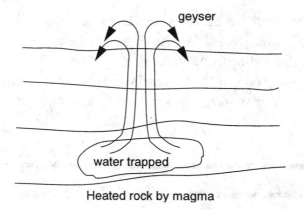

Heated rock by magma

SOLUTION:

A geyser is a hot spring which erupts periodically. As ground water is heated from below, the water deep within the Earth is heated past its boiling point because of the great pressure at such depths. The ground water now expands and forces water up through the overlying rock. As the water exits the Earth, it decreases the pressure on the ground water deep in the Earth, causing it to evaporate to steam. This sudden change leads to the remaining water and steam in the geyser being forcibly ejected from the Earth's surface. Water now begins to fill the geyser again, bringing the cycle back to the beginning.

What is subsidence?

SOLUTION:

Subsidence is the sinking of land due to the removing of an excess amount of water. Holes can be caused by overpumping of water from a well. Land sinking can also be caused by lack of water in an area or a drought.

What is a sinkhole?

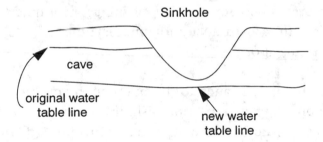

Sinkhole

SOLUTION:

A sinkhole is a depression caused by an underground cave collapsing. The collapse is caused by underlying limestone rock dissolving or by a decrease in ground water levels. The downward force of the soil above the cave causes the collapse. This collapsing of the cavern can cause damage to property.

SHORT ANSWER QUESTIONS FOR REVIEW

Choose the correct answer.

1. The biosphere is (a) land and water surfaces that support life. (b) land that supports life. (c) living parts of the atmosphere. (d) water surfaces that support life.

2. According to the passage, water, as in the ocean or sea, is (a) blue-green. (b) red-brown. (c) blue. (d) green.

3. The most shallow of the seas, measuring 108.4 feet, is the (a) Baltic Sea. (b) Baltic Ocean. (c) Arctic Ocean. (d) Pacific Ocean.

4. The oceans supply man with a variety of things, including (a) a place for water sports. (b) a natural site for photosynthesis. (c) a means of transportation. (d) All of the above.

5. The ocean can be of assistance to the maintaining of the ozone layer by (a) being a breeding area for more fish. (b) being a site of increased photosynthesis. (c) acting as a weather controller. (d) decreasing evaporation processes.

6. Hot springs occur mainly (a) in colder regions of the nation. (b) in warmer regions of the nation. (c) in faulted or folded rock and tornado regions. (d) in faulted or folded rock and volcanic regions.

7. The control of flood waters is important for (a) the survival of coastal habitats. (b) the survival of wading birds. (c) providing recreational areas. (d) All of the above.

8. Tides are caused by (a) the moon. (b) the Earth. (c) the sun. (d) All of the above.

9. The continuous cycle of alternating rise and fall of the sea level observed along the coastlines and bodies of water connected to the sea is called (a) the tide. (b) moon exercises. (c) a waterfall. (d) a tidal wave.

10. Tides are caused by the gravitational interaction between the sun, moon, and (a) Mars. (b) the oceans. (c) Earth. (d) Jupiter.

11. Low water is the (a) trough. (b) crest of the wave. (c) lowest tidal cycle. (d) bottom of the water.

12. The minimum height water can reach during the falling tide is called the (a) high water. (b) cold water. (c) low water. (d) forced water.

13. Tides are classified as (a) one high and low water. (b) two high and one low water. (c) semidiurnal. (d) antidiurnal.

14. Tides are classified as diurnal if they are composed of (a) two high waters and two low waters. (b) one high water and one low water. (c) one high water and two low waters. (d) two high waters and one low water.

15. Currents prevent extremes of temperature by (a) eroding the land. (b) stabilizing the climate over water areas. (c) stabilizing the climate over land areas. (d) wind movement.

16. Currents are influenced by the (a) moon and planets. (b) sun and wind. (c) sun and gravity. (d) moon and Coriolis force.

17. Currents are (a) movements in a horizontal or vertical flow occurring at all depths. (b) movements in a horizontal flow occurring at all depths. (c) movements in a vertical flow occurring at all depths. (d) movements in horizontal or vertical flow occurring at one certain depth.

18. Water tends to flow from an area of (a) low density to high density. (b) high density to low density. (c) hotness to coldness. (d) None of the above.

Items 19 to 21 refer to the following map.

It has been known that ocean conditions influence the weather on land. Look at the following map showing circulation patterns in the oceans and answer the following questions.

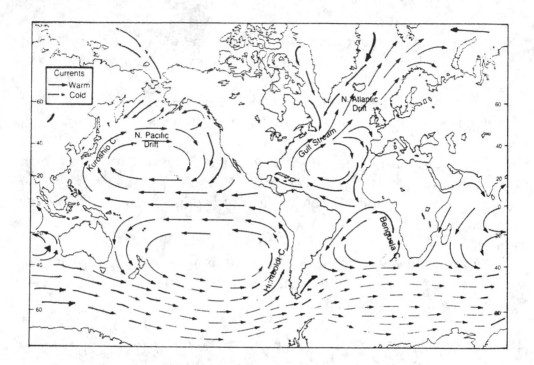

19. Which statement is true? (a) The east coasts of the continents are usually washed by warm currents. (b) The west coasts of the continents are usually washed by warm currents. (c) The east coasts of the continents are washed by cold currents. (d) No pattern exists.

20. Both London, England, and Hudson Bay, Canada, are on the same north latitude, yet London's winters average 35°F warmer. What could account for this difference? (a) England is an island. (b) The waters of the Gulf Stream wash the English coast. (c) Latitude is not a factor in determining temperature. (d) Warm winds from France moderate the weather in England.

21. A bottle with a message is tossed into the ocean on the east side of Japan. Where can it be expected to wash ashore? (a) Australia (b) Western North America (c) Eastern Mexico (d) Western South America

Items 22 to 24 refer to following diagram.

An artesian well system is based on the fact that a water-bearing rock layer (aquifer) is trapped between two impermeable rock layers.

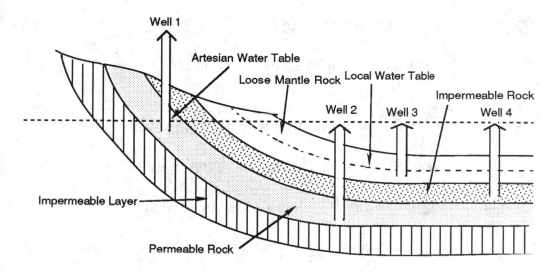

22. Which well is an artesian well that will flow out under its own power? (a) Well 1 (b) Well 2 (c) Well 4 (d) None of the above.

23. Which well is an aquifer well that would require a pumping stem to bring water to the surface? (a) Well 1 (b) Well 2 (c) Well 4 (d) None of the above.

24. Which well is a common well subject to regional weather conditions? (a) Well 1 (b) Well 2 (c) Well 3 (d) Well 4

Fill in the blanks.

25. The percentage of the Earth's surface that is water is _____.

26. The two things that shorelines are made of are _____.

27. An area that is always detached from a shore would be a _____.

28. An indirect source of food for all marine plants is _____.

29. The trench with the greatest depth is located off the coast of _____.

30. Some hot springs are produced by _____.

31. One natural flood control device is the _____.

32. Waves are normally caused by the _____.

33. A tidal cycle along the Gulf coastline will occur about every _____ hours.

Determine whether the following statements are true or false.

34. The hydrosphere is land surrounded by bodies of water.

35. Marine animal behavior is greatly affected by sunlight.

36. Water in the ocean dates about 4 billion years old.

37. Hot springs are naturally occurring bodies of water.

38. An extremely large amount of water flowing into a given area faster than it can leave the area describes a tidal wave.

39. Capillary waves occur in all types of water.

40. Whitecaps usually begin to occur when the wind is moving at varying speed.

41. The maximum height reached by a rising tide is called a hurricane.

42. Mixed tides are either diurnal or semidiurnal.

ANSWER KEY

1. a
2. c
3. a
4. d
5. b
6. d
7. d
8. d
9. a
10. c
11. c
12. c
13. c
14. b
15. c
16. d
17. a
18. a
19. a
20. b
21. b

22. b
23. a
24. c
25. 70%
26. mud and silt
27. rocky reef
28. sunlight
29. Guam
30. geysers
31. sand dune
32. wind
33. 24
34. false
35. true
36. true
37. true
38. false
39. true
40. false
41. false
42. true

CHAPTER 9

ASTRONOMY

Forms of Energy in Space

The weakest force in nature is responsible for the total collapse and demise of the most massive of stars. Identify this energy force which also happens to permeate all of space.

SOLUTION:

Even though it is the weakest force in nature, the gravitational force is responsible for the implosion of the most massive of stars. Newton's Law of Universal Gravitation states that the force of attraction between any two bodies is directly proportional to the product of their masses and inversely proportional to the square of the distance between them. This implies that the strength of gravitational energy fields, while decreasing with increasing distance, approach, but never reach, zero. Thus, these energy fields reach across the vastness of the entire Universe.

● PROBLEM 9-2

On what forms of energy do Earth-based observatories rely?

SOLUTION:

Earth-based observatories use optical telescopes (refractors and reflectors) to gather visible light waves and radio telescopes to gather radio waves. Long wavelengths, such as infrared, microwave, and radar, and short wavelengths, such as ultraviolet, e-ray, and gamma rays, are generally absorbed by various elements in the Earth's atmosphere so they do not reach the ground. These wavelengths are now detected by satellites that go above the Earth's atmosphere, such as IRAS, ROSAT, IUE, GRO, and COBE.

● PROBLEM 9–3

The Universe is filled with electromagnetic radiation (EMR) left over from the initial expansion of the Hot Big Bang. In which region of the EMR spectrum is this background radiation most intense?

SOUTION:

This cosmic background radiation is most intense in the microwave region of the elctromagnetic spectrum and is referred to the microwave background radiation. It was first observed in 1965 by Arno A. Penzias and Robert W. Wilson of the Bell Telephone Laboratories. In 1989, the Cosmic Background Explorer satellite (COBE) made measurements indicating that this background radiation has a temperature of approximately 2.7 Kelvin.

The Types of Telescopes

● PROBLEM 9–4

Name the three basic types of optical telescopes?

SOLUTION:

The three basic types of optical telescopes are refractors, reflectors, and catadioptric. Refractors employ lenses as the main light-collecting element located at the front of the instrument. Reflectors use a concave mirror as their main light-collecting element located at the back of the instrument, and catadioptric systems employ a combination of lenses and mirrors in their optics design.

In the diagram below, which of these is a reflecting telescope?

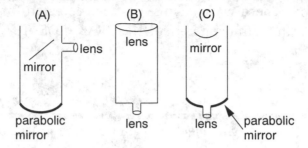

SOLUTION:

Both (A) and (C) are diagrams of reflecting telescopes, while (B) is that of a refracting telescope.

Reflectors are characterized by the use of a parabolic mirror at the base of the telescope to gather light and reflect it to a secondary mirror, which then reflects it to an eyepiece (viewing lens). (A) is known as a Newtonian reflector; (C) is a Schmidt-Cassegrain reflector.

● **PROBLEM 9–6**

Why aren't all telescopes designed to observe in the optical (visible light) range of the spectrum?

SOLUTION:

Astronomical objects emit radiation in various regions of the electromagnetic spectrum. This means that a specific body does not have to radiate its energy within the optical range of the spectrum and would therefore go undetected using optical instruments. Other frequency ranges in which astronomical telescopes operate include: radio, infrared, ultraviolet, x-ray, and gamma ray.

● **PROBLEM 9–7**

Why is it advantageous to put ultraviolet and infrared telescopes into orbit, rather than to rely on orbiting radio telescopes?

SOLUTION:

Our atmosphere interacts in different ways with the different forms of radiation hitting it from outer space. It tends to absorb most of the ultraviolet (UV) and infrared (IR) radiation, while it lets most of the radio waves pass through. Thus, most of the radio waves can be detected on the Earth's surface, while UV and IR telescopes receive little radiation unless they are put into orbit above the Earth's atmosphere.

● PROBLEM 9-8

Provide a description of the Schmidt telescope.

SOLUTION:

The Schmidt telescope consists of a spherical mirror with a specially shaped thin correcting lens mounted in front of it. Thus, it combines both refracting and reflecting elements in the objective. The correcting lens is used to overcome spherical aberrations and helps make the Schmidt ideal for wide-field images.

The Schmidt telescope

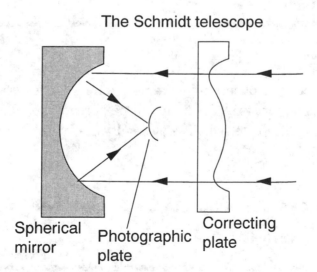

Spherical mirror   Photographic plate   Correcting plate

Shown below are two possible arrangements for focusing the light impinging on a convex mirror:

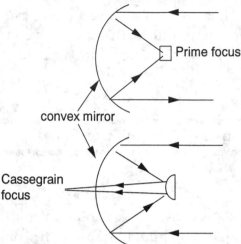

Recall that the focal length of a mirror determines the size of the image. The Cassegrain arrangement has an effectively longer focal length and has therefore a larger image size. Which of the above two arrangements is better suited for observing extremely faint galaxies and why?

SOLUTION:

For the purpose of observing extremely faint galaxies, the prime focus arrangement is better since the light will be spread over the smallest area of the photographic plate, which will result in a better image of the very faint galaxy.

The Influences Between the Earth and the Moon

● PROBLEM 9-10

With what force does the Earth attract the moon?

SOLUTION:

By the Universal Law of Gravitation, we have

$$F_G = G\frac{M_m M_e}{r_m^2}$$

where G is the gravitational constant: $G = 6.67 \ 10^{-8}\left(\dfrac{\text{dyne}\times\text{cm}^2}{g^2}\right)$, r_m is the average distance between the Earth and moon, M_m and M_e are the masses of the moon and the Earth respectively:

$r_m = 3.84 \times 10^{10}$cm
$M_m = 7.35 \times 10^{25}$g
$M_e = 5.98 \times 10^{27}$g

Thus,

$$F_G = \left(6.67\times10^{-8}\frac{\text{dyne}\times\text{cm}^2}{g^2}\right)\times\frac{\left(7.35\times10^{25}\,g\right)\times\left(5.98\times10^{27}\,g\right)}{\left(3.84\times10^{10}\,\text{cm}\right)^2}$$

$= 2.9\times10^{25}$ dynes.

● **PROBLEM 9–11**

Which astronomical body has the greatest effect upon Earth's tides?

SOLUTION:

Tidal effects are caused by the differences in the gravitational attraction upon a body between bodies. Both the sun and moon effect tides on Earth and even though the sun is many times larger than the moon, it is the moon that has the greater effect on the tides. The tide-generating force of the moon is stronger than that of the sun because this force decreases with the cube of the distance (inverse cube law) and the sun is many times farther away than the moon. Note, however, that the sun's direct gravitational pull on Earth is much stronger than the moon's because this force decreases with the square of the distance (inverse square law) and thus decreases much slower.

● **PROBLEM 9–12**

What is meant by the statement, "the moon is in a captured rotation"?

The statement "the moon is in a captured rotation" (synchronous rotation) means that the moon's rotational spin is synchronized with its orbital period. In other words, one complete rotation of the moon on its axis occurs in the same length of time as it takes for it to make one trip around Earth. The end result is that the same side of the moon's surface always faces the Earth. This is not a coincidence but a consequence of the Earth's continued tidal forces on the moon, thus the moon's rotational period has been slowed and currently matches its sidereal orbital period of $27^1/_3$ days. Many natural satellites (moons) of other planets are also in a captured rotation.

● **PROBLEM 9–13**

When the sun and moon lie along a straight line, the solar and lunar tides act in the same direction, producing unusually high tides called "spring" tides. What must be the phase of the moon when the Earth is experiencing spring tides?

SOLUTION:

There will be spring tides when the moon is new *and* when it is full.

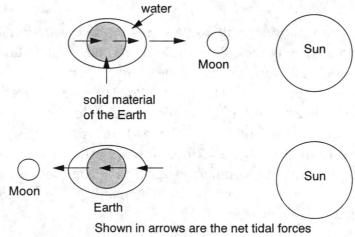

Shown in arrows are the net tidal forces
of the moon and sun

● **PROBLEM 9–14**

What are differences between spring tides and neap tides?

SOLUTION:

Spring tides occur when the moon is in full or new phase and is in a direct line with the Earth and sun. Neap tides occur when the moon is at first quarter or last quarter phase and the moon and sun are at right angles with Earth. Tides are caused by the gravitational pull of the moon on waters of Earth and spring and neap tides also are caused by the moon's pull, as well as the sun's gravitational effect on Earth's waters. Since the moon is so much closer to the Earth, its gravitational effect is greater than the sun's except in spring and neap tides when both bodies effect the tides. Neap tides occur twice each month, as do spring tides.

Phases of the Moon

● PROBLEM 9–15

Why does the moon appear to change its shape?

SOUTION:

The moon shines by reflecting the sun's light and one-half of the moon's surface is always lighted by the sun. Depending on where the moon is in its monthly orbit around Earth, we observe varying amounts of light from its surface. It is this increasing and decreasing amount of observed light from the moon's surface that causes the moon to appear to change its shape. This series of observations result in what is known as phases of the moon.

● PROBLEM 9–16

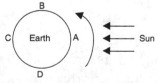

Give the position of the moon when it is new, first quarter, third quarter, and full.

SOLUTION:

When the moon is new, it is in position A; when it's in first quarter, it's in position B; when it's in third quarter, it's in position D; and when it's full, it's in position C.

● PROBLEM 9–17

A solar eclipse occurs when the new moon blocks our view of the sun from Earth and the moon's shadow is cast on the Earth. A lunar eclipse occurs when the full moon passes through the Earth's shadow.

If we have a new moon and a full moon each month, then why isn't there a solar and lunar eclipse occurrence monthly?

SOLUTION:

The moon's orbit is slightly tilted with respect to the Earth's orbit. It is at about an angle of 5° with respect to the ecliptic plane. Thus, the new moon will be slightly displaced when passing between the Earth and the sun and its shadow will be projected into space beyond the Earth. The full moon will also be displaced from the Earth's shadow.

● PROBLEM 9–18

Identify the following moon phase.

A. half moon
B. last quarter
C. third quarter
D. first quarter

SOLUTION:

The foregoing moon phase is described as first quarter, and it occurs when the moon has moved one-quarter around its orbit following new moon. The terms third quarter and last quarter are used interchangeably and appear after the moon has moved three-quarters of the way around its orbit. This phase shows the previously darkened half of the moon illuminated with the other half now darkened. "Half moon" is an incorrect term and should not be used when describing any of the moon phases.

What are the conditions necessary to have a total lunar or solar eclipse?

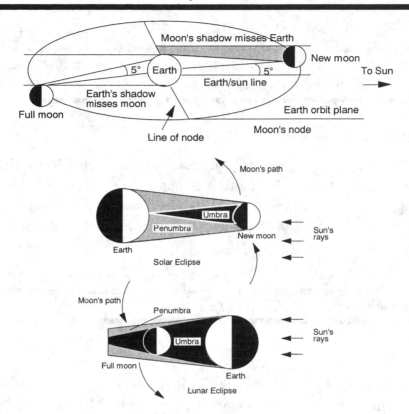

SOLUTION:

To have a total solar eclipse, the new moon must be at perigee, at or near one of the nodes of its orbit, and the sun direction lies along or nearly along the line of nodes. To have a total lunar eclipse, the full moon is at or near a node of its orbit and it must pass through the Earth's umbra.

Planets' Moons

PROBLEM 9-20

Which two planets do not have natural satellites (moons)?

SOLUTION:

Mercury and Venus are the only planets that do not have natural satellites. The term natural satellite refers to an orbiting body there by nature or natural causes. This is in contrast with artificial satellites which are manmade orbiting bodies such as weather and communication satellites. Earth has one natural satellite and its name is "moon."

● PROBLEM 9-21

The largest planet in the solar system has the largest natural satellite. Name this planet and its moon.

SOLUTION:

Jupiter is the largest planet in the solar system, and it has a diameter of about 11 times that of Earth. Ganymede is one of Jupiter's 16 moons and happens to be the largest of all natural planetary satellites. It has a diameter of about 1.5 times that of Earth's natural satellite, "Moon."

● PROBLEM 9-22

What planet do the Galilean moons orbit?

SOLUTION:

The Galilean moons orbit the planet Jupiter. They were discovered by Galileo in the 1600s and are Jupiter's largest moons. In order of distance from the planet, they are Io, Europa, Ganymede, and Callisto. *Voyager* I and II gave us clear pictures of these moons. Io has the most volcanic activity of any body in space caused by the tidal pull of Jupiter and the other Galilean moons.

Io, the innermost moon had more than ten active volcanos and its surface material is most probably powdered sulfur with some sulfur dioxide. Europa is covered with a frozen ocean that might be liquid below the surface. Ganymede, the largest moon in our solar system, was discovered to have evidence of geologic activity like plate tectonics on Earth.

In 1995 the *Galileo* spacecraft will reach Jupiter and will investigate these satellites with extended observations to answer questions such as: What is the chemical nature of the volcanic activity on Io?; How geologically active is Europa?; What are the composition and physical nature of the regoliths (surface material) of Ganymede and Callisto?

The *Galileo* spacecraft launched in October of 1989 has two parts, an instrumented probe and an orbiter. The orbiter will have a highly elliptical orbit about Jupiter for 20 months and will have encounters with the Galilean satellites 100 times closer than those attained by *Voyager*.

● PROBLEM 9–23

In the table below, the properties of Jupiter's four largest moons are given. How would gravity on the surface of these satellites compare with gravity on the moon?

Satellite	Equatorial Diameter (km)	Mass (kg)	Orbital Period (days)	Distance from Planet (in 1,000 km)
Moon	3,476	7.35×10^{22}	27	384
Io	3,630	8.94×10^{22}	1.77	422
Europa	3,138	4.80×10^{22}	3.55	671
Ganymede	5,262	1.48×10^{23}	7.16	1,070
Callisto	4,800	1.08×10^{23}	16.69	1,883

Gravity is proportional to the mass and inversely proportional to the square of the radius: $G \alpha \dfrac{M}{R^2}$; so the ratio

$$\frac{G_{Satellite}}{G_{Moon}} = \frac{M_{Satellite}}{M_{Moon}} \times \frac{R^2_{Moon}}{R^2_{Satellite}} = \frac{M_{Satellite}}{M_{Moon}} \times \frac{D^2_{Moon}}{D^2_{Satellite}}$$

where D is the diameter ($2 \times R$).

Using data from the table, we obtain:

Satellite	$G_{Satellite}/G_{Moon}$
Io	1.1
Europa	0.9
Ganymede	0.9
Callisto	0.7

Thus, they all have about the same gravity as the moon, with Io having a slightly stronger gravity and the rest slightly weaker.

In the figure below, the "miniature solar system" of Jupiter and its satellites is shown. Orbits of the four large Galilean moons are shown, as well as two groups of outer moons. How would the periods of the four large moons be related to their distances from Jupiter?

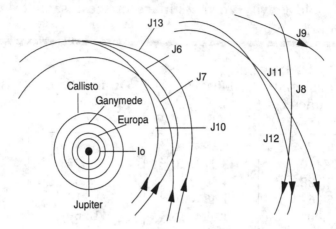

SOLUTION:

The four moons Callisto, Ganymede, Europa, and Io revolve on circular orbits around Jupiter, and can be likened to the planets revolving around the sun—thus the expression "miniature solar system." Thus, we can apply Kepler's third law to answer the question: (replace sun by Jupiter and planet by moon). The squares of the periods of any two moons are proportional to the cubes of their mean distances from the sun.

Kepler's Three Laws

● **PROBLEM 9–25**

State Kepler's Three Laws of Planetary Motion.

SOLUTION:

The first law is the "Law of Orbits"; the second law is the "Law of Equal Areas"; and the third law is the "Law of Orbital Periods."

Kepler's first law states that all planets move along closed orbits called ellipses. The sun occupies one focus position of the ellipse and the other is empty.

Kepler's second law states that the radius vector joining the sun and a planet sweep out equal areas in equal intervals of time.

Kepler's third law states that the square of a planet's orbital period is directly proportional to the cube of its semimajor axis.

Which law of Kepler describes the shape of a planet's orbit?

SOLUTION:

The first law which states: Each planet moves about the sun in an orbit that is an ellipse, with the sun at one focus. The first law not the second or third because: Kepler's second law (known as the Law of Areas) states: the straight line joining a planet and the sun sweeps out equal areas in space in equal Intervals of time.

Kepler's third law (Harmonic Law) states: the squares of the sidereal periods of the planets are in direct proportion to the cubes of the semimajor axes of the orbits.

$$P^2 = a^3 \ (P^2 = Ka^3)$$

K = Earth's distance from the sun in Astronomical Units which is IAU.
P = sidereal period of the planet.
a = semimajor axis of its orbit in AU.
Example: Mars

$$a(\text{AU}) = 1.524$$
$$P^2 = (1.524)^3 = 3.537$$

$$P = \sqrt{3.537} = 1.881 \text{ years} = 686 \text{ days}$$

● PROBLEM 9-27

Of the following planetary periods, which one is representative of the closest planet to the sun?

A. 29.46 years   C. 0.241 years
B. 16.48 years   D. 0.615 years

SOLUTION:

The correct answer is choice C, 0.241 years. Kepler's Third Law states that the square of a planet's orbital period is directly proportional to the cube of its semimajor axis. This implies that the greater the distance to the sun, the longer the period.

• PROBLEM 9–28

An asteroid is observed to move around the sun with a period of eight years. What would its average distance from the sun be in A.U.?

SOLUTION:

Measuring the period P in years and the distance D in astronomical units, Kepler's Third Law becomes
$$P^2 = D^3$$

This law applies also to asteroids since they are minor planets in orbit around the sun.

Given $P = 8$ years, we obtain
$$D^3 = 8^2 = 64$$
and
$$D = \sqrt[3]{64} = 4 \text{ A.U.}$$

Characteristics of the Nine Planets

• PROBLEM 9–29

Explain how rings may have formed around such giant planets as Jupiter and Saturn from previous moons.

SOLUTION:

The rings of Saturn, Jupiter, and Neptune were probably formed by the fragmentation of moons that were orbiting too close to the planet, and which were torn apart by tidal effects. The debris of such fragmentation then formed ring patterns.

• PROBLEM 9–30

Four of the major planets are gaseous and the remaining five are solid bodies. Name the four gaseous planets?

SOLUTION:

Jupiter, Saturn, Uranus, and Neptune are the four gaseous planets and because of their size they are often referred to as the giant gas planets. These planets are also known as the jovian or Jupiter-like planets and all have ring systems around them.

● PROBLEM 9–31

Explain what is meant by the term terrestrial planet; name these planets.

SOLUTION:

The term terrestrial planet refers to Earth-like planets. These are the smaller planets that have a fundamental rocky structure similar to Earth. There are four such planets and they are identified as follows: Mercury, Venus, Earth, and Mars.

● PROBLEM 9–32

Which two planets are associated with the Great Red Spot and the Great Dark Spot? What are these phenomena?

SOLUTION:

Jupiter is associated with the Great Red Spot and Neptune with the Great Dark Spot. These are huge oval shaped anticyclonic storm systems found in the cloud layers of these planets. The Great Red Spot is about three Earth diameters across and the Great Dark Spot about half that size.

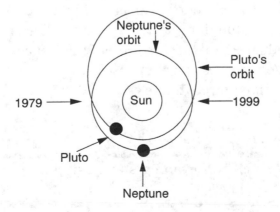

Most planets rotate in a counterclockwise direction known as prograde or direct; however, there are three planets that rotate in the opposite direction described as retrograde. Name these three planets.

SOLUTION:

Venus, Uranus, and Pluto all rotate retrograde (backwards).

What effect does the highly eccentric (flattened) shape of Pluto's orbit have upon the orbit of Neptune?

SOLUTION:

Of all the planetary orbits, Pluto's is the most eccentric. Because of this high eccentricity, Pluto's orbit occasionally brings it inside of Neptune's, thus resulting in Neptune being farther from the sun than Pluto. This occurrence takes place every 20 years out of Pluto's 248-year orbit around the sun. Between 1979 and 1999 Neptune is the farthest planet from the sun.

Which planets exhibit phases similar to those of the moon?

SOLUTION:

As seen from Earth, the inferior planets exhibit a cycle of phases similar to those of the moon. Inferior planets are those planets whose orbits lie closer to the sun than Earth's. There are only two such planets and they are Mercury and Venus. These planet phases are not visible to the unaided eye but can be observed through a telescope.

Are the morning star and evening star really stars? What are their proper names?

SOLUTION:

Neither the morning star nor the evening star are actually stars. They are either the planet Venus or the planet Mercury. When one of these planets appears in the eastern sky in the early morning shortly before sunrise, it is called the "morning star." If it is visible in the western sky right after sunset, it is called the "evening star."

● PROBLEM 9-37

Which planet is often referred to as the "red planet"? Why does it appear red?

SOLUTION:

Mars is known as the red planet because of its rusty color appearance. Most of this planet's surface is covered with red dust (iron oxides). Wind storms throw surface dust high into the Martian atmosphere, thus giving the sky its reddish hue.

● PROBLEM 9-38

Some astronomers have characterized Jupiter as "almost a star." Discuss the specific features of Jupiter that set it apart from the rest of the planets and give it star-like properties.

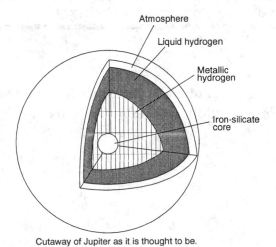

Cutaway of Jupiter as it is thought to be.

SOLUTION:

It is known that Jupiter gives off substantially more energy in the form of heat than it receives from the sun. Thus, unlike the rest of the planets, it is not just a passive reflector, but has its own source of energy. Jupiter is the largest planet, but its mass is still more than 10 times too small for it to generate energy by means of nuclear fusion as real stars do. It is believed that its source of energy is the heat of its original condensation and its turbulent, boiling interior carries this energy outward by a process known as convection.

● PROBLEM 9–39

What are the common characteristics of the gas giants?

SOLUTION:

They all are large in mass, have frozen atmospheres consisting of primarily hydrogen and helium, ring systems, numerous satellites, and rotate much faster than Earth, i.e., Jupiter 10 hours, Saturn 10.5 hours, Uranus 17 hours, and Neptune 16 hours.

The Asteroid Belt

● PROBLEM 9–40

Locate the asteroid belt with respect to the rest of the solar system.

SOLUTION:

The asteroid belt consists of small bodies (minor planets) whose orbits lie near the plane of the ecliptic between the orbits of Jupiter and Mars.

Members of the asteroid belt are found orbiting the sun

A. packed close together.
B. sparsely separated.
C. having different orbital periods.
D. Both B and C.

SOLUTION:

The correct response is choice D (Both B and C). Asteroids are sparsely separated and because they orbit the sun at varying distances, they have different orbital periods. Those asteroids closest to the sun travel at higher speeds and therefore take less time to orbit the sun. That is, they have shorter orbital periods.

Observations of minor planets in the asteroid belt can yield accurate astronomical data. In 1931, the minor planet EROS' distance to Earth was measured quite accurately to be 26 million km. Its distance in astronomical units was known quite well (from Kepler's Laws) to be 0.17 AU. How many kilometers would this indicate that there are in an astronomical unit?

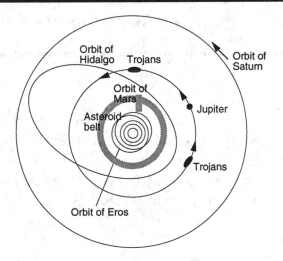

SOLUTION:

Using the figures given, there is 0.17 AU in 26 million km, therefore, 1

AU corresponds to $\dfrac{26}{0.17}$ = 152.94 million km.

Meteoroids, Meteorites, and Meteors

● **PROBLEM 9–43**

Give definitions for each of the following: meteoroid, meteorite, and meteor.

SOLUTION:

Meteoroid: A particle in space, generally smaller than a few meters across.

Meteorite: An interplanetary rock or metal object that strikes the ground.

Meteor: A rapidly moving luminous object visible for a few seconds in the night sky (a "shooting star").

● **PROBLEM 9–44**

If a meteorite is observed to pass through the atmosphere and is tracked and recovered, it is called a meteorite **fall**. On the other hand, if it is found on the ground but is not known to have freshly fallen, it is called a meteorite **find**. It is known that about 70% of the meteorite **finds** are irons, whereas over 90% of the **falls** are stones. What is an obvious reason for this?

SOLUTION:

Stones are so similar to Earth rocks (especially after undergoing weathering and erosion) that after a time they are very difficult to distinguish and so are not noticed. Irons, on the other hand, are very distinctive and easily recognized. Thus, meteorite finds are more likely to be irons, even though the majority of meteorites are rocks.

Name the three successive phases of a shooting or falling star that reaches the Earth's surface?

SOLUTION:

Phase 1 is a meteoroid, a piece of rock or dust in space with the potential of becoming a meteor. Phase 2 is a meteor, the brief streak of light seen in the sky as the meteoroid burns on entering Earth's atmosphere. Phase 3 is a meteorite, a meteoroid that has survived passage through Earth's atmosphere and reached its surface.

What is the typical size of a meteoroid that produces a visible meteor (i.e., shooting star or falling star)?

A. The size of a small star
B. The size of a large boulder
C. The size of a 12-inch rock
D. The size of a grain of sand

SOLUTION:

The correct answer is choice D, the size of a grain of sand.

Which of the following is believed to be debris left over from the formation of the solar system?

A. Asteroids
B. Comets
C. Meteoroids
D. All of the above

SOLUTION:

The correct answer is choice D, all of the above.

What causes the annual meteor showers observed from Earth?

SOLUTION:

It is now believed that the debris left in a comet's orbit as it approaches perihelion is the source of annual meteor showers. The Eta Aquarids seen in May and the Orionids in October are caused by a swarm of particles moving in the orbit of Halley's Comet which comes to perihelion every 75 years.

The Origins of the Comets

Comets are leftover debris from the formation of the solar system. These icy bodies reside in two regions of the outer solar system; name these regions.

SOLUTION:

Comets reside in the Kuiper belt and the Oort cloud regions. The Kuiper belt extends from the orbit of Neptune past that of Pluto. The outer region of the Kuiper belt merges with the Oort cloud where the vast majority of comets reside. Occasionally, one of these comets may experience a gravitational tug that causes it to move towards the inner planets.

The Dutch astronomer Jan Oort observed that comet orbits are inclined at nearly random angles to the plane of the solar system and concluded that comets populate a roughly spherical volume of space around the sun. Describe how this relates to where comets originate.

SOLUTION:

The extensive spherical swarm of comets, known as the Oort cloud, is where comets spend most of their time. It is about 50,000 AU from the sun. Comets drift slowly at these great distances along elliptical, nearly parabolic, orbits. When its orbit takes it to the inner solar system, the comet usually spends only a few months near the sun and then swings back toward the Oort cloud where it may spend hundreds of years.

Major Comets in our Solar System

● PROBLEM 9–51

In 1704 the English astronomer Edmond Halley discovered that comets travel on long, elliptical orbits around the sun and that certain comets reappear. One such comet, which was named after him, is known to have a period of 76 years and its most recent approach to Earth occurred in 1986. Halley predicted the reappearance of this comet in his lifetime. Which year did the comet reappear?

SOLUTION:

Since the comet last reappeared in 1986, and since it has a period of 76 years, we can calculate the years in which it visited the Earth's neighborhood in its recent past. Thus, its last visit before 1986 was in 1910, and before that in 1834 and before that in 1758 and before that in 1682.

Thus Halley's prediction, which was made after 1704, was that the comet would return in the year 1758, 17 years after his death.

● PROBLEM 9–52

What is the name of the famous comet of 1910 and last seen in 1986?

SOLUTION:

Halley's comet is the most famous of all periodic comets and is named in honor of astronomer Edmond Halley. Although Halley wasn't the first to observe this comet, he was the first to recognize the connection between this comet (which he saw in 1682) and earlier sightings separated by 76-year intervals. He correctly predicted the return of this comet in 1758, 17 years after his death. Historical records indicate that Halley's comet has been observed for more than 2,200 years.

The Revolution of a Comet

● **PROBLEM 9-53**

In the figure below, a comet is shown orbiting the sun. Describe the changes in the appearance of the comet and discuss why such changes take place.

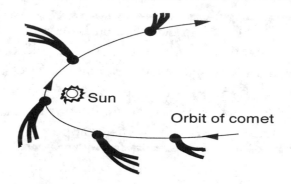

SOLUTION:

As the comet approaches the vicinity of the sun, it appears to be larger and its tail (the coma) gets longer and there may be more than one tail present.

The tail tends to point away from the sun, trailing the nucleus of the comet as it approaches the vicinity of the sun; however, when the comet is leaving the vicinity of the sun, the tail precedes the nucleus. These changes are due to the effects of solar radiation (light) pressure and the solar wind (particles ejected from the sun) which release gas and dust from the nucleus into space in a direction pointing away from the sun.

● **PROBLEM 9-54**

The orbits of comets, unlike those of planets, are oriented at random in space. Many comets appear to approach the sun from one direction as from another. It is believed that most, if not all, comets are members of the solar system, and that they travel on elliptical orbits, most of which are extremely long and have eccentricity near unity. A comet can be observed from the Earth only when it is at the part of its orbit that takes it to perihelion. When is the comet moving most rapidly?

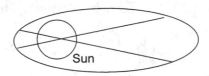

Sun

SOLUTION:

We need to apply Kepler's Second Law (the radius vector sweeps out equal areas in equal times), or in other words that the rate of change of the area is constant. It is clear that when the distance of the comet to the sun is small, the area swept in a given time period is small. For the same angular displacement, and when the comet is at a large distance from the sun, the area swept is large. Thus, in order to satisfy Kepler's Second Law, the comet must move more rapidly when it is near the sun, and must move more slowly when it is far from the sun. The rate of change of the area swept will thus be constant.

● PROBLEM 9–55

Periodic comets travel in closed orbits and non-periodic comets travel in open orbits. What kind of orbit describes Halley's comet?

SOLUTION:

From question 9-52, Halley's comet was observed in 1910 and 1986. It travels in a closed orbit with a period of approximately 76 years. Another sighting is expected around the year 2062. Non-gravitational forces such as gas jets emitted from comets can cause uncertainty in predicting exact return dates.

● PROBLEM 9–56

A typical comet in Oort's cloud has a semimajor axis of about 40,000 AU. How often would it return to the inner solar system? Use Kepler's Third Law: $P^2 = a^3$, where a is the semimajor axis (in AU) and P is the period (years).

SOLUTION:

The period of the comet is the time that separates its visits to the inner solar system.

If a = 40,000 AU = 4×10^4AU, then by Kepler's Third Law $P^2 = a^3 = 64$ $\times 10^{12}$ and $P = \sqrt{64 \times 10^{12}} = 8 \times 10^6$ or P = 8 million years.

The Layers of the Sun

● PROBLEM 9–57

Describe the surface layers of the sun and the activities that take place there.

SOLUTION:

The surface layers, or photosphere, from which the light we see comes, are some hundreds of kilometers thick. Manifestations of solar activity, such as sunspots and flares, occur in these layers. The layer over the photosphere is the chromosphere, visible as a glowing pinkish ring during a total solar eclipse. The thinnest, outermost layers forming the solar corona merge into the interplanetary medium.

● PROBLEM 9–58

How is energy transferred from the core of the sun to its surface?

SOLUTION:

Throughout most of the sun's volume, energy is transferred by radiation. In the region just below the photosphere, however, energy is transferred by convection. See figure below.

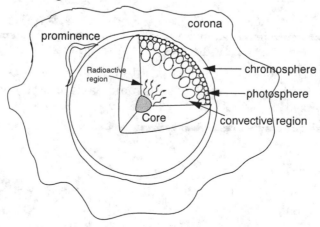

High-resolution images of the sun's photosphere reveal a cellular pattern known as granulation. What is the physical cause of this effect?

SOLUTION:

Granules are bright regions in the photosphere caused by rising hot gases from deeper and hotter layers and darker, cooler gases falling from upper layers. This phenomenon, known as convection, is the main method of energy transfer in the photosphere.

Nuclear Fusion on the Sun

● PROBLEM 9–60

Which of the following astronomical bodies produce their own light?

A. Venus
B. Sun
C. Moon
D. All of the above

SOLUTION:

The correct answer is choice B, the Sun. Planets (e.g., Venus) and natural satellites (e.g., the Moon) cannot produce their own light and therefore shine by reflecting the sun's light. Stars like the sun produce their own light through thermonuclear fusion.

● PROBLEM 9–61

Thermonuclear fusion is how the sun generates its energy. In this process, into what element is hydrogen converted?

SOLUTION:

Thermonuclear fusion in the sun occurs principally through two methods: the Proton-Proton chain and the Carbon cycle. The Carbon cycle is also known as the CNO or Carbon-Nitrogen-Oxygen cycle. In both of these methods, four hydrogen nuclei are consumed, thereby producing one helium nucleus with the simultaneous release of energy. An enormous number of these reactions are taking place each second within the sun; yet the sun has enough hydrogen to fuel itself for another five billion years.

● **PROBLEM 9–62**

The proton-proton nuclear chain reaction is the dominant source of energy in stars with core temperature of less than about 15 million degrees kelvin. It involves the three steps shown below, along with the energy released in each step:

$$p + p \rightarrow D^2 + e^+ + \nu \ (1.44 \ M_eV)$$

$$D^2 + p \rightarrow H_e^3 + \gamma \ (5.49 \ M_eV)$$

$$H_e^3 + H_e^3 \rightarrow H_e^4 + p + p \ (12.85 \ M_eV)$$

What is the total nuclear fusion energy released by this chain reaction?

SOLUTION:

First observe that since the third reaction uses two H_e^3 particles, the creation of one ^4H_e nucleus necessitates that the first and second reactions each occur twice. Thus, the total energy released is 2(1.44 + 5.49) + 12.85 = 26.71 M_eV.

● **PROBLEM 9–63**

Shown in the figure is the so-called triple-alpha process, which involves three helium nuclei, or alpha particles. Write down the nuclear-reaction equations for this process and explain how it can create energy.

$$^4_2He + {}^4_2He \rightarrow ({}^8_4Be)^*$$
$$^8_4Be + {}^4_2He \rightarrow {}^{12}_6C + \gamma$$

SOLUTION:

The process can be described by two equations:

$$_2^4He + _2^4He \rightarrow \left(_4^8Be \right)$$

$$_4^8Be + _2^4He \rightarrow _6^{12}C + \gamma$$

The beryllium nucleus is unstable, thus the second reaction must follow immediately for the process to occur. The three helium nuclei together have a greater mass than the resulting carbon nucleus, and this difference in mass is converted to energy: $E = mc^2$.

● PROBLEM 9-64

The sun radiates about 4×10^{33} ergs of energy per second into space. How much mass of matter is consumed each second, assuming that the energy source of the sun's energy is the conversion of mass into energy?

SOLUTION:

In order to determine the mass equivalent of the energy radiated by the sun in a second (4×10^{33} ergs), we must make use of Einstein's formula $E = MC^2$.

$E = MC^2 \qquad E = 4 \times 10^{33}$ ergs $\qquad C = 3 \times 10^{10}$ cm/sec

$$M = \frac{4 \times 10^{33}}{\left(3 \times 10^{10} \right)^2}$$

$$M = \frac{4 \times 10^{33}}{9 \times 10^{20}}$$

$$M = \frac{4 \times 10^{13}}{9} = 4.4 \times 10^{12} \text{ grams or almost } \frac{41}{2} \text{ tons}$$

● PROBLEM 9-65

Describe how nuclear fusion in a star helps maintain the equilibrium between the forces within the star.

SOLUTION:

Radiation from the star's center exerts outward pressure that supports the star against the inward gravitational force (see figure). This pressure lasts as long as nuclear reactions create the energy which is radiated from the core.

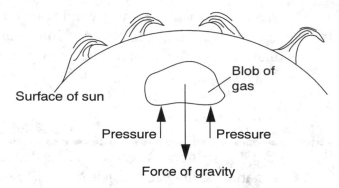

The Formation of Stars

● PROBLEM 9–66

Why do stars form in groups or clusters instead of individually?

SOLUTION:

Stars form from the gravitational collapse of a diffuse interstellar cloud; however, fragmentation is an almost inevitable consequence of the cloud collapse process. Since each large cloud, containing many star masses, breaks up into subclouds that form stars, many stars form together.

● PROBLEM 9–67

Interstellar clouds and hot, luminous (and therefore young) main-sequence stars are very often associated with each other. How can this fact help construct a theory of star formation?

SOLUTION:

The basic idea in the theory of star formation is that the gas cloud condenses and fragments into smaller clouds which then collapse to form stars. This can explain why clusters of young stars are associated with gaseous clouds. It remains to find the forces that could squeeze a cloud down to the point where it collapses under its own gravitational attraction. Two possible scenarios are shown in the figure below. A cloud may find itself near a hot star, and the radiation pressure of the star tends to compress the cloud. Or two clouds might collide and initiate the collapse.

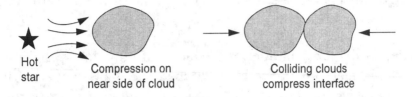

Hot star   Compression on near side of cloud   Colliding clouds compress interface

● PROBLEM 9–68

What physical processes are important in the formation of stars?

SOLUTION:

Gravitational contraction and energy generation through nuclear fusion. The material of the protostar condenses and collapses due to gravity. The core heats up through the release of gravitational energy until the temperature is high enough for the nuclear fusion of hydrogen into helium to take place. This provides the radiation energy of the star's light and the pressure to prevent collapse.

● PROBLEM 9–69

Stars are born from clouds of dust and gas. What is the principal gas in this stellar formation?

SOLUTION:

Stars are formed from huge interstellar clouds of dust and principally hydrogen gas. Stars such as the sun are relatively abundant in heavier elements and are known as population 1 stars. They are the younger stars and are confined to the plane of the galaxy. Those stars less abundant in heavier elements are called population 2 stars and are older. These stars are found in a spherical halo around the center of the galaxy.

Magnitude of Stars and the Hertzsprung-Russell Diagram

● PROBLEM 9-70

The figure below shows a Hertzsprung-Russell diagram of the young star cluster NGC2264.

Give a possible explanation for the fact that only the stars in the upper part of the main sequence have reached the main sequence, whereas the stars in the lower part have not yet reached the main sequence.

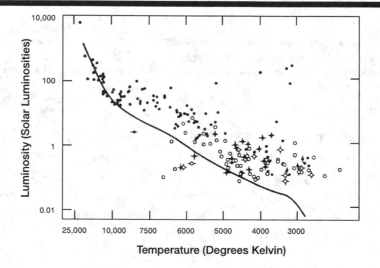

SOLUTION:

The stars in the upper part of the H-R diagram are more massive than the stars in the lower part of the diagram. Because they are more massive, the force of gravity is stronger, and they tend to contract more rapidly.

● PROBLEM 9-71

Many star clusters are observed to have Hertzsprung-Russell diagrams with a turn-off branch (see figure). This turnoff is due to the most massive stars in the cluster having exhausted their hydrogen fuel (after only a few million years) and moving away from the main sequence and into the red giant region. As more time passes, the lower-mass stars will likewise begin to leave the main sequence.

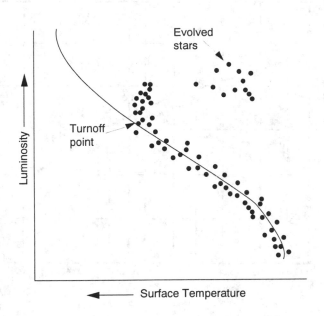

How is the age of the cluster related to the position of the turn-off point?

SOLUTION:

The main-sequence stars at the turn-off point indicate the age of the cluster. The lower the turn-off point, the older the star cluster, since stars on the lower main sequence take longer to exhaust their hydrogen fuel.

● **PROBLEM 9–72**

Assuming that a star is a main-sequence star and that its temperature has been measured to be 10,000 K, what would its luminosity and mass be in terms of the sun's luminosity and mass? Refer to the Hertzsprung-Russel diagram on the following page.

SOLUTION:

Starting from a point on the surface-temperature axis, at 10,000 K, and going up vertically to intersect the main-sequence curve, the mass can be estimated to be about 2.7 solar masses. Drawing a horizontal line from that point to intersect the vertical axis, we obtain a luminosity of about 70 solar luminosities.

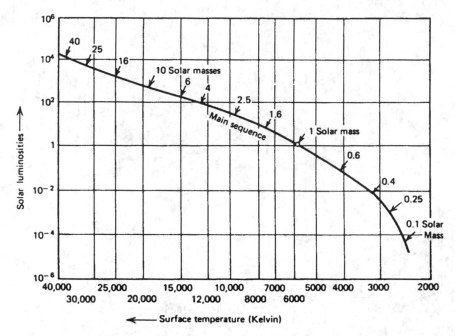

Two stars, S_1 and S_2, lie on the main sequence in different parts of the H-R diagram as shown below:

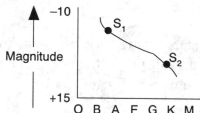

Which is more luminous?

Which is hotter?

Which is more massive?

Which is larger?

SOLUTION:

The H-R diagram shown is plotted as magnitude versus spectral class. It should be recalled that (absolute) magnitude decreases with increasing luminosity and temperature. Spectral class O, for example, corresponds to a typical temperature of 40,000 degrees Kelvin, and spectral class M corresponds to a temperature of about 3,000 degrees Kelvin. Thus, S_1 is hotter and more luminous than S_2 which also makes it more massive and larger than S_2 (on the main sequence, size is correlated with mass).

The Lifecycle of a Star

● PROBLEM 9-74

How does the main-sequence phase of a star's life depend on the mass of the star?

SOLUTION:

During the main-sequence phase of a star's life, hydrogen burning in the core continues until the fuel supplies are exhausted. The timescale of this process is reduced dramatically with increasing mass. The sun has a main-sequence lifetime of 10 billion years as compared with only 500 million years for a star three times as massive.

● PROBLEM 9-75

Would an old star, in its last stage of evolution, have a larger or smaller proportion of hydrogen, relative to heavier elements such as helium and carbon, than main sequence stars?

SOLUTION:

The old star would have a smaller proportion of hydrogen than a main sequence star since it had already converted much of its hydrogen to helium and carbon.

● PROBLEM 9-76

A main-sequence star has about 10 times the mass of the sun and, therefore, has about 10 times as much potential nuclear fuel. Why then does it have a main-sequence lifetime only $1/100$ as long as that of the sun?

SOLUTION:

The more massive star burns its fuel more rapidly and with a process that requires this higher rate. From the H-R diagram in the previous question, a 10 solar-mass star has a luminosity of the order of 1,000 solar luminosities. So it loses 1,000 times as much energy per second but has only 10 times the fuel. Thus, it would remain on the main sequence for $\frac{10}{1,000} = \frac{1}{100}$ of the corresponding time for the sun.

Quasars, Pulsars, and Black Holes

● **PROBLEM 9–77**

Identify the following objects:

A. Objects that show very large red shifts
B. Rapidly rotating neutron stars
C. Stars that have undergone complete gravitational collapse

SOLUTION:

A. Quasars are objects that show very large red shifts and are believed to be the active nuclei of early galaxies. They are very bright for their small angular size.

B. Pulsars are rapidly rotating neutron stars. They are the remnants of supernova explosions having a mass less than three solar masses.

C. Black holes are stars that have completely collapsed on themselves and thus been crushed out of the visible universe. What is left behind is a region of space where the gravitational force is so strong that nothing can escape, not even light.

● **PROBLEM 9–78**

The pulses detected from a pulsar are best modeled by

A. a strobe light.
B. a rotating beacon.
C. electrons intermittently giving up their energy in phase.
D. an expanding and deflating object.

SOLUTION:

The correct answer is choice B, a rotating beacon. As a pulsar rapidly spins, it is emitting a continuous flow of radiation. Because of its very high rate of rotation, however, a pulsar's sweeping radiation is detected as pulses.

If nothing is powerful enough to overcome the gravitational attraction of a black hole, then how can they be detected?

A. Use of optical telescopes to observe a hole in space
B. Through a companion star
C. Use of special instruments that can detect sound energy emitted from black holes
D. Black holes cannot be detected.

SOLUTION:

The correct answer is choice B. X-ray telescopes detect x-radiation given off by the black hole's companion star as material from the surface of the star is being pulled towards the black hole.

A pulsar is a rotating neutron star whose synchrotron radiation from its polar regions is detected as a regular signal (or pulse) on Earth. What physical law causes the pulsar's rotation to speed up if, as a result of a "starquake," the star collapses slightly?

SOLUTION:

The physical law is known as the conservation of angular momentum. The angular momentum is proportional to the square of the radius and to the angular speed of rotation. Thus, when the radius is reduced under collapse, the angular speed must increase in order to keep the angular momentum constant. This is the same principle that explains why a figure skater's spin increases when she pulls her arms in.

A quasar is observed to vary in brightness by a factor of three in only three days. What is its maximum size?

SOLUTION:

The quasar can only be as big as light can travel across it. The change in brightness indicates that light takes three days to travel across it, and thus the quasar is three light-days (or about one hundredth of a light year) across. Compare this to hundreds of light years for typical galaxies.

Explain how black holes help us understand the enormous energy output of a quasar.

SOLUTION:

A quasar is a very distant extragalactic object that is exceedingly luminous for its size. Observations show that the central energy source in quasars is confined to a very small volume. Matter falling into supermassive black holes has been proposed as an explanation for this exceptionally high energy production. The loss of gravitational potential energy is given off as radiation.

There are no observed pulsars whose periods exceed a few seconds. What is the possible reason for this fact.

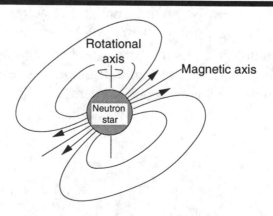

SOLUTION:

As the rotating neutron star slows down, it loses energy. It will probably reach a point at which it has too little energy left to power the pulsar.

● **PROBLEM 9-84**

Black holes can never be observed directly: their existence can only be inferred from their effects on a nearby companion. Explain how the study of a binary system can show the existence of a black hole.

SOLUTION:

The existence of a black hole can only be inferred from its gravitational effect on a nearby object (a star in a binary system with the black hole as the second member of the system), as well as the radiation emitted by material falling into the black hole. Observations of the visible star make it possible to determine the orbit and mass of its dark companion. Hot x-rays result from energy released as matter streams onto the compact star.

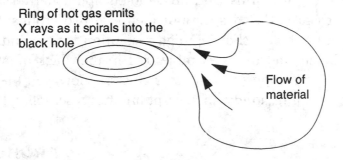

Ring of hot gas emits
X rays as it spirals into the
black hole

Flow of
material

● **PROBLEM 9-85**

The mass of a star affects its fate. Those most massive become black holes and those a little less massive become neutron stars. What is the fate of even less massive stars like the sun?

SOLUTION:

After billions of years, a sun-sized star becomes unstable and expands to become a red giant star. After radiating for millions of years, it then blows off part of its atmosphere and becomes what is described as a planetary nebula. This star then begins to contract and becomes a planet-sized star called a white dwarf. Eventually, this star ceases to shine and is known as a black dwarf.

The Main Types of Galaxies

● **PROBLEM 9-86**

Name the different types of galaxies.

SOLUTION:

One of the earliest and simplest classifications of galaxies still used today was invented by Edwin Hubble in the 1920s. He instituted three principal classification sequences: Ellipticals, Spirals, and Barred Spirals. The Irregular Galaxies formed a fourth class in his system of classification. He used E0 to E7 to classify ellipticals according to their ellipticity or flattening. Spirals were denoted by S and a,b,c, were used to indicate the tightness of the spiral arms, and SB denoted Spiral Barred Galaxies also using a,b,c. Irregular Galaxies were divided into two groups: Irr I galaxies which consist of objects showing high resolution into O and B stars and emission nebulae, and Irr II resemble Irr I in their lack of symmetry but they display no resolution into stars or clusters; however, they do display spectra that are continuous with absorption lines resembling type A5 stars.

● **PROBLEM 9-87**

Using the Hubble classification scheme of galaxies, classify the galaxies shown in the figure below.

SOLUTION:

Galaxy A is an E0 galaxy (spherical elliptical).

Galaxy B is an Sa galaxy (spiral with tight arms).

Galaxy C is an SBb galaxy (barred spiral with fairly tight arms).

Galaxy D is an S0 galaxy (a transition between an elliptical and a spiral, lacking clear spiral arms).

Galaxy E is an Sc galaxy (a spiral with loose arms).

A   B   C   D   E

● PROBLEM 9–88

Which type of galaxy tends to be the biggest and the brightest?

SOLUTION:

The largest and brightest galaxies, although rare, are probably giant ellipticals. Although some spiral galaxies may be larger than giant ellipticals, they are usually not as bright.

● PROBLEM 9–89

Which galaxy is closest to our galaxy, the Milky Way?

SOLUTION:

The large Magellanic Cloud followed by the Small Magellanic Cloud are the closest galaxies to us. Both of these galaxies are satellite galaxies of the Milky Way. They can only be seen from the Southern Hemisphere.

● PROBLEM 9–90

Name the most distant object visible to the unaided eye?

SOLUTION:

At a distance of just over 2 million light years, the Andromeda Galaxy is the most distant object visible to the unaided eye. On a clear dark night, it appears as smudge in the sky. The light we see today from this galaxy began its journey more than 2 million years ago.

The center of our galaxy lies in the direction of the constellation Sagittarius. When we look in this direction, is it possible to see the visible light of the stars at the center of our galaxy? Why or why not?

SOLUTION:

The answer is no, and the reason is that interstellar dust obscures our view of the galactic center. As shown in the figure below, between us and the center of the Milky Way lie spiral arms made up of stars and interstellar material. Visible light cannot penetrate this galactic dust, but infrared light can. In fact, the center of our galaxy was first observed using infrared detectors developed in the late 1950s.

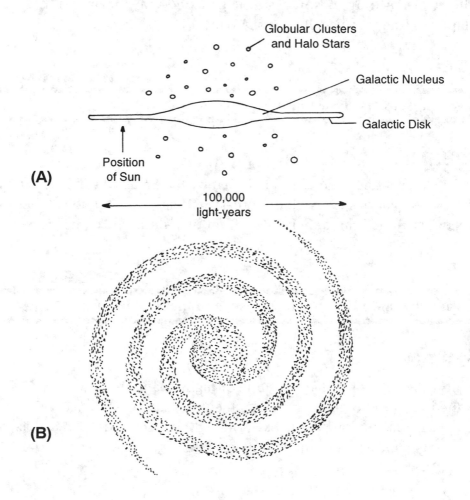

How might the velocity-distance relationship be used to estimate the distance to a galaxy? See figure below.

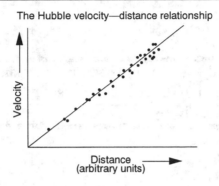

The Hubble velocity—distance relationship

Velocity ⟶

Distance ⟶
(arbitrary units)

SOLUTION:

In order to be able to use the Hubble velocity-distance relationship to get a galaxy's distance, we first need to determine its velocity. This is done by analyzing the Doppler shift of common spectral lines in the spectrum of the galaxy. Once its velocity has been established, we enter the velocity-distance relationship graph from the vertical axis, draw a horizontal line to intersect the Hubble line, and then draw a vertical line from this intersection to intersect the distance (horizontal) axis. We thus get the distance of the galaxy.

The Major Theories of the Formation of the Universe

● PROBLEM 9-93

What are the two main theories for the origin of the Universe?

SOLUTION:

The Hot Big Bang theory and the Steady State theory are the two main theories for the origin of the Universe.

The Hot Big Bang theory states that there was a time when all of the matter in the Universe was close together. At this time the Universe was extremely hot and very dense from which it began a rapid expansion. The Universe has been expanding ever since and is currently described by this model.

The Steady State theory says that the Universe did not evolve and that it is the same everywhere for all observers at all times. In order to maintain the density of the Universe as it continues to expand, this model proposes that matter is being created continuously. This model was popular through the 1950s and most of the 1960s.

● PROBLEM 9–94

Astronomers observed early in this century that galaxies are receding from us in every direction. Does this necessarily imply that we are in the very center of the Universe?

SOLUTION:

The conclusion that we are in the center of the Universe is incorrect. In fact, it is not difficult to show that any observer in an expanding Universe would see the same thing. It is helpful to use a simple analogy to illustrate this point. Consider galaxies in the Universe to be like the raisins in a raisin cake that is baking in an oven. As the cake bakes, it expands uniformly and each raisin in the cake recedes (gets farther) from every other raisin. Furthermore, the larger the distance between two raisins, the more rapidly they will move away from each other. Hence, if you were located on *any* raisin and observing the other raisins, you would see them all moving away from you, just as we observe the galaxies in the Universe receding from us. Thus, it is not necessary for us to be at the center of the Universe to observe this.

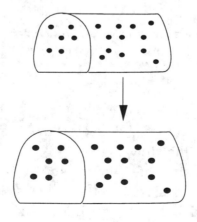

The steady state cosmological theory states that, essentially, the Universe looks about the same at all times. Why is this theory NOT supported by our knowledge of quasars?

SOLUTION:

Observations of quasars show that these extremely luminous quasi-stellar objects are more numerous at great distances, hence existed at earlier times. Thus, the Universe must have been different at earlier times, which contradicts the steady state theory.

The Big Bang Theory

The Big Bang Theory grew out of Edwin Hubble's discovery in the 1920s that the galaxies are flying apart from one another and that the farther away a galaxy is, the faster it moves. This theory also states that the entire Universe was once packed into a point of infinite density and extraordinarily high temperature. The Big Bang created not only the Universe and all matter in it, but also the space that makes up the Universe and time itself. As the Universe expanded, it cooled. The temperature was too hot for atomic nuclei to capture electrons. Photons of light could travel only short distances before interacting with free electrons, but after 300,000 years the temperature fell below 5,000 Kelvin and atoms formed. Radiation could now travel freely because the electrons were tied up in atoms and the Universe became transparent to light. What evidence has been found to support the Big Bang Theory?

SOLUTION:

In 1964 Arno Penzias and Robert Wilson, Bell Labs researchers, detected remnant microwave radiation which was predicted as a result of the Big Bang. Launched in 1989 the Cosmic Background Explorer's (COBE) Differential Microwave Radiometers discovered tiny variations in the temperature of the microwave background which were declared to be imprints of tiny ripples in the fabric of space-time put there by the primeval explosion. Note: Penzias and Wilson received the Nobel Prize in Physics for their work.

● PROBLEM 9-97

Cite three observations that give support to the Hot Big Bang theory.

SOLUTION:

One piece of evidence that supports the Hot Big Bang is the currently observed expanding Universe.

A second piece of evidence is the presence of the microwave background radiation.

A third piece of evidence is the abundance of the light chemical elements and isotopes resulting from the early hot and dense state of the Universe.

● PROBLEM 9-98

Why do most astronomers support the Big Bang Theory as the leading theory for the formation of the Universe?

SOLUTION:

The discovery of the 3 K microwave background radiation, which was predicted by the Big Bang Theory, is a strong piece of evidence in favor of this theory. This theory proved to have more predictive power than any other theory.

Unmanned Space Probes

● PROBLEM 9-99

Which of the following is the unmanned space probe: *Galileo, Magellan, Voyager,* or *Viking?*

SOLUTION:

All of the foregoing are unmanned planetary probes. The *Galileo* probe is scheduled to reach Jupiter in 1995 to learn more about the planet, its rings, and its natural satellites. *Magellan* was a probe to Venus that successfully mapped the majority of its surface by means of radar in 1991. The two *Voyager* probes revealed information about the jovian planets Jupiter, Saturn, Uranus, and Neptune; and the two *Viking* probes visited Mars in 1976 and sent back a wealth of data for years.

● **PROBLEM 9–100**

In 1973, NASA launched the unmanned space probe Mariner 10 to study the planets Venus and Mercury. Its orbit sent it to a close encounter with Venus, whose gravity assisted in putting the space probe into an orbit around Mercury with a period of twice that of Mercury (which is known to be 88 days). See figure below. The space vehicle first passed close to the planet on March 29, 1974, and it was scheduled to be in three more rendez-vous with Mercury. What is the date of Mariner 10's last rendezvous with Mercury?

The Orbit of *Mariner* 10

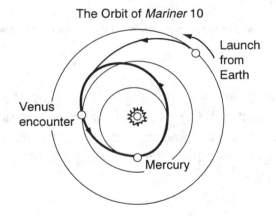

SOLUTION:

First let us determine *Mariner 10*'s orbital period. This must be 2 x 88 = 176 days. According to the figure showing the orbit, the rendez-vous with Mercury occurs once during an orbital period. Hence, if the date of the first rendez-vous was March 29, 1974, the following encounters must have taken place on September 21, 1974, then on March 16, 1975, and finally on September 8, 1975.

Galileo is a NASA spacecraft launched in October 1989 from the space shuttle; however, it was impossible to obtain sufficient power by means of the shuttle launch for a direct journey to Jupiter. How did the NASA engineers exploit the gravitational force of other planets in order to give *Galileo* enough energy to reach Jupiter?

SOLUTION:

NASA engineers designed a gravity-assisted flight plan, whereby the spacecraft was accelerated by close passages by Venus and twice by the Earth during the first three years of *Galileo*'s journey.

Manned Space Probes

● **PROBLEM 9–102**

What is the name of the successful NASA program designed to put a man on the moon before the end of the 1960s?

SOLUTION:

NASA's Apollo program was successful in putting the first human (a man) on the moon in July 1969. A total of six manned moon landings took place from 1969 to 1972. Two landings occurred in 1969, two in 1971, and two in 1972. The Apollo program has allowed for a total of 12 humans to actually set foot on the lunar surface.

● **PROBLEM 9–103**

What is the most important obstacle to manned space exploration?

SOLUTION:

The most important obstacle to manned flights is economics. Manned space flights are very expensive. Our race to land the first man on the Moon cost $40 billion and the planned Space Station Freedom, proposed during the Bush administration, has gone from $100 billion to one now estimated to cost $17 billion. NASA has already spent $11.9 billion since the early 1980s on this space station. In 1994 under the Clinton administration, Congress barely passed a $17 billion allocation for the Freedom Space Station which has been dubbed the "Orbiting Pork Barrel" by opponents of this manned program. The proposed "Ares" manned mission to Mars, at a cost of $300 billion, has been scrapped. Other proposals have been made, which have reduced this cost to about $50 billion. The benefits of manned space exploration will not only include advances in computer technology, the advancement of knowledge about the "Red" planet, and a better understanding of the future of the Earth, but we also may find that we are not alone in the Universe.

● PROBLEM 9–104

What sort of special space suit design would be needed if astronauts were to be able to walk on Venus?

SOLUTION:

Venus' atmosphere is composed almost entirely of carbon dioxide, and the surface pressure is more than 90 times that of the Earth. It also has an exceptionally high temperature of 450°C.

A spacesuit on Venus must keep the atmosphere out and stop the pressure from crushing the wearer. It would also need to have a very efficient cooling system. Present astronaut suits would not work on Venus.

SHORT ANSWER QUESTIONS FOR REVIEW

Choose the correct answer.

1. The sun crosses the celestial equator going north on March 21. This is known as the (a) solstice. (b) lunar eclipse. (c) solar eclipse. (d) spring equinox.

2. If the moon completely covers the sun as seen by an earthbound observer, there is a (a) total lunar eclipse. (b) total solar eclipse. (c) partial lunar eclipse. (d) partial solar eclipse.

3. Kepler's Second Law says, essentially, that (a) force equals mass times acceleration. (b) the square of the period is proportional to the cube of the semimajor axis. (c) the orbits of the planets are ellipses with the sun at one focus. (d) the line from the sun to a planet sweeps equal areas in equal times.

4. In order of increasing distance from the sun, the terrestrial planets are (a) Mars, Venus, Earth, and Mercury. (b) Mercury, Venus, Earth, and Mars (c) Jupiter, Saturn, Uranus, Neptune, and Pluto. (d) Mercury, Venus, Mars, and Earth.

5. If Star X appears to be 2.5 times as bright as Star Y, then the two stars differ in magnitude by (a) 0. (b) 1. (c) 2.5. (d) 0.5.

6. The sun's galactic motion in the Milky Way can be described as (a) radial motion towards the center of the galaxy. (b) radial motion away from the center of the galaxy. (c) motion along a very elongated ellipse. (d) motion in a circular orbit.

7. Elliptical systems appear to lack spiral arms but possess (a) round bodies. (b) square bodies. (c) rectangular bodies. (d) oval bodies.

8. The Milky Way contains (a) clusters of stars forming their own distinct pattern. (b) clusters of dust forming their own distinct pattern. (c) clusters of planetoids forming their own distinct pattern. (d) clusters of comets forming their own distinct pattern.

9. The first quasar was located in 1959. Since that date, scientists have located more than _____ quasars. (a) 20,000 (b) 1,000 (c) 100,000 (d) 100

10. Upon entering the atmosphere, metallic masses glow due to friction with the atmosphere and cause the mass to glow; hence, we are able to see a(n) (a) sun. (b) meteor. (c) star. (d) eclipse.

11. Damage to the Earth by meteorites occurs (a) at the changing of the moon. (b) at times of devastation. (c) seldomly, but could be devastating. (d) at changing of the seasons.

12. To determine the origins of the Universe and the solar system, one could study (a) mentors. (b) meteorites. (c) mentalities. (d) oceans.

13. The sun has a mass of 750 times greater than (a) all terrestrial planets. (b) the four largest planets. (c) the Earth, moon, and sun combined. (d) all planets combined.

14. Asteroids are irregularly shaped objects orbiting between Jupiter and Mars that are _____ in size. (a) tiny (b) large (c) small (d) medium

Items 15 to 18 refer to the following diagram.

Diagram of the major constellations

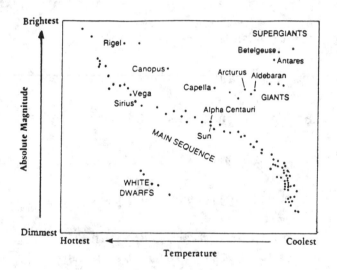

15. Most stars represented belong to which group? (a) Giants (b) Main Sequence (c) White Dwarfs (d) Alpha Centauri

16. Compared to our sun, Sirius is (a) cooler and dimmer. (b) cooler and brighter. (c) warmer and dimmer. (d) warmer and brighter.

17. Which star is matched with an incorrect group? (a) Vega—main sequence (b) Aldebaran—giant (c) Betelgeuse—Supergiant (d) Canopus—white dwarf

18. Which statement is correct? (a) Our sun is similar to most other stars

in the Universe. (b) Our sun is very unique among stars. (c) Distances between stars can accurately be determined from this diagram. (d) Our night sky looks like this diagram.

Fill in the blanks.

19. When the Earth passes between the sun and the moon, this causes an occurrence called an _____ .

20. The planet closest to the sun is _____ .

21. The path of the sun across the celestial sphere is called the _____ .

22. Declination is from the _____ coordinate system.

23. Astronomers call the visible surface of the sun the _____ .

24. Icy worlds with a size of a few kilometers across are _____ .

25. We can find the temperature of a star by measuring its _____ .

26. Galaxies are groups or systems of _____ .

27. The Earth is a planet in the galaxy called the _____ .

28. Located in the center of our solar system is the _____ .

29. The known galaxy that resembles the Milky Way most is _____ .

30. A star's mass is indicated by its _____ .

31. A group of stars is called a _____ .

32. A place where stars are viewed and studied is called a _____ .

33. A meteor is sometimes called a _____ .

34. Meteorites are _____ matter.

35. The farthest planet from the sun is _____ .

36. The largest planet in our solar system is _____ .

37. Asteroids orbit between Jupiter and _____ .

38. One rotation of the Earth takes _____ .

Determine whether the following statements are true or false.

39. Meteoroids are chunks of iron resulting from collisions between planetoids.

40. The projection of the Earth's axis on the sky is the celestial poles.

41. The coordinate right ascension is usually measured in kilometers.

42. The parallax of a star is its temperature divided by its mass.

43. If a star has a parallax of 0.1 second of arc, its distance is 10 parsecs.

44. Jupiter is closer to Earth than the sun.

45. The AU is the average distance of the Earth from the sun.

46. Venus has no natural satellites.

47. The first person to study astronomy was Plato.

48. A planet could possibly have begun as a nebula.

49. The difference between a nebula and an eddy would be their shape and movement.

50. Galaxies are located billions of light years from the Earth.

51. The Earth is a star.

52. The Milky Way is an elliptical galaxy.

53. The discovery of quasars has been aided by radio astronomy.

54. The band of starlight coming from our own galaxy forms the Milky Way.

55. What appears as star movement is actually the spinning and placement of the sun.

56. A meteor is another name for a falling comet.

57. A meteor will glow for a few years.

58. The Earth-like planets are made up of oxygen and carbon dioxide.

59. The moon's gravitational pull produces the tides.

ANSWER KEY

1. d
2. b
3. d
4. b
5. b
6. d
7. a
8. a
9. b
10. b
11. c
12. b
13. d
14. c
15. b
16. d
17. d
18. a
19. eclipse
20. Mercury
21. ecliptic
22. equitorial
23. photosphere
24. comets
25. spectrum
26. stars
27. Milky Way
28. The sun
29. Andromeda
30. brightness

31. constellation
32. planetarium
33. shooting star
34. extraterrestrial
35. Pluto
36. Jupiter
37. Mars
38. 24-hours
39. false
40. true
41. false
42. false
43. true
44. false
45. true
46. true
47. false
48. true
49. true
50. true
51. false
52. false
53. true
54. false
55. false
56. false
57. false
58. false
59. true

CHAPTER 10

THE EFFECT OF MAN AND TECHNOLOGY ON THE ENVIRONMENT

The Growing Population of the Earth and Cities

● PROBLEM 10-1

What are expected trends in human population growth into the next century?

SOLUTION:

Best estimates for global populations claim that 3.0 billion humans lived on Earth as of 1960. By 1990 the estimates were at 5.3 billion, and by 1993 the number had grown to 5.5 billion. One prediction states that by 2075, 14 billion people will be living on planet Earth. The stresses that human populations are exerting on the environment today effect many different areas in various ways. The hydrosphere is placed in peril as fresh water demands outstrip supply in many areas, and the oceans must adjust to the dumping of wastes and garbage. The biosphere and atmosphere are placed in a delicate balance due to the needs of growing populations and the quest for a higher quality of life by those populations. There is little reason at this point in time to predict that the growth curve for humans will stabilize soon. But many are starting to take a hard long look at these trends.

Speculate as to the factors that allow for such rapid increases in global populations.

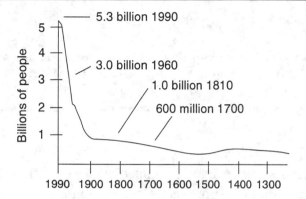

SOLUTION:

The dramatic rise in the human population can be attributed to a combination of causes. People are living longer today than ever before due in part to advances in the sciences. Improved medical knowledge, practices, and worldwide communication have effectively reduced the death rate in many corners of the globe. Better agricultural practices produce more foods through irrigation, fertilizers, pesticides, insecticides, and improved seed genetics. New technologies also allow for better sanitation and hygiene among large populations. All these factors have contributed to the population "explosion" of the twentieth century.

Renewable and Non-Renewable Resources

● PROBLEM 10-3

Considering dwindling supplies of world reserves of petroleum, what is "new" oil?

SOLUTION:

Currently about 50% of the oil in a given site is recovered. Due to the technology of the times, the remaining oil is economically untouchable. The rising cost of oil may make the recovery of the remaining petroleum in a field cost effective and even necessary. Very viscous (thick) oil could be recovered through the injection of high pressure hot water or carbon dioxide gas. The remaining oil may be extracted by pumping water into existing oil fields to cause migration of the lighter density oil. New technology combined with rising petroleum prices may make the recovery of this "new" resource necessary in the future.

● PROBLEM 10–4

Identify the location of water supplies on Earth. Where is water found and how much is found there?

SOLUTION:

Oceans are estimated to contain just over 97% of the total volume of terrestrial water available. This means approximately 3% of the remaining water on Earth is fresh water. Of the small percentage of total water left, about 2.1% is locked in glaciers and polar icecaps. The remaining .6% is found mostly in underground aquifers, with trace amounts left for lakes and rivers, and even less for the atmosphere and biosphere. The small volume of total fresh water available within the hydrologic cycle is of concern due to the increased demands being placed on it.

● PROBLEM 10–5

Briefly outline the hydrologic cycle of planet Earth.

SOLUTION:

The cycle of water on Earth depends on the ability of water to easily change states of matter. Evaporation, transpiration, and precipitation are important pathways of water within this endless cycle. Evaporation of oceanic and fresh water combined with water transpired by soil and vegetation provides a source of liquid for condensation and precipitation. The fall of rain and snow provides water for the formation of glaciers, ponds, and streams. This accumulation in turn feeds rivers and ground water. The rivers eventually flow into the oceans to start the cycle again. Ground water on the other hand infiltrates aquifers to supply plants and animals with needed springs and soil moisture. The hydrologic cycle continues as water transforms from one state to another throughout any part of the process.

● PROBLEM 10-6

What do scientists mean by the mercury cycle?

SOLUTION:

The heavy metal mercury is a natural element found in the crust of the Earth. Out gassing from volcanoes has been shown to contribute small amounts to the cycle. Mercury is also found in trace amounts in crustal rocks, with slightly higher concentrations found in granitic rocks of magmatic origin. The concentration levels found in the ecosphere are acceptable at a natural level. The problems arise, however, when human activity begins to concentrate various amounts of mercury in the environment. This metal is toxic to the biosphere even at small concentrations. The food chain tends to concentrate this toxic element as organisms ascend the chain and eventually lead to toxic levels in consumers at the top of the food chain. In the hydrosphere, mercury will be eventually deposited in sediments and if left undisturbed will become restricted from the biotic cycle by sedimentary entrapment.

● PROBLEM 10-7

Compare the lead cycle to the mercury cycle.

SOLUTION:

Lead, also a toxic heavy metal, can be concentrated in the environment as it is released into the air, water, or soil. Once in the biosphere, lead can be absorbed by plants or animals and then be concentrated through the food chain. The same can be predicted for any and all metals used in industrial applications. Examples include: mercury, cadmium, arsenic, and nickel. In natural concentrations these metals may not be considered a hazard. When concentrated due to industrial and technological applications, they pose significant hazards to the biosphere. Special care must be taken when considering lead problems and issues as this toxic metal has already obtained widespread exposure in the human environment. Examining exposure of the young of an area is especially important since the critical young developmental years are impaired by this heavy metal.

Contrast the resource consumption on developed and non-developed countries.

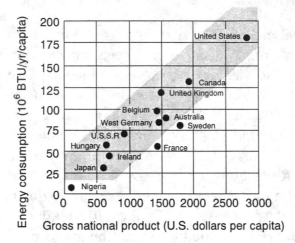

SOLUTION:

Approximately 17-19% of the total land surface of Earth is used for agricultural purposes, yet 20% of Earths' population live with hunger and in poor conditions. First world (developed) countries contain slightly less than 25% of the estimated global population. These nations use a great percentage of the fuel resources and produce 85% of the goods. They use these resources to generate shelter, food, and an acceptable standard of living for their citizens. Seventy-five percent of the population of Earth at this point exist without the benefit of the use of these resources. If lesser developed third world nations were to achieve technological equality and an equal standard of living, the ecosphere might not be able to handle the stresses.

What steps might science take to augment the recovery of mineral deposits so essential to the economic life of a technological country?

SOLUTION:

One area showing future recovery promise is that of seabed resources. Long ago the Greeks and recently the Japanese have extended their mines under the sea in search of valuable resources. Interest in sea floor mining is rising as reserves on land dwindle and prices for those reserves rise. Common and age old techniques include dredging and claw/clam scoop sampling. By scraping and scooping the resources on the sea floor, their recovery becomes similar to that of a land-based strip mine. The process is cost effective, yet is not environmentally acceptable to many. Drill corers may also be effective where mineral concentrations are great, but these deposits seem to be few and far between on the sea floor. As costs rise and prices for resources increase, a much harder look will be taken at seabed resources. Should production costs of offshore resources come in line with those of land-based resources, then international competition for sea floor riches will become intense indeed.

● PROBLEM 10–10

In general, what types of resources are available on the ocean floor?

SOLUTION:

The following is an incomplete inventory of all of the mineral resources considered economically important, but the list is still impressive nonetheless. Of primary use from the sea floor is sand and gravel which have been dredged for thousands of years to supply civilization with needed landfill in low lying areas. Utilization of this resource is about 1.1 million metric tons annually. Phosphorite could be mined from offshore sands and muds. The extracted phosphates can then be used for agricultural fertilizers. Coal, oil, and natural gas are resources that are commonly thought of when discussing sea bed riches. Yet sulfur and sulfides of zinc, gold, iron, copper, silver, lead, chromium, and platinum can be harvested as well. Also available are manganese nodules. These nodules in some areas contain the following resources and their percents: manganese 30%, copper 1-2%, nickel 1.5%, cobalt 0.25%. The estimated natural production of these nodules is between 15 and 17 million tons per year on the sea floor. Other possible reserves to consider are biomedical chemicals, as well as agriculture, fish farming, and algae production for human consumption.

Debate who, if anyone, holds the rights to sea floor riches? What steps could be taken to secure them for all nations?

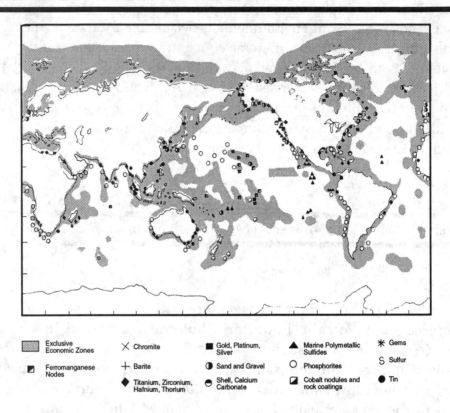

▦ Exclusive Economic Zones	✕ Chromite	■ Gold, Platinum, Silver	▲ Marine Polymetallic Sulfides	✳ Gems
▨ Ferromanganese Nodes	＋ Barite	◐ Sand and Gravel	○ Phosphorites	S Sulfur
	◆ Titanium, Zirconium, Hafnium, Thorium	◓ Shell, Calcium Carbonate	▧ Cobalt nodules and rock coatings	● Tin

SOLUTION:

The majority of these riches are found in international waters. The United Nations in 1982 proposed the Law of Sea Treaty. This treaty would allow the U.N. to grant license to private companies to do limited mining and then share a portion of their profits. The United States did not sign the 1982 treaty but instead joined France, West Germany, Japan, Italy, and several other countries in signing a separate treaty in 1984. High sea bed mining costs combined with low metal prices will limit how much action is taken in the near future. Undeveloped land-based resources have yet to be tapped, and this makes current sea mining costs prohibitive.

Alternative Energy Sources

> Detail the possible advantages and disadvantages of the expanded use of the following energy sources: direct solar rays, biomass, hydroelectric and geothermal. What are the incentives for pursuing these alternative energy sources considering the abundance of coal, oil, and natural gas?

Distribution of Solar Rays

20% Absorbed by Clouds and Atmosphere

50% Absorbed by Surface

5% Reflected by Surface

25% Reflected by Clouds and Atmosphere

SOLUTION:

a) DIRECT SOLAR RAYS: Most people picture photovoltaic cells converting sunlight to electricity as solar energy. Perhaps one pictures a solar farm with mirrors or lenses to concentrate the solar spectrum at a single point for the intended purpose of creating steam. This type of solar collector can be both cost effective and energy efficient under the right conditions. The picture of solar energy can be looked at from a much larger perspective if one considers active and passive solar heating as well. Should a structure such as a home be designed to use sunlight for heating, then the consumer could expect to reduce their energy bills in winter, as well as reduce their consumption of other fuel sources. Active solar collectors can be placed on a wall or roof to convert the solar rays to heat. In any case, it is a smart bet to take advantage of direct and indirect solar energy in the construction of any building. One of the only disadvantages of this energy source is that constant dependable sunlight is needed and

301

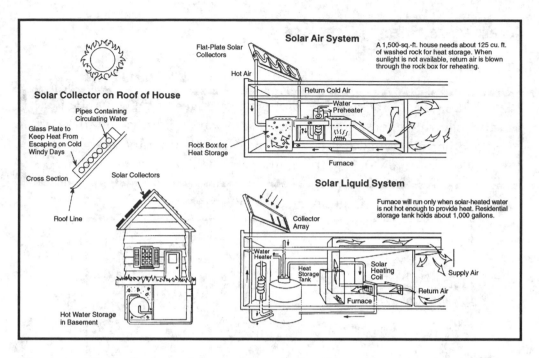

climate and weather can become an adverse factor in some areas.

b) BIOMASS: Material that is biologic in origin is indirectly a type of solar energy that is collectively called biomass. Wood has been an old staple in the energy cycle of humans. Several variations of biomass are now being investigated as alternative energy sources. One of these sources is agricultural in origin. Grains and sugars can be burned directly or converted to the liquid fuel alcohol. Municipal waste can be used also with the added advantage that any garbage converted to methane or burned directly will not end up as extra volume in a landfill. For these alternative sources, the overall technology is effective, but costs as of yet are not completely competitive with fossil fuels. Another drawback for agricultural biomass is that land originally used for food crops are now taken out of production for that purpose. Those acres must now be managed in the same way that they were before, yet nourishment for the populous is not produced. At the same time water, fertilizers, insecticides, and possible runoff pollution are all kept in the production equation. The use of wood to produce energy could be looked at as positive, taking the strain off fossil fuels; however, deforestation and the effects of plant loss on the atmosphere must be considered first. This area called biomass has many key issues to be considered before major steps will be taken.

c) HYDROELECTRIC: The force of gravity on fluids as they flow through the water cycle can produce an abundance of energy. Rainfall anywhere on a land mass will start the process. As water works itself to base level (sea level), the kinetic energy it picks up can be dammed and stored as potential energy and later used to turn turbines and create power. This source is natural, renewable, and possibly as old as the oldest rocks of earth. Problems associated with hydro power start as soon as a dam is constructed to trap the water. Sediments carried as load in the streams or rivers will settle out of suspension in the slow moving pool created by the dam. Over time these sediments will reduce the efficiency of the reservoir as the total volume is decreased. To keep the dam working, the sediments must eventually be dredged and relocated. This poses the problem of where to put the dredged sediment. A second possible problem is that flooding upstream will occur as the former river valley is drowned in dam backwater. Flooding can occur far upstream in heavy rains and down stream of the dam, water volume is reduced and the area may experience environmental changes associated with the reduction in river volume.

d) GEOTHERMAL: Energy generated from magmatic heat within the Earth is not currently in widespread use worldwide. New Zealand, Iceland, Italy, and the United States are among the nations which produce energy from geothermal sources. San Francisco receives approximately one-half of its total energy needs from magma. At a conversion efficiency of only 1%, it has been estimated that global reserves of geothermal energy would equal 14 billion barrels of oil per year. Should new technology produce a productivity of 50%, then geothermal energy could become an important energy source. In areas where magmatic heat is near the surface, artificial fields can be created to expand the total area in which geothermal energy can be produced.

Regardless of how efficient, dependable, or widespread, all of these alternative energy supplies need to be investigated and embraced in one form or another. This will allow for the conservation of fossil fuels. These energy sources can free the United States from dependence on other countries. They can reduce the amount of capital spent on importing foreign energy. They can help to create new job markets and supplement the economy of the U.S. They can also help protect the environment from many harmful forms of pollution.

● **PROBLEM 10–13**

Explain the process of energy production from geothermal sources.

The process seems to be a simple one. Use the natural heat within the Earth to turn water into steam. The steam can then run turbines to produce electricity. In areas where rock has been previously exposed to magmatic events, the temperatures may be hot enough to make energy. Rock at +180 degrees C will heat pressure-injected water enough to produce the desired results. Near San Francisco in an area called the Geysers, the electrical needs of almost two million people are met through such technology. The problems experienced include: possible corrosion of machinery by magmatic waters, dissolved ions and metals in water, and exposure to amounts of sulfuric gasses; however, the pluses of this alternative energy source must be considered as many areas of the world could obtain at least part of their energy needs from geothermal sources.

Pollution of the Earth, Water, and Air

• PROBLEM 10–14

Summarize the steps that might be taken if developed nations should choose to reduce their resource consumption and production of pollutants.

SOLUTION:

The United States alone produces about 180 million tons of garbage annually. Approximately 73% of this refuse is deposited in landfills. These numbers alone are staggering, yet when combined with the consumption and wastes of other developed nations the problem becomes gargantuan in proportion. One alternative is for developed nations to revert back to simpler and more environmentally friendly ways. Reduction would be key in this concept as smaller and less is better. Smaller homes filled with less consumable goods. Less air conditioning, less rich foods from high up on the food chain, simpler packaging, and greater use of recycling and reuse are proposed as just some of the methods that could be embraced. On paper the concepts sound good, but the economic feasibility of reduced economic growth would for most nations be unsuitable. Would the people of an advanced nation give up their creature comforts in an attempt to level the playing field for people of a lesser developed nation? Perhaps a leveling of population growth coupled with increases in science and technology will help to even the field of play for all nations of Earth.

Examine current solid waste practices in the United States. What suggestions could be made as possible solutions to the dilemma?

Estimate of World Wastes Produced per Year		
Type	Millions of metric tons	%
Municipal solid waste	1,500	36.2
Dry sewage sludge**	65	1.6
Dredged material	1,075	26.0
Industrial wastes	1,500	36.2
TOTAL	4,140	100.0

**Produced by treatment plants.

SOLUTION:

How can we get rid of our garbage? Out of sight out of mind has been the norm in the past. This solution has just now come back to haunt us. Americans discard about 180 million tons of solid waste each year with 73% of it reaching landfills. The following are all possible solutions that used in combination could greatly reduce the amount of waste disposed in landfills. Source reduction by cutting back the volume of packaging that retail stores and factories use could be a large step in the right direction. Recycling of all types of packaging would also be a great help. Currently only 13% of solid waste is recycled in the U.S. Waste incineration for energy production is but another direction that can be taken with solid wastes that typically are deposited in landfills. About 14% of solid wastes are being burned for fuel in this country today. In our municipal waste is a mixture that consists of 20% plastic, 34% paper, 12% metals, and 2% glass. Clearly much of this material, which is destined for landfills, could be recycled and reused in the marketplace.

● **PROBLEM 10–16**

Compare and contrast the "good news and bad news" in the fight to clean up the atmosphere.

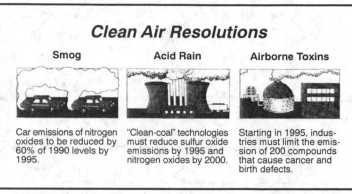

Clean Air Resolutions

Smog

Car emissions of nitrogen oxides to be reduced by 60% of 1990 levels by 1995.

Acid Rain

"Clean-coal" technologies must reduce sulfur oxide emissions by 1995 and nitrogen oxides by 2000.

Airborne Toxins

Starting in 1995, industries must limit the emission of 200 compounds that cause cancer and birth defects.

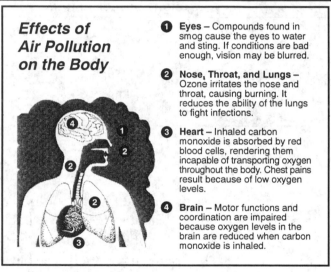

Effects of Air Pollution on the Body

1 Eyes – Compounds found in smog cause the eyes to water and sting. If conditions are bad enough, vision may be blurred.

2 Nose, Throat, and Lungs – Ozone irritates the nose and throat, causing burning. It reduces the ability of the lungs to fight infections.

3 Heart – Inhaled carbon monoxide is absorbed by red blood cells, rendering them incapable of transporting oxygen throughout the body. Chest pains result because of low oxygen levels.

4 Brain – Motor functions and coordination are impaired because oxygen levels in the brain are reduced when carbon monoxide is inhaled.

SOLUTION:

Most all people will agree that cleaning the environment is a good thing. The obvious negative impacts on human health and the ecosystem of Earth are well understood. Yet there are other underlying consequences to be studied as well. The government of the United States has requested voluntary action from citizens and industry, but it has also legislated action as well. An example of this is the 1990 Clean Air Act. The good news is, this law requires that emissions into the air meet certain standards which will help clean up the environment. Under this act, cars would have to reduce emissions of nitrous oxides by 60%. "Clean coal" technologies would also have to reduce harmful emissions. Industry is required to reduce emissions of over 200 compounds that are known to cause health problems and must do so starting in 1995. The act targets auto exhausts, factory emissions, acid rain, and ozone depletion. The down side of any such act is the cost of compliance. Estimates of consumer costs for a cleaner environment go as high as $50 billion per year. The result of such extra costs could include loss of jobs, rising consumer prices, and possibly a slowing of the economy.

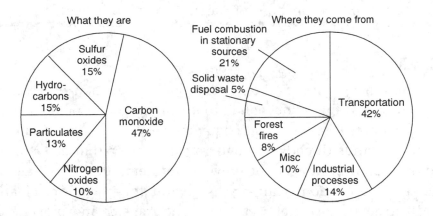

Describe current American waste management techniques as they relate to coastal oceans.

SOLUTION:

Currently about one-half of the population of Earth lives near coastal regions. This number is also true for the United States as well. A major problem with such concentrations is the disposal of sewage and municipal wastes from such a large number of people. Currently New York and the surrounding cities discharge over 8 million tons of sludge per year alone; most of it is deposited directly into the Atlantic Ocean just a few miles offshore. Bays and ports must be dredged to keep them open or they may fill with sediments and be forced to close. Over 25% of all dumping at sea is sediment of this type. Garbage, sewage, and heavy metals (lead, mercury, and cadmium), pesticides, solvents, insecticides, fertilizers, radioactive wastes, and plastics of all types and sizes all contribute to the problem. Alternative solutions to ocean dumping are few and expensive and so alternatives are not economically feasible at this time. An old saying is that the solution to pollution is dilution. This may have been the case in the past but today dilution does not seem to be an attractive solution when compared to the many environmental problems that arise.

Earth, the "blue marble," depends on water for many processes. Describe some of the functions of water in the natural world.

SOLUTION:

In the biosphere, perhaps the most important function of water is in photosynthesis and the production of food and oxygen. It naturally occurs in all three states of matter (solid, liquid, gas). Water is important to all living things either directly through respiration or indirectly through metabolic ingestion. Indirectly it provides nutrients through weathering, erosion, and deposition. Humans use water for irrigation, cleaning, cooking, and many forms of recreation. The transfer and movement of water through the hydrologic cycle is important to study and understand due to the enormous impact that water has on the biosphere of planet Earth.

● **PROBLEM 10–19**

What is the water table and why is it important to examine and understand?

SOLUTION:

The water stored naturally within the subsurface of the Earth keeps a level similar to that of a lake. Hydrologists call this the water table. This underground "lake" stores water in substances of various porosity. The input of water to the water cycle causes a surplus of water supply; the depletion by extraction or lack of input causes a deficit of water supply. For human populations, this fluctuation of water level can be a cause for alarm due to the dependence of agriculture and technology on a "clean" supply of water for the production of crops and goods.

● **PROBLEM 10–20**

Examine the consequences involved with the possible depletion of a water table in a given area.

SOLUTION:

The water stored underground in large pools is enormous but not infinite. The demands of increasing populations, industry, and agriculture have put a tremendous strain on these reservoirs. The input of water needs to be monitored so that the output does not cause a deficit for any given region. If more water is taken out than goes in, the "well" will start to lose water and the supply will eventually be depleted. The process of depletion may take years, decades, or centuries depending on the size of the aquifer and the rates of fluid extraction. In a way the water in any given aquifer can be considered to be a nonrenewable resource in that the rate of recharge is far below the rate of extraction.

● PROBLEM 10-21

Consider the implications of site selection for construction with respect to environmental considerations.

SOLUTION:

Far too often cost or location are the primary consideration of an agency when contemplating a future construction site. Chance development with an eye for profit margins causes development in areas not suitable for construction. Aspects of agriculture, ground water, recreation, transportation, and urbanization should be considered before any sites are selected for construction. Will ground water be affected? Can the slope or site handle the change in water runoff characteristics? Will ground water supplies handle population stresses? Will ground water supplies be safe from contamination? As one can see, many considerations should be made before construction is initiated.

● PROBLEM 10-22

How should toxic waste be approached as an environmental issue even though our civilization and technology depend on it for our very survival?

SOLUTION:

Prevention of any contamination would be a preferred option, but much of the problem occurred before people understood the full scope of the actions they were undertaking. Legislation did not fully define guidelines or limits and thus the damage was done. Pesticides, herbicides, fertilizers, metals, sewage, cyanide, PCBs, mine drainage, and low level radiation are just some of the toxic problems that surface in environmental circles today. Former sites of disposal will be difficult at best to clean up. To seal the site as securely as possible may be the only answer for today. Ground water monitoring and evaluation of contamination may help. The best solution seems to be the identification and monitoring of past dump sites and the use of new technology to create safer sites for future disposal.

● PROBLEM 10–23

The production of undesirable wastes and chemicals is a necessary evil of our society. Emphasize ideas that will improve future landfill sites for these wastes.

SOLUTION:

The sanitary landfill is primarily designed to contain our organic wastes. Each day a layer of topsoil covers the fill to reduce odors and also prevent wastes from blowing away. These landfills are typically lined with concrete, plastic, or clay to provide an impermeable barrier to any contaminants. Problems with respect to landfills include: plastics that will not degrade, cans, batteries, cleaners, solvents, medicines, and paints. Most of those items should be recycled and reused rather than dumped. To encourage recycling and precycling, by law if necessary, would encourage intelligent disposal of these items. With landfills nationwide running out of room and new sites in short supply, the future is questionable for the continued use of landfills for disposal of the discarded surplus of civilization.

● PROBLEM 10–24

Several nations have expressed concerns about the number of small projectiles in orbit around Earth. What considerations are being given to all this "garbage in space"?

SOLUTION:

The North American Aerospace Defense Command (NORAD) estimates at least 3,800 "objects" orbit the Earth. These objects amass a total weight of more than six tons with 60% being found in geosynchronous orbit 22,300 miles above the planetary surface. The remaining 33% pose a more immediate threat in low earth orbit at a distance of 120 to 300 miles. Estimates suggest that since 1957, more than 9,700 objects have fallen from orbit with the largest being the American space station Skylab at 77.5 tons (it fragmented as it disintegrated in the upper atmosphere). In 1978 a nuclear powered Soviet satellite weighing five tons crashed across the Canadian tundra. In 1965 a collision between two satellites destroyed both. In 1981 a Russian satellite was fragmented into 135 pieces as a result of a low orbit collision. An early space shuttle mission documented a pea sized crater on a front windshield. The responsible "agents" include oxygen cylinders, nuts and bolts, spent rocket boosters, food containers, sewage, and a white glove from a 1960s space walk. Suggested solutions include space collection junkyards, collection of debris and forced deposition in Earth's oceans, collection and ejection from orbit into deep space or toward the sun. In any case a collision of a spacecraft with any orbiting "junk" could spell disastrous results for the crew members of that mission.

● PROBLEM 10–25

What is the major form of land pollution?

SOLUTION:

Solid waste is the major form of land pollution. Substances that are not biodegradable, such as plastic and glass, do not decompose over time. These substances are nearly permanent in the landscape.

Sanitary landfills, where solid waste is covered by dirt, are the most common form of solid waste disposal; however, many landfills are being shut down since their capacity has been reached. These landfills can pose future problems for the land and water of the area.

● PROBLEM 10–26

Examine what effects cities might have on local weather patterns.

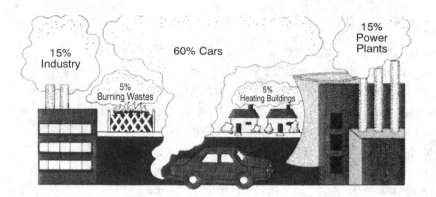

SOLUTION:

Although not fully understood, weather data suggests that urban industrial centers modify weather surrounding them. Sometimes known as "heat islands," cities can produce unstable air masses especially at night. The thermal radiation can cause local wind disturbances. Measurements indicate that pollution increases at night possibly from low level contaminants from many smaller, less regulated heat sources. Larger sources such as factories and power plants face tighter regulation and also disperse their load through tall smokestacks. Auto exhausts add many compounds to the air resulting from incomplete combustion of petroleum products. These gases plus the dust and particulate matter produced may affect local cloud formation and precipitation. Also measurable is the increase in background pollution. Local pollution can be combined with distant contaminants transported by wind and air masses. These factors have been shown to affect local weather patterns. More research in this area is needed and new findings are sure to be published as populations increase and cities grow.

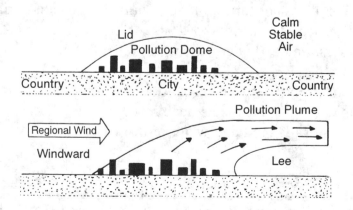

The Greenhouse Effect and Global Warming and its Consequences

• PROBLEM 10-27

Explain the carbon cycle of the Earth.

SOLUTION:

Carbon is an essential element found in the biogeochemical reaction of Earth. Carbon is found in the atmosphere, biosphere, hydrosphere, and lithosphere (crust). Carbon is important in biotic tissue building and energy release. Photosynthesis uses carbon to produce food and release oxygen. Carbon is stored in fossil fuels and in the biosphere; it is stored in the oceans, rocks, and air. It cycles from sphere to sphere naturally at different rates. Carbon bonded with oxygen (CO_2) is found in the atmosphere and makes up a very important greenhouse gas. The variations in the total percentage of CO_2 in the atmosphere are believed to have played a major role in past climate changes. The burning of deforested areas and fossil fuels can add extra carbon to the cycle and could possibly play a role in climatic changes in the future.

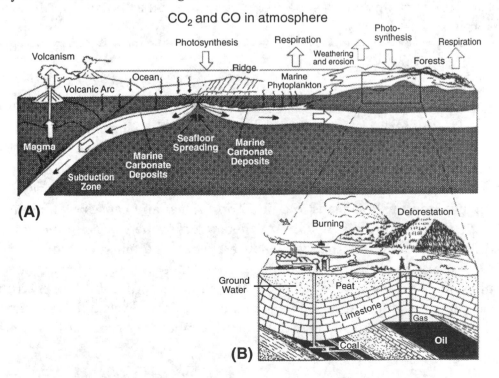

313

Relate current events dealing with Antarctica and Earth's ozone layer.

SOLUTION:

Synthetic chlorofluorocarbons, or CFCs, have been shown to contribute to ozone depletion. The freon group of CFCs have in the past been used as propellants and refrigerants. Their use for these purposes has declined since the 1970s. In the late 1980s major chemical groups in the United States agreed to phase out CFC production and use. It has been shown that the thickness of the protective ozone layer is diminished and in some high latitude areas is almost nonexistent. The depletion of ozone by CFCs can cause the Earth's surface to be exposed to excessive ultraviolet radiation. The effects of excessive UV radiation on the biosphere could be traumatic. A thinning ozone layer can also affect the growth rates of ocean phytoplankton. This could accelerate the greenhouse effect since phytoplankton take large amounts of carbon dioxide out of the atmosphere.

Relate the similarities between a greenhouse and a planetary atmosphere.

SOLUTION:

A greenhouse functions by allowing the full spectrum of solar radiation to enter through large windows in the walls and ceilings. As the interior of the greenhouse absorbs the sun's energy, it heats up and begins to radiate energy in the infrared portion of the spectrum. The glass windows are opaque to this wavelength of radiation and reflect most of it back into the greenhouse. This leads to a build-up of heat and causes temperatures in the greenhouse to increase. A planetary atmosphere which functions in this way is exhibiting the "greenhouse effect." The full spectrum of solar radiation reaches the planet's surface. The planet absorbs the energy, heats up, and begins to radiate energy in the infrared portion of the spectrum. Certain gases in the atmosphere are opaque to this wavelength of radiation and function like the glass windows of a greenhouse and reflect this energy back to the planet's surface. All things being equal, this will cause a build-up of heat and lead to increasing temperatures in the planet's atmosphere.

● PROBLEM 10-30

Generalize about the atmospheres of Earth and Venus.

SOLUTION:

These terrestrial "twin" planets share similar sizes, mass, and lithospheric composition according to spectrometers and surface lander data. The difference involves the enormous amounts of carbon dioxide found in the thick atmosphere of Venus. The CO_2, combined with water vapor, trap the solar radiation in a runaway greenhouse effect. In fact the surface of Venus is hotter than the surface of Mercury even though it is further from the sun. It appears that CO_2 in the atmosphere of Venus is not cycled or removed as it is on Earth. On Earth most of the CO_2 is held in the lithosphere in carbonate rocks such as limestone. Still, other amounts are found in the waters and plants of Earth. Carbon cycles throughout the ecosystem and balances over the geologic history of Earth have taken care of themselves naturally. The accelerated burning of fossil fuels when combined with deforestation have raised concerns about the possible acceleration of the greenhouse effect on Earth.

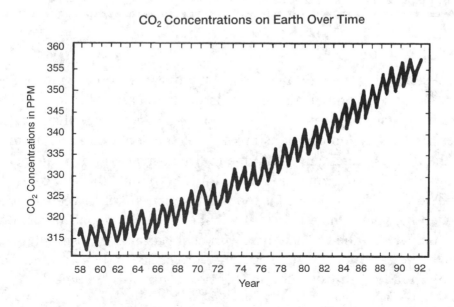

CO_2 Concentrations on Earth Over Time

Analyze the possible future effects of tropical deforestation on the atmosphere of Earth.

SOLUTION:

The reduction of forested acreage could allow an increase in greenhouse gases in the atmosphere. The resultant rise in global temperature due to a thickening of the atmospheric blanket could result in many global side effects. Warmer temperatures could affect climate and rainfall across the surface of the planet. Reduced or excess moisture in the soil would affect plant growth, crop production, and global biomass. Warmer temperatures could also cause the melting of glacial ice. The addition of the melted water to the oceans could cause sea level rises to several hundred feet depending on the severity of the temperature rise. Even a limited rise in temperature could start a warming chain reaction that may take decades to counter or reverse. Most major Western industrial nations have agreed to stabilize or reduce their greenhouse emissions in this decade. This is considered an important step in the right direction in controlling the escalation of greenhouse gases released into the atmosphere.

● **PROBLEM 10–32**

Evaluate trends in global temperatures as observed in the past.

SOLUTION:

All recent data points to increases in many gases in the atmosphere of Earth. Carbon dioxide is but one constituent measured but is a major player in the environmental drama. Other factors include methane, nitrous oxides, and chlorofluorocarbons or CFCs. Predictions of temperature rise over the next 50 years range from one to five degrees. Though the increase seems small, it is unknown just how much variation the environmental system can absorb. How much is too much is not entirely agreed on within the scientific community. It is well documented that global temperatures have fluctuated in the geologic past with cool glacial and warm interglacial periods. The efforts of climatologists, meteorologists, and environmentalists will continue to shed new light on this very controversial subject.

Describe the role of the hydrosphere in the global warming dilemma.

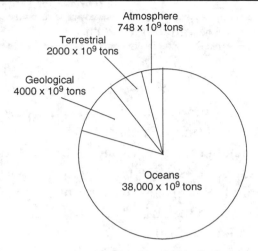

Atmosphere
748 x 10^9 tons

Terrestrial
2000 x 10^9 tons

Geological
4000 x 10^9 tons

Oceans
38,000 x 10^9 tons

World carbon dioxide distribution

SOLUTION:

With the start of the industrial revolution two centuries ago, human dependence on the burning of fossil fuels has escalated. At the start of the revolution, estimates in parts per million of carbon dioxide in the atmosphere were at 295ppm. By the end of the twentieth century, estimates predict 375ppm, and +600ppm late in the twenty-first century. It is estimated that the oceans can absorb about 40% of the CO_2 increase. This percent equals approximately 2 billion tons per year entering the oceans and ocean sediments. It is debated that the increase of CO_2 in the atmosphere will be absorbed by the hydrosphere and the carbon cycle will continue to be naturally buffered. Some expect that increases in CO_2 will stimulate photosynthesis in phytoplankton which will help to absorb extra carbon and heat released by increasing industrialization. Much research needs to be undertaken to fully understand the role of the hydrosphere in global warming.

International Weather Modification

Generalize the factors that affect global climate.

SOLUTION:

The role of climate is complex and involves many factors. According to the rock and fossil record, radical changes have occurred in the past. We should expect those changes and adjustments to continue as well. The role of the sun and the output of solar energy is critical. We know that the rate of output changes and that orbital patterns of all planets fluctuate with relation to their distance to the sun. Also to be considered are interactions between the hydrosphere, atmosphere, lithosphere and also the interaction of the changing biosphere. Changes in a system so large and complex take much time to occur and thus may take much research and thought to understand. We know that the surface of the Earth, like a living thing, is moving and adjusting due to tectonics and mantle convection. Computer models can attempt to map out the various scenarios, but such modeling at this point cannot cover the full spectrum of a system so massive and interactive.

• **PROBLEM 10–35**

Describe some possible problems that may arise from human attempts to modify weather.

SOLUTION:

Science had demonstrated limited success in the area of weather modification. Experiments in cloud seeding have been shown to reduce both the size and frequency of hail. The reduction of hail damage, which costs Americans hundreds of millions of dollars annually, is agreed to be a good thing. On the down side though, reduction of hail output from a storm system may increase the volume of rainfall from that system. The resultant flooding caused by excess precipitation may be just as costly as the hail would have been. Cloud seeding to produce rainfall may increase the moisture that one area needs but the extra moisture that seeding squeezes from the system will then not be available to other areas the weather system visits next. Should droughts occur in one state because of seeding in another, heavy legal and political consequences must be considered. The modification of hurricanes has been an age old goal of science. We have just begun to understand the consequences of modifying hurricanes. It is understood that hurricanes are one of nature's systems to help transfer heat to higher latitudes from the equatorial regions. Should this heat transfer be reduced, it is not known what predicted weather climatic modifications could occur. The global distribution of energy, called the heat budget, could be affected if hurricanes are reduced in strength or eliminated. Any attempt to change one part of an environmental system is sure to effect another part of the system. Potential problems may arise as modifications in weather patterns in one area might adversely affect the weather in another location.

● PROBLEM 10-36

What points of emphasis would a seismologist consider when predicting an earthquake for a given geologic area?

SOLUTION:

The location of the predicted quake would be of primary importance to residents of a seismologically active area. Also of importance would be the magnitude of the predicted seismic event and the specific time the shaking would occur. As with the prediction of the weather, anything less than perfection will be looked upon with ridicule and scorn from the general population. On the other hand, accurate earthquake predictions will provide some interesting complications to the mind sets and economic pocketbooks of people in prediction site areas.

● PROBLEM 10-37

Discuss the "good news, bad news" with respect to earthquake prediction.

SOLUTION:

As with any scientific evaluation the pluses and minuses must be evaluated. Evaluation of modern data suggests that several observable changes occur before an earthquake strikes. Microseisms or multiple small quakes have been recorded preceding some events. The release of stress along a fault line may include swarms of micro-quakes as rock units strain and crack before the pressure of "the big one." Surface deformation indicated by ground surface tilting is one factor to be considered. Any rapid increase in ground tilt suggests a seismic event in the immediate future. Variations in the following have in past events also suggested pending seismic events:

Increases *and* decreases in well water levels.

Increased or decreased conductivity of rock along the fault.

Changed magnetism within rock along the fault line.

Increases in radon gas in areas near faults.

Any measurable changes in the physical properties in rocks.

Good news includes the possibility that people can prepare for the worst or at least get out of a predicted quake area. On the bad news scene, jobs, insurance rates, and short-term economics may be effected by quake predictions. The resulting economic slowdown could cripple a given area, and if a predicted quake does not occur, the scientific community loses credibility for the next prediction.

● PROBLEM 10–38

Predict the implications to society if science can directly cause earthquakes.

SOLUTION:

The ability to cause earthquakes was discovered serendipitously (a lucky accident recognized for its importance through experiments near Denver, Colorado) in the early 1960s. As waste water was injected under high pressure into deep wells, swarms of small earthquakes began to occur. As water disposal levels increased so did the earthquakes. When disposal levels were decreased seismic activity decreased as well. This accidental experiment was duplicated in a Colorado oil field. How would a metropolitan area react to such an experiment? The ability to cause many smaller earthquakes may reduce the pressure on a given fault area and allow tectonic forces to be continually released in a controlled manner. The major concern is that the experiment could set off a series of events that may be uncontrollable. Could the lubrication of a major fault with water cause a chain reaction mega quake? If so, who would be responsible and what action if any could be taken?

Regarding seismic prediction and monitoring, what new work is being done with regard to tsunami (tidal wave) prediction and warnings.

SOLUTION:

Large earthquakes on the seafloor or volcanic eruptions can cause tidal waves. Since they are not caused by the moon/sun tidal action, they are scientifically called seismic sea waves, or tsunamis. The wavelength of a tsunami can extend to 100 miles combined with a velocity of up to 450 miles per hour. The speed of these waves combined with their height as they compress when approaching shallow beaches produces a wave that can reach enormous height and velocity. The tsunami can hit coastal areas at speeds of 300 miles per hour and reach heights in excess of 100 feet. Worldwide communication and warnings make tsunamis a far less deadly force today then they have been in the past. Communications from local seismic events will alert sites of impending tsunami events.

Nuclear Accidents

● PROBLEM 10–40

List the history of nuclear accidents worldwide.

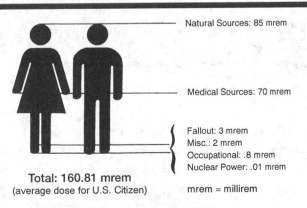

Natural Sources: 85 mrem

Medical Sources: 70 mrem

Fallout: 3 mrem
Misc.: 2 mrem
Occupational: .8 mrem
Nuclear Power: .01 mrem

Total: 160.81 mrem
(average dose for U.S. Citizen)

mrem = millirem

SOLUTION:

Several accidents have been documented well before today's current headlines shocked the publics awareness of this issue. In 1957 a British air-cooled graphite reactor used in weapons production experienced problems when it caught fire and some of the fuel cladding melted. Amounts of volatile products were released into the surrounding environment. The plant was taken out of service soon after as was a twin unit. The most openly publicized event occurred near Harrisburg, Pennsylvania in March 1979 at the Three Mile Island Reactors. Due to system malfunction and human error, between one-third and one-half of the core melted. The containment vessel maintained its integrity and kept the radioactive debris within the vessel. A large volume of gaseous material escaped the vessel but was trapped by the containment building surrounding the vessel. The radiation released as a sum total was almost undetectable against normal background radiation. In April 1986 at the Chernobyl nuclear power plant in Russia during a test which violated standing reactor safety regulations, the reactors' emergency water cooling system was shut off. Several steam-induced explosions shattered the containment system and was followed by a third chemical explosion that started a series of fires. The magnitude of the explosion ejected radiation to high altitudes. Dozens died in the initial disaster, and persons within 30 km were evacuated. Radioactive fallout circled the globe with the heaviest fallout in western Russia and parts of Europe. The core was later covered by sand to absorb energy and prevent further release of radiation, then it was smothered in cement to prevent any further energy escape.

● PROBLEM 10–41

Document the developmental history of nuclear powered reactors in the U.S. What is the scope of and future for energy produced in nuclear power plants in America?

SOLUTION:

In the 50 plus years since the discovery of nuclear fission, the U.S. has become the largest consumer of nuclear energy. In 1990, about 20% of the total electricity consumed in this country came from nuclear power. Only coal which contributes 55% is a larger source in the U.S. There are 108 operating plants as of 1990 with 416 plants worldwide. There has not been an order for a new plant in the U.S. since the 1970s. This trend follows worldwide trends that mark the slowdown in national nuclear programs. With the accidents at Three Mile Island and Chernobyl, construction costs have risen due to new requirements and construction delays have

KEY

●   Reactors With Operating License

○   Reactors With Construction Permit

△   Reactors On Order

THE URANIUM-238 DECAY CHAIN*

Radiation Emitted			Radioactive Elements	Half-life		
Alpha	Beta	Gamma		Minutes	Days	Years
●		●	⇐ Uranium-238			4.5Bill
			⇩			
	●	●	⇐ Thorium-234		24.1	
			⇩			
	●	●	⇐Protactinium-234	1.2		
			⇩			
●		●	⇐ Uranium-234			247,000
			⇩			
●		●	⇐ Thorium-230			80,000
			⇩			
●		●	⇐ Radium-226			1,622
			⇩			
●			⇐ Radon-222		3.8	
			⇩			
●	●		⇐ Polonium-218	3.0		
			⇩			
	●	●	⇐ Lead-214	26.8		
			⇩			
●	●	●	⇐ Bismuth-214	19.7		
			⇩			
●			⇐ Polonium-214	0.00016 second		
			⇩			
	●	●	⇐ Lead-210			22
			⇩			
●	●		⇐ Bismuth-210		5.0	
			⇩			
●		●	⇐ Polonium-210		138.3	
			⇩			
NONE			⇐ Lead-206		STABLE	

expanded the length of time it takes to get a reactor online. Today it may take a reactor 10 to 15 years from planning to actual final construction. Special interest groups have played a large role in the rising costs and delays that have been experienced in the nuclear industry. Their legal actions on behalf of the environment have been a key factor in major construction delays. Currently, new nuclear plant costs are not competitive with those of coal plants due to rising costs and legal difficulties.

Oil Spills and Other Environmental Accidents

● PROBLEM 10–42

What are potential sources of environmental contamination from petroleum?

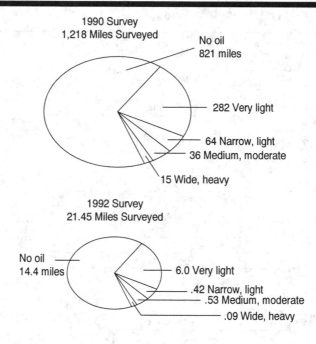

1990 Survey
1,218 Miles Surveyed
No oil
821 miles
282 Very light
64 Narrow, light
36 Medium, moderate
15 Wide, heavy

1992 Survey
21.45 Miles Surveyed
No oil
14.4 miles
6.0 Very light
.42 Narrow, light
.53 Medium, moderate
.09 Wide, heavy

SOLUTION:

Any time a product is transported from one point to another, the potential exists for accidents. As for oil, the resources are found far from the marketplace, making transportation imperative. Estimates claim that for every one million tons of oil moved, about one ton is lost to spillage. The loss can occur anywhere between the pipelines, trucking, and shipping tankers. Loss can also happen at the source as rigs and wells experience blowouts and leakage. In the last decade it is estimated that an average of 340 million gallons per year have been lost in transport. Large scale spillage will always grab the headlines such as the estimated 300 million gallons lost during Kuwait oil rig fires in the Gulf War. The spill in Prince William Sound in Alaska resulted in 11 million gallons being lost. The need for energy from petroleum is great and the transportation of that oil is essential. Caution, improved transportation measures, and improved cleanup measures can lessen the impact of such disasters.

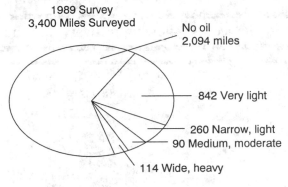

1989 Survey
3,400 Miles Surveyed

No oil
2,094 miles

842 Very light

260 Narrow, light
90 Medium, moderate

114 Wide, heavy

1991 Survey
315.5 Miles Surveyed

No oil
238.1 miles

58.5 Very light

9.8 Narrow, light
8.0 Medium, moderate
1.1 Wide, heavy

● **PROBLEM 10-43**

Describe measures that can be used to clean up an oil spill.

SOLUTION:

Since large scale spills occur on or near water in coastal areas, most recovery technology focuses on those types of recovery. Cold water deluge involves pumping clean local water into areas that have been exposed to the spill. Gravity will pull the oil down to the waterline where it can be trapped by booms floating on the surface. The trapped oil can be skimmed and recovered. This method is used often to pick up large volumes of oil in bulk spills. Warm water washing is similar in method except that the washing water is first heated to 140°F in an attempt to rinse clean a higher percentage of the spill. Bioremediation involves adding nitrogen and phosphorus to stimulate bacterial growth. The bacteria feed on the hydrocarbons in oil and naturally degrade the spill into CO_2 and water. Mechanical and manual treatment require machines and human labor to physically expose contaminated areas and remove oil with shovels, rakes, and absorbent materials.

• **PROBLEM 10–44**

Define environmental concerns following recovery from a spill.

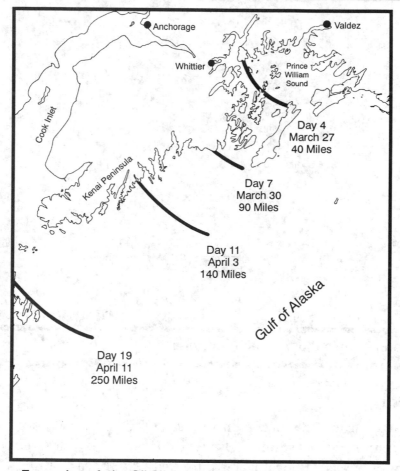

Expansion of the Oil Slick from the Exxon Valdez Accident

SOLUTION:

The impact of a spill can cut much deeper than just the loss of wildlife or intrinsic beauty. Scenic degradation causes economic loss from reduced tourism to the afflicted region. Fishing industries dependent on viable stocks of fish may suffer huge economic losses. Coastal waters rich in shellfish, clams, and oysters are adversely affected and commercial beds may have to be closed until recovery is complete. In tropical waters, coral reefs could be damaged beyond the point of recovery. The sum totals of clean-up costs as well as economic losses are difficult to estimate. It is safe to assume that any spill is going to be a loss for the people and environment of the area.

SHORT ANSWER QUESTIONS FOR REVIEW

Choose the correct answer.

Items 1 to 3 refer to the following map.

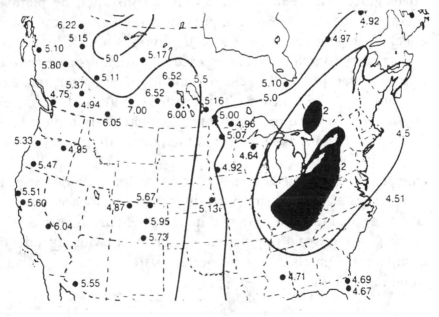

ANNUAL MEAN VALUE OF pH IN PRECIPITATION
IN NORTH AMERICA FOR 1980

1. Which part of the United States and Canada has the most serious acid rain problem? (a) Northern (b) Northeast (c) Southern (d) Northwest

2. The Great Lakes in most serious danger from acid rain are (a) Superior and Huron. (b) Huron and Michigan (c) Michigan and Erie. (d) Erie and Ontario.

3. Which factor could not account for variation in pH readings? (a) Forest cover (b) Industry (c) Population densities (d) Rainfall variations

4. The product of cellular respiration that has the most direct impact on the atmosphere and promotes the greenhouse effect is (a) O_2, the oxygen molecule. (b) CO_2, the carbon dioxide molecule. (c) H_2O, the water molecule. (d) B and C only.

5. Through photosynthesis, plants help to counteract the greenhouse effect by consuming _____ from the atmosphere. (a) oxygen (b) carbon dioxide (c) water (d) nitrogen

6. If the same amount of carbon dioxide that is produced when breaking down glucose in cellular respiration is consumed by plants in the production of glucose through photosynthesis, why is the greenhouse effect escalating so rapidly? (a) The combustion of fossil fuels and other energy sources is releasing excessive amounts of carbon dioxide into the atmosphere. (b) The greenhouse effect is not related to the amount of carbon dioxide in the atmosphere and would escalate anyway. (c) Through the Earth's gravity field, carbon dioxide is being drawn into the atmosphere from outer space. (d) None of the above.

7. One reason man needs to clear tracks of forest is because (a) wild animals live in the forest and pose a threat to local villages. (b) the land is needed to meet food and housing demands realized as a result of the growing world population. (c) forests are not a productive use of the land. Man clears them to make better use of his resources. (d) None of the above.

Item 8 refers to the following passage.

Cancer is the result of mutations in the DNA of cells. Through these mutations, cells escape normal control mechanisms that direct cell division. These mutations cause cells to divide uncontrollably and form tumors. Carcinogens are cancer-causing agents and are found in tobacco and many pollutants.

8. What would be a logical pathway for a pollutant dumped legally in small amounts into the ocean to become concentrated enough in people to cause cancer? (a) People swim for short periods of time in

the ocean and absorb large quantities of the pollutant through their skin. (b) Through large fish feeding on many small fish with trace amounts of the cancer-causing pollutant. Humans then consume many of the large fish resulting in toxic levels of pollutants. (c) There is no logical pathway. Ocean water evaporates into the air and concentrations never become high enough to cause a threat to humans. (d) None of the above.

Items 9 to 12 refer to the following passage.

Iodine-131 is a radioactive isotope with a half-life of 8 days. Iodine-131 decays by way of beta decay. The half-life of a radioactive isotope is the time it takes for half of the sample to decay. In 8 days, only 5 grams of a 10-gram sample of iodine-131 would be left: the other 5 grams would have decayed.

9. How much of an 8-gram sample of iodine-131 would be left after 16 days? (a) 2 grams (b) 4 grams (c) 8 grams (d) 10 grams

10. If we started with a 4-gram sample of a radioactive isotope with a half-life of 6 years, how long would it be until there was only 1 gram left. (a) 24 years (b) 6 years (c) 12 years (d) None of the above.

11. The half-life of uranium-238 is 4.5 billion years which is close to the estimated age of the Earth. How old will the Earth be when half the uranium-238 that exists now decays. (a) 4.5 billion years old (b) 9 billion years old (c) 13.5 billion years old (d) None of the above.

12. Many radioactive isotopes cause serious damage to our cells. What would be the effect of a plutonium-239 "spill"? Plutonium-239 has a half-life of 24,000 years. (a) There will be a short-term effect. Luckily plutonium-239 decays quickly. (b) There will be a long-term effect. Even if we were able to "clean up" the spill, a long-term and safe storage area would be needed to store the contaminated matter until it was no longer radioactive. (c) Undecided. (d) None of the above.

Items 13 to 15 refer to the following passage.

A bioassay is a laboratory test to measure harmful levels of toxic chemicals in places such as streams and sewage waste sites. The "LC50" (lethal concentration) value is the concentration of a toxic substance needed to kill 50% of the exposed organisms.

Copper sulfate ($CuSO_4$) is a chemical used in the metal plating industry. Suppose a tanker truck carrying copper sulfate crashed and spilled the chemical into a lake. Would this be a serious pollution problem.

Here are the results of a bioassay to find the LC50 value for copper sulfate.

Concentration of $CuSO_4$ ppm (parts per million) in a solution	% of water fleas dead from exposure to the solution
00.0	0
0.03	66.7
0.06	100
0.12	100
0.25	100
0.50	100

13. From the results of the experiment, what minimum concentration of $CuSO_4$ proved to be a lethal concentration (equal to or greater than the LC50 value)? (a) 0.12 ppm (b) 0.06 ppm (c) 0.03 ppm (d) 0.00 ppm

14. The LC50 value for water fleas when exposed to $CuSO_4$ must lie between (a) 0.00 and 0.06 ppm. (b) 0.00 and 0.03 ppm. (c) 0.06 and 0.50 ppm. (d) 0.50 and 1.00 ppm.

15. What would be the impact of a major spill resulting in a high concentration of $CuSO_4$ into a lake? (a) Ecosystems of the lake would be seriously effected. (b) The results from the bioassay show that organisms will not be substantially effected. (c) The results from the bioassay are not conclusive concerning the toxicity of $CuSO_4$ on organisms. (d) None of the above.

16. Solar energy can be collected and converted directly to electrical energy without intermediate mechanical devices using (a) direct processing. (b) photovoltaic process. (c) heat translators. (d) windmills.

17. Humans appeared late in the Earth's history but were ultimately able to modify the Earth's environment by their activities by escaping environmental constraints that limited other species and by changing the environment to meet their needs. This fact has presented a much larger problem that we call (a) technology. (b) pollution. (c) environmental response. (d) environmental management.

Fill in the blanks.

18. Deforestation is the process where man clears forest area to use the land for other purposes such as cattle ranching. A cheap and easy way to clear the forest is to burn it down. If a rancher cleared a track of forest to raise cattle, the atmosphere would be effected in many ways. By burning the trees, _____ would be released into the atmosphere. The cattle raised on the land will release _____ into the atmosphere through the process of _____.

19. One reason the rate of cancer has risen dramatically since the industrial revolution is because man is now exposed to many pollutants which cause mutations in _____.

20. If the use of industrial CFCs were stopped today, it would take _____ for the ozone to be completely free of industrial CFCs.

Determine whether the following statements are true or false.

21. If the number of plants on the Earth continues to be reduced, one effect will be more oxygen in the atmosphere and an increase in the greenhouse effect.

22. Two factors that contribute to the greenhouse effect are respiration and photosynthesis.

23. The least available renewable resource is petroleum.

24. Pollution affects the quality of life and natural functioning of our ecosystems.

ANSWER KEY

1. b
2. d
3. d
4. b
5. b
6. a
7. b
8. b
9. a
10. c
11. b
12. b
13. c

14. b
15. a
16. b
17. b
18. carbon dioxide, carbon dioxide, respiration
19. cell DNA
20. 95 years
21. false
22. false
23. false
24. true

INDEX

Numbers on this page refer to PROBLEM NUMBERS, not page numbers.

Numbers on this page refer to PROBLEM NUMBERS, not page numbers.

REA's Test Preps
The Best in Test Preparation

- REA "Test Preps" are **far more** comprehensive than any other test preparation series
- Each book contains up to **eight** full-length practice tests based on the most recent exams
- **Every** type of question likely to be given on the exams is included
- Answers are accompanied by **full** and **detailed** explanations

REA publishes over 60 Test Preparation volumes in several series. They include:

Advanced Placement Exams (APs)
Biology
Calculus AB & Calculus BC
Chemistry
Computer Science
Economics
English Language & Composition
English Literature & Composition
European History
Government & Politics
Physics B & C
Psychology
Spanish Language
Statistics
United States History

College-Level Examination Program (CLEP)
Analyzing and Interpreting Literature
College Algebra
Freshman College Composition
General Examinations
General Examinations Review
History of the United States I
History of the United States II
Human Growth and Development
Introductory Sociology
Principles of Marketing
Spanish

SAT II: Subject Tests
Biology E/M
Chemistry
English Language Proficiency Test
French
German

SAT II: Subject Tests (cont'd)
Literature
Mathematics Level IC, IIC
Physics
Spanish
United States History
Writing

Graduate Record Exams (GREs)
Biology
Chemistry
Computer Science
General
Literature in English
Mathematics
Physics
Psychology

ACT - ACT Assessment

ASVAB - Armed Services Vocational Aptitude Battery

CBEST - California Basic Educational Skills Test

CDL - Commercial Driver License Exam

CLAST - College Level Academic Skills Test

COOP & HSPT - Catholic High School Admission Tests

ELM - California State University Entry Level Mathematics Exam

FE (EIT) - Fundamentals of Engineering Exams - For both AM & PM Exams

FTCE - Florida Teacher Certification Exam

GED - High School Equivalency Diploma Exam (U.S. & Canadian editions)

GMAT CAT - Graduate Management Admission Test

LSAT - Law School Admission Test

MAT - Miller Analogies Test

MCAT - Medical College Admission Test

MTEL - Massachusetts Tests for Educator Licensure

MSAT - Multiple Subjects Assessment for Teachers

NJ HSPA - New Jersey High School Proficiency Assessment

NYSTCE: LAST & ATS-W - New York State Teacher Certification

PLT - Principles of Learning & Teaching Tests

PPST - Pre-Professional Skills Tests

PSAT - Preliminary Scholastic Assessment Test

SAT I - Reasoning Test

TExES - Texas Examinations of Educator Standards

THEA - Texas Higher Education Assessment

TOEFL - Test of English as a Foreign Language

TOEIC - Test of English for International Communication

USMLE Steps 1,2,3 - U.S. Medical Licensing Exams

U.S. Postal Exams 460 & 470

RESEARCH & EDUCATION ASSOCIATION   website: www.rea.com
61 Ethel Road W. • Piscataway, New Jersey 08854 • Phone: (732) 819-8880

Please send me more information about your Test Prep books

Name _____

Address _____

City _____ State _____ Zip _____